COME HOLY SPIRIT

COME HOLY SPIRIT

Sermons

BY KARL BARTH
PROFESSOR OF THEOLOGY IN THE
UNIVERSITY OF BONN, GERMANY

AND

EDUARD THURNEYSEN
MINISTER OF THE REFORMED
CHURCH, BASLE, SWITZERLAND

English Translation by

PROFESSOR GEORGE W. RICHARDS, D.D., LL.D., D.TH.
THEOLOGICAL SEMINARY OF THE REFORMED CHURCH
IN THE U. S. A., LANCASTER, PA.

REVEREND ELMER G. HOMRIGHAUSEN, S.T.M., TH.D.
MINISTER OF THE REFORMED CHURCH, INDIANAPOLIS, IND.
PROFESSOR-LECTURER IN BUTLER UNIVERSITY.

PROFESSOR KARL J. ERNST, PH.D., D.D.
MISSION HOUSE THEOLOGICAL SEMINARY,
PLYMOUTH, WIS.

TRANSLATION READ AND APPROVED
BY KARL BARTH

———————

WIPF & STOCK · Eugene, Oregon

Wipf and Stock Publishers
199 W 8th Ave, Suite 3
Eugene, OR 97401

Come Holy Spirit
Sermons
By Karl Barth and Eduard Thurneysen
ISBN 13: 978-1-60899-237-9
Publication date 10/30/2009
Previously published by Round Table Press, 1933

THE TRANSLATORS' PREFACE

These sermons were prepared from 1920 to 1924. Professor Barth preached some of them while he was minister of the Reformed congregation in Safenwil, Canton Aargau, Switzerland; others in the Reformed Church in Göttingen while he was professor of theology in the University. Pastor Thurneysen at that time preached to the congregation in Bruggen, near St. Gall, Switzerland. The sermons were written not for special occasions but for the regular Sunday morning service, and were addressed to such men and women as one will find in any village or city church—to men and women in the struggle for life, waiting and seeking for God.

Pastor Thurneysen selected the sermons and arranged them according to a scheme that may be indicated by the words Promise, Christ, Christian Living. These titles, however, do not appear either in the table of contents or in the context. The motive of the sequence of the sermons is suggested by the choice of texts. For the first six sermons these are taken from the Old Testament—from the Psalms, Proverbs, Ecclesiastes, Isaiah; for the next eleven sermons, from the New Testament, six from the Gospels and five from the Epistles; for the last eight, one from the Epistle to the Philippians and seven from the Second Epistle to the Corinthians. The sermons are, therefore, to be considered as forming an organic whole

v

setting forth the different aspects of the Word of God in prophecy, in the Christ, in the Christian. Their sequence is not logical, nor biological, but theological, Christological, soteriological.

Four editions in German have been published. This is the first volume of sermons from the Barthian school to appear in English. The translators found it difficult to put into clear, fluent English the distinctive thought, the paradoxical statements, and the idioms of the original text. They tried to be true to the authors, to the content of their discourses, and to the English reader. To what extent they have succeeded the reader will have to determine.

These sermons are not popular, clever, eloquent pulpit discourses such as the modern audience is accustomed to hear and to applaud. They probably would not receive large space in an American Monday morning newspaper. They cannot be easily comprehended, because they are so different in form and content from any sermons that have ever been published in this or any other age. They must be read and pondered, reread and pondered again, until the truth in them becomes spirit and life in the reader.

The aim of the sermons is to give God's answer to man's primary needs—his deep, inward, spiritual needs—which must be satisfied before any other needs can be satisfied. The sermons, therefore, do not soothe or please or flatter the reader. He may lay them aside without reading them to the end, because he is made to feel, as never before, his worthlessness and helplessness—the worthlessness even of the best that he thinks and does. Not only the sinner but the righteous man is brought to judgment and must cry for mercy. There-

fore the reader may say to himself: "Can I do nothing
that is acceptable to God?   Nothing that is worthwhile?
Does not this lead to hopeless despair?   Am I not
robbed of all power of moral endeavor?"

That is precisely the effect that the preachers intend
to produce in the reader, or the hearer. For man must
be overcome, humbled to the dust, before God can
lay hold of him, lift him up, mold him to and for His
eternal purpose. Only when man is brought into the
condition of the publican facing the blaze of the holiness
and righteousness of God, or of the prodigal who in
coming to himself comes to his father, is he in a condition to become a child of God, to cry Abba Father, to
enter upon the work of God, to be co-worker with God
in His Kingdom. One who has already prepared his
program and wants God to ratify it, who has already
found God and defined Him, who is bent on building
the Kingdom of God into the hearts of men with
modern techniques and the wisdom of science, will find
little in these sermons to please him, unless by the grace
of God the truth of the sermons will change his mind.
Man's response to the gospel is the response of repentance and of faith working in love through the patience
of hope. This is the beginning of life, of the abundant,
the eternal life.

Yes, here hope is inspired such as one finds nowhere
else excepting in God as revealed in the Scriptures; for
here an infinite vista is opened before the soul through
the prophets and the evangelists, a vista that ends in
eternity. Yes, here is power, the power of omnipotent
love given to man through Christ crucified, risen, glorified. Yes, here is optimism, the optimism that is based
upon the abounding grace of God in Jesus Christ, from

which will come the new heavens and the new earth in
which dwelleth righteousness.

Again, the reader may be disappointed because he
does not find on these pages wise sayings or ingenious
pronouncements on the things that now disturb and interest men, discussions of the problems of life from the
standpoint of common experience and in the light of the
highest moral and social values. One looks in vain
for sociological or political harangues, for literary mas-
terpieces captivating the cultured reader with their fas-
cinating rhetoric, for subtle theological speculations or
philosophical acumen based on recent scientific discoveries, for satisfactory explanations of the contradiction
between science and religion.

These sermons simply proclaim God, but not as a
static absolute far removed from the world, not as an
immanent essence entangled with the world; they
preach the good news of God "in action," of a living
person who is wholly other than the world and yet
Creator, Upholder of the universe, Savior and Sancti-
fier of men, as He is revealed in the prophets, incar-
nated in the Christ, working through His spirit in the
fellowship of believers, the Church. They proclaim
the purpose that has been in God through eternity and
is now made manifest in Christ, that in the end His will
of justice and love is to prevail as in heaven so upon
earth. This and this alone is assumed to be the power
of God unto salvation unto all them that believe.

Perhaps in sermons like these we may catch a glimpse
of what Spengler was groping after and could not find,
when he wrote:

"In this very century, I prophesy, the century of
scientific-critical Alexandrianism, of the great harvests,

of the final formulations, a new element of inwardness will arise to overthrow the will-to-victory of science. Exact science must presently fall upon its own keen sword. First, in the 18th Century, its methods were tried out, then, in the 19th, its powers, and now its historical role is critically reviewed. But from Skepsis there is a path to 'second religiousness,' which is the sequel and not the preface of the Culture. *Men dispense with proof, desire only to believe and not to dissect."* [1]

October, 1933,
Lancaster, Pa.

[1] The Decline of the West, I, 424. (Italics ours.)

CONTENTS

THE SERMONS OF KARL BARTH

By Joseph Fort Newton

Why do people go to church, if they do go? What do they really want to hear, though they may not have formulated their need clearly in their own minds? What is the unasked question for which they are seeking an answer? Why do they go again and again, in spite of many disappointments, yearning deeply, listening intently, as if the word they want to hear may any moment come to birth and bring the blessing they seek?

They do not go to church to hear about science, philosophy, economics, or art, useful as such studies may be. Nor do they go to hear the preacher tell of his faith, his feelings, his experiences, much less his opinions on life and its problems. No, they go sorely needing and sadly seeking something else, something more primary and profound—longing to hear a voice out of the heavens, telling them the things eye hath not seen nor ear heard. They go seeking, as of old, the healing touch which makes them know that they are not alone in their struggle for the good; wanting to hear the forgiving, redeeming, all-inclusive, all-solving Word of God which embraces the whole of life—"the one Word alongside of which there is and can be no other."

Such is the vision of preaching in the soul of Karl Barth, out of which his theology was born, not as an academic adventure, but as a response to divine urging

in contact with aching human need; an effort "to tell
that God becomes man, but to tell it as the Word of
God, as God Himself tells it,"—nothing less, nothing
else. If we are to understand his theology, he tells us,
we must hear all through it the question which the
preacher puts to his own soul and tries to answer, "What
is preaching?" It was while in the pastorate, looking
into his own heart and into the expectant faces of his
people, that he discovered that preaching, as he had
been trying to practice it—the preaching of spiritual
values, based on his own inner experience or that of
others, seeking to satisfy religious needs—is not enough,
and was indeed no longer possible for him. Hence his
quest for a Word more authentic, more authoritative,
more intimately personal, more inviting, in which the
contradictions of human life are reconciled; an answer
to the cry of the soul not for truths, but for Truth, not
for solutions but for the Solver, not "for something
human, but for God as Saviour even from humanity."

What, then, is preaching? "It is thirty minutes to
raise the dead in," said Ruskin; and only the living
word of the Living God can work such a wonder. So
defined, it is an august and impossible undertaking,
"an act of daring," as Barth admits, and only the man
who would rather not preach, he adds, and cannot
escape from it, ought ever to attempt it. Who, alas,
is sufficient for these things? The answer is that our
sufficiency is from God, who has spoken to us in His
Word, and who has commissioned us to preach. Else,
thinking up against these facts, no man could muster
either knowledge or courage enough for the task, even
if the right to attempt it could be claimed. But the
preacher is under orders; he preaches because he must.

It is the paradox of his office that he must "dare the impossible," as Barth puts it, aware of an imperfect human instrument; but he can do no other, since his office is qualified as obedience, coming under the sign of the highest responsibility and promise.

For the preacher, to say it once more, is not a lecturer, nor a teacher, nor an exhorter; he is an ambassador of authority, a herald bearing tidings. His word is not his own. He has his message, as he has his office, not by virtue of a poetic temperament, a dynamic personality, or a mastery of fine phrases, but as a witness of the Word of God. A Christian preacher, says Barth, "does not speak in the way of a clever conversationalist who wants only to be listened to, or as a teacher who claims only attention, or an agitator who seeks only agreement, or as a person of importance who desires only acquiescence." If he were any or all of these, men might well require his credentials, or regard him as an officious meddler and adventurer whom they have good right to warn off. No, the preacher is a bringer of the Divine Word, so far as human lips can upbear it, not denouncing men like the prophet, but calling for faith, repentance, obedience, and proclaiming the Gospel of Reconciliation in which warning is blended with "the wooing note" of love.

Here, then, in a swift sketch, is what Karl Barth means by preaching, and no one in our generation has done more to exalt the preaching office, alike in theory and in practice. It is remote from the artificial conception of preaching which regarded sermon-making as a literary act, and the sermon itself as an object to be achieved, if not an end in itself; a legacy from the Sophists, as Hatch taught us in a famous lecture. It is far more momentous and thrilling than the old evangelical three R's, Ruin, Redemption and Regeneration preached with Animation, Affection and Application. It is too big for our current academic and homiletic definitions, in that it makes the sermon really an extension of God's revelation of Himself, and of the record of His Word in the Bible; and therefore a sacrament in very truth.

By the same token, as will be discovered in the sermons here to be read, the vision of what preaching is determines the method and art of the preacher, so direct in its approach, so disarming in its earnestness, so deceptive in its simplicity. The sermons are unique both in matter and in manner, and no one can read them without feeling that we have in them a living Word of God in the midst of our confusions, when the soul of man is astray in its own life, and the nations grope in the dark without goal or guide. May the vision grow and abide.

St. James's Church,
Philadelphia.

COME HOLY SPIRIT

OPEN WIDE THE GATE!

The earth is the Lord's and the fulness thereof; the world and they that dwell therein. For he hath founded it upon the seas and established it upon the floods. Who shall ascend into the hill of the Lord? And who shall stand in his holy place? He that hath clean hands and a pure heart: who hath not lifted up his soul unto vanity [loose doctrines], nor sworn deceitfully. He shall receive a blessing from the Lord, and righteousness from the God of his salvation. This is the generation of them that seek him, that seek thy face, O God of Jacob. Lift up your heads, O ye gates; and be ye lift up ye everlasting doors: and the King of glory shall come in. Who is the King of glory? The Lord strong and mighty, the Lord mighty in battle. Lift up your heads, O ye gates; even lift them up ye everlasting doors; and the King of glory shall come in. Who is this king of glory? The Lord of hosts, he is the King of glory.—*Psalm 24.*

"The earth is the Lord's and the fulness thereof, the world and they that dwell therein." Is not all that we humans need to know really said to us in this word of the Psalmist? Is it not true that if we could rightly speak and understand such a Word, if we could say it and hear it so that it would rise and come out of the Bible and work in us, we should be helped immediately? But what does that mean? Certainly nothing else than that it would be so spoken and heard, not

I

as a pleasing word of man, but as the Truth, even as
the word that God speaks to us.

We are all seeking for such a word, one that is
not simply another word. How often each one of us
has longed for just this right word in sorrow or in
some other situation! If we but bear a little of the
burden and the hope of these times upon our hearts,
we shall become humans who longingly look for the
redeeming word. For the anxiety and the hope of
today is due to the want of this word, and we can
not rest in our quest for it. The variety of prophets
today who profess to know something, and the
thronging of men who desire to find something—
these are proofs of this questing and questioning.
And the worse the need becomes, the closer it ap-
proaches the one universal need which, like a flood,
covers the whole earth, and from which no one can
escape. The fewer the islands become which are not
threatened by this flood of need, the more all the barriers which we have thrown up against it are burst
because they are puny structures of man—the more do
we feel that this redeeming word must be a primary,
all-inclusive word which must embrace the whole
world; it must be the *one* word along side of which
there is and can be none other, even God's word. Today we see clearly how all need hangs together. To
really help a single unemployed family would mean
that we have to create work. But to create work
today would mean to solve the whole European problem of labor. Thus, that which apparently is a small
thing is the greatest. Thus all need, even the smallest, is tragic—the cry of the hungry child is a terrible

and fearful matter. These little means of ours can no longer help. Always and in everything we have to do with the total situation. And the help for the need must have a powerful character, the most powerful there is. The need today reaches as far as our portion of the earth, and still farther. "Europe"— that is the extent of our misery today; the "world" will increasingly be the name for need. How can any name be spoken that is smaller, less powerful than the name of God, the name of the Lord?

And now He is named. "The earth is the Lord's and the fulness thereof, the world and they that dwell therein." Here the two meet, the need and He who can satisfy the need; earth and heaven; man and God. Here God reaches forth His hand and says: "The earth in her need—that is mine!" And when God says that, can it mean anything else than: "I will help, I will redeem, I will have mercy, I, the Lord!" This is *the* help. To look for help means to look for it, to inquire whether this proffered help is authentic, whether it is true, whether it is spoken into the wind, or, whether it is in reality God's word. Or do we need something other than the promise that "the earth is the Lord's and they that dwell therein," and that the will of God will be executed in spite of the unreasonableness of men? Would we not have all that we need to carry on, if we were really certain of this promise? Would we not be certain, that while men put through their own wills, while they seek their own glory, while they worship their own gods, that God is doing His work? And is the work of God anything else than that he puts forth His hand upon them and that with all the doing of their own wills they will not get away from His will, and in all their seeking for glory, His will finally will triumph?

And does the will and the glory of God mean anything else than that in the depth of their need men acknowledge Him as Lord, as He whom they should call upon to relieve their need? Does the will and the glory of God mean anything else than that men acknowledge how all need has in common the fact that men in their need have not called upon God as they should? So that eventually they may come out of the midst of their worship of false gods, to the place where they call upon Him and fear Him? God so works in the achievements of men against the achievements of men, whilst he awakens and illuminates until men's eyes are opened and they see these achievements in their terrible reality and cry out: "God be merciful to me a sinner!"—until we acknowledge that our need is a judgment that has come upon us because we have forgotten God. Again and again men play with God until God reaches in with a powerful hand and reveals Himself as the Lord whose the earth is and all they that dwell therein. And when the lightning flash of this acknowledgment drives through the night of men's lives and men understand their need and seek help, and when they again allow judgment and grace to be true, and also grant that the earth is the Lord's—then the light of a new day streams across the earth. Then there breaks upon us what is termed a new day, for which we wait so longingly.

"The earth is the Lord's and the fulness thereof,
the world and they that dwell therein." Yes, the
right Word is spoken. But why does it enlighten us
so faintly? Why does it not penetrate our ears and
issue from our lips? Why do we not ascend, as it
is said later in our Psalm, "into the hill of the Lord,"
and stand, even amidst the need which surrounds us, in
the holy place? Why is it not true and real to us and
why do we not live by that Word: "the earth is the
Lord's." Why, then, do we live on as though it is
not true, if it *is* true? We know how the whole world
waits to live by it. But we are ourselves "world."
We are never able to accomplish it in our own little
lives, so as to allow salvation and truth to come to
light. We live our days as though not a flicker of
light would reveal itself. How poor our words are,
how darkened are our spirits! How little we seem
able to say to the great need and darkness of our
times. We scold about the newspapers because they
seem to thrash straw in their daily reports, but we
ourselves know no better. Even our Christian words,
our sermons and pious observations, are so helpless,
faltering, lacking in light and spirit. They sound
pious, but from them proceed the same far-distant
hopelessness and perplexity, the same obstinate and
despairing spirit which proceeds everywhere from
books and men. The sad part of it all is that we speak
and hear the word of God as a mere word of man, it
no longer possesses its unique power and meaning.

Here undoubtedly lies the deepest reason of our
need. The word of God is there, it is verified to us
that God is Lord, and if we could accept it we would

be helped. But we cannot. A bolt is fixed in place, it requires certain hands, different hands from our own, to open. "Clean hands" are required for it, say the words of our text. There is a darkness there which robs us of our vision. Even when we have the clearest, divine word of promise before us, it does not tell us anything. And we cannot get anything out of it. It requires men with other hearts than our own to see God's light. He who has "a pure heart," say the words of our Psalm, can "ascend into the hill of the Lord." There is a power of temptation which frustrates us when we would and should believe. "Should God have said . . . ?" and by it our faith is severed at its roots. It requires men in our places who have "not lifted up their souls to *falsehood*," to break the bonds of this temptation, says the Bible.

"He who has clean hands"—this is the primary thing which is told us. Clean, guiltless hands open the bolt that closes the entrance to the redeeming and freeing things which God has to say to us. To understand what is meant we may imagine that all of us, without exception, are sitting, as it were, in a prison which we have erected around ourselves and keep on building through our foolish, frivolous, cruel and unclean living, thinking and doing. And when God lays His hand upon us, when He directs His words to us, it is that He wants to overlook all this; He wants to divorce us from it; He wants to forgive us. "The earth is the Lord's and the fulness thereof." He wants to tell us that all this imprisonment is invalid. It does not belong to you; that is not the real you. That is your imprisonment and God wants to look upon that as removed, as though it did not exist; He wants to look upon you without imprisonment. You are free before Him and through Him. But we must let that be done for us. We must learn to look upon our lives and ourselves that way, look upon them in the light of the judgment and grace of God. We must divorce ourselves from the old existence, we must become ashamed of our imprisonment. Something in us wants to be ashamed of itself. Something in us wants to believe that all this does not really belong to our real selves but that it is an imprisonment. This something we must give its right; it must be helped to break through. We must not be callous or hardened. For what separates us from God is not our sins, but our *unwillingness* to have our sins forgiven! We must really give God our hands when He walks toward us and desires to take them. The hands of men which are taken out of guilt and laid in the hands of God and which He takes are "clean hands," for God forgives sin. Such hands unbolt the door which keeps us from redemption. But he who loves his sins more than God who wants to forgive them—with such a one God cannot speak.

This callousness of heart might happen in the finest and most spiritual manner. For instance, we might assent to all that God's word says, but always apply it to others, to the unfaithful, the godless world. We conceive the strife for God and His things as a strife which *we should direct* against other folks—here the good, there the bad—and we are on the side of God as soldiers of the army of light. Then we shout "the earth is the Lord's and the fulness thereof"; yes, and we shout it with a peculiar enthusiasm and zeal, but in the end we mean *our* own things, the things of *our own* religious party or movement. But in the same measure that we strive against other folks for our own things especially when it becomes important whether we shall keep the upper hand, in that same measure we thicken the walls of our prison and do not have anything more to do with God's word, even if we are ever so familiar with it. God does not ask about the right of our life, He asks about the wrong of our life, for He does not want to help *us* into the saddle, but He wants to *forgive* us so that He alone might be right. Where is our unrighteousness, our sin, our weakness, and where are those sinful, wrong, and weak hands extended to God that He might take and make them into clean hands? This is the main thing, the only thing. As long as we have so many right deeds and habits to impose upon others, just so long are there no "clean hands," and just so long will no active striving help us even if it is the noblest. We are still imprisoned, and God cannot do for us what He wants to do.

The words of our text tell us a second thing. We are perhaps ready to acknowledge and substantiate the truth that the earth is the Lord's and the fulness thereof, but only as a truth at which we have arrived by the power of our own human insight, which we have validated by the power of our own experience. We add perhaps with a dash of pride, that it is a truth in line with all other truths, knowledge, experiences, and convictions which, in the course of life, we accumulate that the darkness of our existence may be a little clarified. But God is a jealous God, for He will be sole validator of what He says, and He will not be considered as a bit of human wisdom in line with others. Words of the Bible are remarkably poor in capacity for falling in line with words from the classics of philosophy and religion. That "the earth is the Lord's" is not a clever saying of man's life-experience, for it is a truth too great for man to express, know and perceive, as he would express, know and perceive other truths. God and the divine is not a subject of our perception or measurement. That He has created the world and that it is His—that is not a scientific fact to be taught, and we must be careful not to allow it to become such. It is true, but true from God and not from us. There is an eternal world, but we cannot see it, not even as a city above the clouds, and we would do well not to forget that when our artists represent it as such to us. Perhaps it would be better for them to let these things be.

As far as our knowledge is concerned, God is hidden. He does not ask, as he draws near to us: "Do you understand me?" But he asks: "Will you, in spite of the fact that you do not perceive me, will you put yourself in my hands and let yourself be led by me, even through the night?" In our own times there is a strong tendency, whether through science or through earnest investigation of the Bible, to get behind the plan, existence, and government of God. Whoever has understanding, who really understands God, will not meddle with these matters. To understand God means to bow before God, to pray to God, to make God authoritatively valid without understand-

ing Him. To come to this position a cleansing of the
desire to understand with one's own powers is required. It requires the insight that only God Himself can place us upon the path that leads to Himself.
It requires the insight that revelation is necessary.
That is what is meant by the "pure heart" which
alone is able to pierce through the darkness in which
God lives. It signifies that a renunciation is necessary which acknowledges that all our knowledge about
God comes from the knowledge that we know nothing,
except what He wills to reveal to us. "Blessed are
the pure in heart, for they shall see God." A person
cannot give himself a new heart, but he can plead
for it. And in this pleading, if it is earnest and humble, there lies concealed the purity of heart. And
in this purity lies the promise, "He shall receive a
blessing from the Lord, and righteousness from the
God of his salvation."

But is it not possible that this knowledge, this perception of the majesty of God and His word, might
be reduced to mere human knowledge?—perhaps to
a teaching, a theology, or a sermon, which we might
possess as we possess other things? Yes, that is possible. It has always and frequently happened in Christianity. Not for nought are we warned, by a third
word in our text, about "falsehood," loose doctrine,
or, literally, that we turn our hearts to that which is
nothing. Nihilistic teaching, loose teaching, that is
the opposite of holy teaching. This warning tells us
that we must, in seeking after God, look upon God
Himself. Not upon our own doctrines, even if they
are ever so pure; not upon what grows in our own

heads or dwells in our own hearts, even if it is ever so spiritual and living. "Who will ascend into the hill of the Lord?" . . . "The generation of them that seek after him, that seek thy face, God of Jacob." Much zealous striving after truth or much praying is in vain, because we will never merely by these ways make it right with God. The holiest thing is lacking, even though we talk much about it: that deep respect for God's majesty, that real reverent respect is wanting, in that God's thoughts in every case are higher and other than our thoughts. There is wanting that earnest prerequisite of knowledge of God: not what I think, intend, say, but only: *Thy* name, *Thy* Kingdom, *Thy* will—*that* is wanting, and when that is wanting it is not merely *something* that is wanting, but *everything* is wanting. When that is wanting then nothing will succeed, everything is loose, empty doctrine, even if it be tenfold pure.

In closing, a great requirement sums up everything: "Lift up your heads, O ye gates . . . ye ancient doors." A great king desires to enter. Our distress is not that there is no help before our gates. The help is there, but the doors are too narrow, too low, too small for help to enter. Our ears are callous and deaf. God can continue to speak His word for a long time, but we do not hear it, we do not understand it as it ought to be understood and in such a way as to help us. "Lift the doors and open the gates"—this is the exhortation which must first of all be heard and obediently followed. Our small, selfish human thinking must be opened wide that it may become a vessel into which God will pour the great, the bright, the streaming content. It is a command to become humble, for only humility can open wide and high the door. Humility means: not I, not my understanding and knowing,—and this "not I," this "not my" understanding and knowing is the lifted door through which God would enter into the least of these. To be humble means to wonder and to wait and to hope for that which is truly great, for that which God desires to do unto us; and wherever this wondering, waiting and hoping is to be found, that which is truly great is not distant.

But can one *summon* this, can one *demand* it? Is this "Lift up your heads O, ye gates, and be ye lift up ye everlasting doors!"—is this really a command? Is it not much rather a proclamation, a promise? Not that we have the capacity to open wide and high our gates, but because the *King comes*, because *He is at our gates*, and because, with His coming and existence, He would present humility to mankind; therefore, the call goes forth: "Lift up your heads O, ye gates!" The King is there, the One who makes us humble, because of whom we are humble at all times, who gives us pure hearts and clean hands. And this thy King comes to thee! Verily, more is expressed here than mere human command and human wisdom. Here Jesus Christ is speaking, the Son of the living God. Here alone one can withdraw the bolt and permit the blindness and foolishness and stubbornness of heart to be forgiven, and become joyful so that what this Psalm says is true, Yea and Amen, in Him. The earth is the Lord's; man is God's! Oh, that our eyes and ears might open soon!

THE GREAT "BUT"

Every man regards his ways as clean in his own eyes; but the Lord weigheth the spirits.—*Proverbs 16:2*.

"But" says the wisdom of the Bible. For one who has once heard and understood this wisdom nothing can surpass this panoramic, significant, heavily-contended, biblical "but." We can never be done hearing and comprehending it. One can divide the readers of the Bible into those who note it and those who note nothing of it. Not all the learned belong to those who note it—nor all the unlearned. All of us belong at times to those who note, oftentimes to those who do not note. "But" means that there is still something that is overlooked and forgotten, still something to be taken into consideration, there is still another possibility at hand. "But" signifies that in all of our thinking and speaking and perceiving and doing we must turn a sharp corner. A ship is traveling at full speed with both happy and sad travellers, with hard-working stokers and sailors aboard, ploughing forward, straight ahead,—"but" the man at the helm swerves the rudder around as he avoids a disaster, because a sandbank lay in the direct path of voyage. One simply cannot always sail straight ahead. A group of hikers are travelling a dusty highway, fretting because of the heat, complaining because of the length of the hike,—"but" one suddenly bends down and in the dust of the highway finds a gold coin. Many

times it pays not to fret and complain, but to keep
your eyes open; something quite different might suddenly appear. But these are only illustrations and
parables. That something different to which the "but"
of the Bible points, is the totally different which is
expectantly waiting upon us, which comes to meet
us, which might instantly appear to us to tell us that
it was always there and that it will always be there.
It may be that when it meets us we shall be filled
with fear, or with joy, but that is not the main issue.
Happy is that servant whom the Lord, when he comes,
finds awake—that is the main issue.

The "but" in the Bible is the great "but" which
is the cause of all these many little and littler "buts"
which are to be found in our lives and in the world.
It is the reason of all reasons, the reason why we
humans must so often turn the corner, the reason why
again and again we must learn to see things in a different light, to think differently and to speak differently. It reminds us of *the* Greatest which is
often overlooked and forgotten, but which is to be
respected, but not only does it remind us of *the* Greatest, but rather of the One and Only. Because we
overlook this One, we overlook so much. Yet if this
One is respected, then everything is respected. The
"but" of the Bible reminds us of the sense of God
which is prior to, behind and above, yet always in,
the sense and the non-sense of man. In every moment it is the altogether new, in every moment it
is the totally different possibility: even God! Shall
we grow hysterical in the face of it? Shall we rejoice about it? Both are possible, sometimes both

at the same time. More important is the question
as to whether we will *heed* it. The Bible can be eye
and ear to us whereby we can see what really is con-
tained within our own lives. God is! This is what
the people of the Bible say. And they ask us: Who
sees? Who hears? Who believes our report, and
to whom is the arm of the Lord revealed? That is
the Bible's "but."

The Lord weigheth the spirits, says our text. One
could say that this is just what the Bible tries to say.
For the Bible does not always say the *same* thing over
and over again, but it does say this *one* thing again
and again: But the Lord weigheth the spirits. This
is the same thing the Bible says on other pages: But
he who dwelleth in the heavens shall laugh, he shall
have them in derision! . . . But my words shall never
pass away . . . But he was wounded for our trans-
gressions and because of our sins was he smitten . . .
But Christ is raised from the dead and has become
the first-fruits of them that slept . . . The "but" of
the Bible proclaims to us the existence and the deeds
of God. Who is God? He who always confronts us
as Lord, incomparable, startling, unforeseen, He who
possesses all and is all, over against whom we are
nothing and possess nothing, and from whom our possessions and existences come as the shadow does from
the light. What does God do? He weigheth the
spirits. The spirits are the spirits of men. We, too,
are on His scales, examined of Him, judged by Him,
put to the test by Him to see how much we are worth
in His estimation. That is our life-situation, as seen
from the point of view of God's existence and deeds.

The next thing of importance is that we are being weighed. We ourselves weigh and are weighed. We make judgments as to good and evil, truth and falsity; we discriminate between the worth and the unworthiness of our experiences in various situations and achievements which confront us, between the words and the deeds of mankind as well as our own. From day to day and year to year we go through our existence with a scale in our hand more or less observantly testing. But where did we get these scales? How do we know what we simply cannot know? That is the novelty: with our tiny scale in hand we are ourselves in the great scale. Not only do we discriminate but we are being discriminated. We not only judge, but are being judged. We not only apprehend, but are being apprehended. An eye that sees me, an ear that hears me, a master who is proving me, a judge who is judging me, a king who chooses me or does not choose me—that is the final, deepest truth of my life and it is not merely my own seeing, hearing, testing, judging, and choosing.

We humans are apt to pass over this truth very often and with great unconcern. That is why we are so vociferous and forcible, especially in our complaints and indictments, as well as in our boastings and assertions. We overlook the fact that what *we* say must not be taken so seriously, no matter how serious it may be to us. What *we* say is not so important, but rather what is being said to us. That is why we are generally so disunited in our weighings, why we mutually contradict ourselves by valuing what *we* say and thus contradict ourselves and involve our-

selves in strife. If we only realized that we are all
being judged, then we must and would judge with
the greatest reserve and eventually cease judging altogether. That is why there is so much error in our
judging and discriminating. Our opinions can be true
only when they proceed out of what God thinks about
us. But if we build our houses so that the peak
of the roof becomes the foundation, we shall surely
experience their downfall. Again and again a vigor-
ous, deliberate thoughtfulness is necessary, and perhaps very bitter experiences, to bring us to the consciousness, whereby we will be quiet and perceive that
before we weigh, we are weighed, that before we let
our little lights shine, we are first in the presence of
a great light.

The Lord weigheth the spirits, it says. We humans
weigh by the gross, as we say. What is life? It is
the journey of man through his allotted time; his
infancy and aging; those pieces of good fortune and
those of ill fortune which befall him; his appearance
which gradually takes on sharper lines until upon the
deathbed these lines finally, intuitively indicate what
his character actually was; the pleasant or unpleasant
impressions which he arouses; his words, whereby we
habitually read his thoughts; his achievements from
which we think we learn what he is or is not capable
of doing; the influence which radiates out from him;
his success which he possesses or does not possess. As
we look upon all this we judge a human life, and
perhaps ourselves, as a fortunate or unfortunate, a
good or bad, a worthy or unworthy person. On the
basis of these things we respect or neglect, love or

hate. What is life? The trek of mankind through the ages; the history of differing epochs or cycles of culture; the variations among mankind; how they labor, feed, clothe and educate themselves; how they separate themselves in war and peace; mankind's great men; their ingenuity and discoveries; the battles won and lost; their monarchies and democracies; their art and science; the untold possibilities of their faith; and finally their gods and idols.

Viewing all this we speak of world history, of progress and evolution, of the glorious past, tragic present and darker future. But the Lord weigheth the spirits. Is this then life? Or what is life in all this? Do we not err' when we weigh in gross? The Lord weighs the true weight, the content. This content is secreted in all sorts of crevices, but what are the crevices without a content? The crevices are not weighed along. The spirits are the essential things weighed. The spirits, the spirits of men are life which surges, moves, creates in all that is called life, whether good or evil. The spirits are the fruits of which it is said—by them shall ye know them, the fruits which are gathered in the eternal granaries of God, as well as the weeds which shall be consumed with eternal fire. The spirits dwell beneath all sorts of countenances, and the countenance does not always correspond to the spirit which dwells beneath. The spirits speak in various languages and not always does the great spirit speak out of the great deed, nor the small spirit out of the insignificant.

All the evil that folks plan does not proceed out of the evil spirit, nor does all good come out of the

good spirit. The spirits dwell in the highest as well
as in the lowest strata of mankind and where they
dwell no one knows. The spirit is the man himself
as God alone knows him. He is the man as he is
penetrated through and weighed of God, as he stands
naked before God, for or against God, honest or dis-
honest, true or untrue, chosen or rejected. The spirit
of man is in the scale of God. The novelty of this
fact is: *Our sins* cannot corrupt us, *our righteousness*
cannot save us, it is the spirit that comes to judgment. The spirit of man that comes to judgment is
the tap-root of man in eternity, the spirit is as an
open window facing Jerusalem, the spirit is as the
question full of answers: how can I gain a merciful
God? The spirit is as suffering pregnant with a hopeful hearing: Thy Kingdom come! What is the significance of anything and everything else, what is
the significance of progress and decadence of the
world's history in the face of this one thing? How
do you stand towards this one thing? *There* life itself becomes a burning question, there is the difference
between life and death, there is the finger which writes
upon the wall: numbered, weighed—and perhaps—
found too light. And it is the *Lord* who weighs the
spirits. God is the Spirit of all spirits and thus their
judge. God's word is the living, powerful, sharp,
double-cutting sword. God is the truth of our lives,
of all life. We cannot be respectful enough, we cannot retreat back far enough, we cannot stand distant
enough so as to even faintly conceive what it means
that God weighs the spirits.

It is possible that whenever we utter the word

"God" we think of something high, great and beautiful, as a goal or ideal which we have set for *ourselves*. But fundamentally that would be a weighing of *ourselves* by *ourselves;* we ourselves would be our own judges and emancipate or condemn ourselves. But God dwells in a light which no man can approach. Even the highest which we think about Him when measured by His true self is still an illusion. He himself is God. He alone knows us. He alone accepts us or rejects us. He alone, He only. Wherever man stands before God he faces a "Halt!" which he cannot escape, a "Halt!" that can be compared only with death. Whatever belongs to our natural lives is not yet really of God. And what has come to us from God is no longer of us. When in life we are laid upon the scales of God, we are confronted by a death-line, a boundary line of judgment, and whatever is on this side of the line must pass away.

But the extremity-line at which we stand and face God is also a beginning; the "Halt!" which is directed at us is also a command to march, "Forward!" The death-line of our existence is also a line of life's beginning, the line of grace. That sharp incision which separates us from God is also the boundary by which we partake of His invisible, everlasting being. Just that quest after God cannot tear us away, it cannot cease, it cannot be discharged, for the quest is the answer. This is the new thing about this truth: we stand in the light of the cross and the resurrection of Jesus, weighed of God, dying His death with Him and living His life with Him. We never come

forth from God and yet we are never forsaken of
God. We cannot get along with Him and yet we
cannot leave off continually questing after Him anew.
Flesh and blood cannot inherit the Kingdom of God
—and yet this corruption must put on incorruption
and this mortality must put on immortality. We are
created beings, but we are created by *God*. We are
dust and ashes in his sight, but we are never without
hope of salvation and glory. Wanderers between two
worlds, travelling from here to yonder, nearing always
the yonder from the here. For the Lord, in whose
hands we are, is the Lord of life, because he is the
Lord of death.

And now: *The ways of a man are clean in his own
eyes.* Here we are in the midst of what we already
understand all too well. Here is where all of us live,
in the circle of our duties and obligations, the cares
and the joys of our life, whether significant or insignificant. Here we live and weigh, each with his
own particular character, with his own particular fortune, with his own particular light, or, it may be, with
his own darkness which is given him. Here is where
we live and compare ourselves unconsciously with
others who are either better or worse off than we, or
who are faring better or worse than we. Here is where
the whole of mankind lives, in the peculiar twilight
of the present moment, in which no one knows whether
the day will dawn or whether it will now become a
darker night; here the nations, parties, classes live with
their particular necessities and particular truths, here
also dwell the multitudinous individuals who go their
lonely ways with their thoughts and aspirations, with

that which they would love to promote and proclaim.
And every man's ways are clean in his own eyes. And
each one thinks that he is justified in walking his
own way and convinced that he must walk in precisely
that way in which he is walking, nursing his inner complaints or his joys in his workaday conduct, his love
or his hate.

We can quarrel with one another about what we
regard in our own eyes. One could say to another:
You do not mean well, or, you have no intention of
meaning well. It is not right for you to weep and
to laugh then and there, to speak and behave thus and
thus. Look and take notice how I regard things in
my own sight. Behold, how clean my way is. One
can also lose his zeal to quarrel about what others
regard as good and clean. But what *is* clean, if every
man can regard *his* way as clean? Does it not all
amount to this, that our ways are all unclean? Behold, that is our life, when faced with the great "but"
of the Bible. In the face of that "but" *all* the life
of mankind is clean and, yet, nothing is clean. *All*
yes and *all* no. Whoever is satisfied in this pride and
doubt in this twilight and fog, does not hear this
"but." Whoever cannot endure this twilight hears
and notices and understands. He places himself in
the unambiguous light which falls upon our lives from
on high.

But the Lord weigheth the spirits. Are our ways
clean or unclean, are we right or wrong in our living,
thinking and speaking, if the Lord weighs the spirits?
We must say, *No*, we are not right. Who can be right
in God's judgment? Who can remain calm and self-

reliant when he is placed in the scales of God? Who
is there that cares to stand before Him? *No*, in His
presence we can but become terrified, become humble;
in His sight all this strife about what is clean in our
own eyes comes to an end, before Him everything
that would stand and remain firm is shattered and
dissolved. But we must say *Yes*, too, for who does
not have the right, who could not secure the right
through the grace of God? Who could not be secure,
calm and hopeful if he is in the scale of *God?* Who
cannot stand in the power of forgiveness? Are we
not His own, known of Him, moved by Him? Does
not the death-line, which is the life-line, pass through
the midst of our life? Why should not our ways be
clean before Him?

No and Yes can be said of us, *No and Yes* is the
truth of our lives. In God there is no opposition
to us. In God we persevere, for in Him is stimulus,
life, hope. There is nothing but Yes and No in God,
only because of the Yes. Those people who have
heard the "but" no longer are disturbed about the
No and the Yes; they pilgrim, they toil, they pray
from one to the other; they have, even as prisoners,
something of the freedom of the coming world within
themselves. Fearful and certain in spirit they are
even now God's witnesses and preparers of the way.
Do not let anyone say, "I cannot hear." Jesus has
spoken, even to *our* life: I am the resurrection and
the life!

THE NAME OF THE LORD

The name of Jehovah is a strong tower; the righteous runneth into it and is safe.—Proverbs 18:10.

I am not sure that we have often prayed, with understanding and sincerity, the first petition of the Lord's Prayer: "Hallowed be thy name!" We presume to understand what is meant by the "kingdom" and the "will" of God, in the second and third petitions. We feel that these and the petitions that follow them directly concern us. But what is meant by the *name* of God? On this point we are *not* in the clear. To be honest, does not the term sound strange and distant to us? Have we not secretly asked ourselves what really is the vital and weighty thing in the word 'name'? We found no answer, in spite of the excellent definition of the term in the Lutheran and Heidelberg Catechisms. This is a fact worthy of consideration. For the petition, "hallowed be thy name," was the first that Jesus put into the mouth of his disciples; and it is the gate of entrance to all the others. If we do not enter by this gate we shall be perplexed and confused when we offer the other petitions, however well we may think we understand them. This is not merely a so-called "religious" question. For as one prays so one lives and walks and behaves.

He who prays our Lord's Prayer aright will be

heard; in difficult and adverse circumstances his way will become clearer, more steady, more perfect, as perfect as the way of a man can be. Indeed we do not see many men walking so perfect a way. Even we ourselves are not men of this sort. Perchance the real trouble in our difficult times is that we are so dull of hearing and that in our lives so little of the perfect way is manifest. On this account we are restless and like the disciples we are driven to ask Jesus: "Lord, teach us to pray!"—to pray so that we shall be heard. Both they and we have been taught how to pray; therefore we are not to learn something new, but to apply and practice what we have been taught. To speak honestly, we stumble, as it were, into the Lord's Prayer, when we offer the petition, "hallowed be thy name!" and when we think we are advancing into the other petitions, which we presume to understand better than the first, we are actually standing still. Our failure to listen attentively, our uncertain and disorderly conduct, the want of answers to our prayers, is evidence of this fact; and, if we are not to sink like Peter into the waves of the sea, we must begin anew with the cry, "Lord, help us!" yea, with the simplest and profoundest thing—with the beginning, with the name of the Lord.

But what is meant by the name of the Lord? The answer of the text is not learned, not pious, not ingenious; but short and complete as the answers of the Bible usually are: "The name of the Lord is a strong tower." We are quite right when we feel that here we have to do with something alien, that we are standing on the outside, as it were, against an

astounding other which is not in any way a part of
ourselves.

The name of the Lord does not come from the
heart, the head, or the conscience.   One cannot experience Him, that is, take Him into one's life so that
He becomes a part of oneself.   The name of the Lord
is and remains far rather a contradiction that is raised
against us, a hostile bridge-head in the midst of our
land.   Jesus teaches us to pray: "Our Father who
art in heaven!"   With these words the deepest things,
the only thing necessary, all is said, that we can say
to God and that has the promise of being heard.
Upon these four words: "Our Father in heaven,"
one's life can be based, by them one can live and die
—providing we say these words after Jesus as He
has said them for us.   Because this truth is not self-evident, Jesus spoke more than these four words.

The first and the most direct is a call to halt! halt,
for you have taken the name of God upon your lips.
Do you know what ye have done?   Perhaps the noblest thing that a man can do, perhaps the meanest;
perhaps the saving act of humility and knowledge,
perhaps the act of immeasurable conceit and haughti-
ness.   What have we to do with God?   Praying is not
a work like other works.   "Put off thy shoes from off
thy feet, for the place whereon thou standest is holy
ground!"   The name of the Lord is to be hallowed.
Otherwise prayer is not prayer.   Pray that you may
pray aright, that you will actually pray to God.   Then
perchance you will learn further how to pray; and,
while you pray, ye are heard already because you have
prayed to God.

One cannot walk so easily on a straight and even
path, into the presence of the Father in heaven, not
even through Christ—above all, *not* through *Him!*
Only when one has become severely and unequivo-
cally serious with the hallowing of the name of God,
then in Him, that is in Christ can he come to the
Father. The name of God is the name of *God.* It is
repellent, stern, yes, terrifying. That is the "strong
tower" of our text. Later we are told one can flee
to it and be exalted by it. But first one must have
discerned how like a tower, like a rock, how threaten-
ing He rises ahead of him. He who has never fled
before Him, cannot flee *unto* Him. And he who there
has *not been humbled,* cannot there *be exalted.* But,
once again, what is meant by "the name of the Lord"?
The name of a thing or a man is the symbol by which
we are taught that this is this, he is he; the limits by
which we distinguish persons or things, that are equal
or similar, from one another. So it is with the name
of God. It is the mark of God's separateness and
otherness over against everything that is not God. He
who speaks the name of God makes use of this mark.

But there is another trait peculiar to the name of
God. In the beginning of the Bible (and what we
read there is full of meaning) we are told that man,
by God's command and yet by his own free and rational judgment, gave names "to all cattle and to the
birds of the heavens and to every beast of the field;"
and finally he named the woman, the creature of his
own kind. That reminds us that the names we give,
the limits and distinctions we draw (between the creatures themselves and between men and other crea-

tures) are valid or invalid according to the accuracy
or the error of our insight. They are not worthless
but meaningful and useful; we must not be astonished,
however, because these limits are so easily defaced
and changed, and, in the last resort, so questionable
and frail that the names we give and those we hear
are not holy but in the end—here the poet is right—
are mere sound and breath. But one is wrong when
one says this of the name of God. For man did
not, and does not, give God His name. The distinctive thing that separates God from every other,
also from us men, man is not able to measure; nor
can he see the mark that indicates the distinctive thing
in God, that divides God's land from man's land.

The divine right of giving names belongs not only
to man. But as the Bible tells us (again rich in meaning): Only God Himself can call Himself by name,
and when men know His name, they know it only
(with fear and trembling) because God Himself has
revealed it to them—first to Abraham: "I am God
almighty!" then to Moses: "I am that I am!" But
God has not revealed it that men, again unafraid,
may take the name of God upon their lips; but that
when men give a name to God according to their
own, free, rational judgment, however well or ill they
may understand it, they at the same time can and
shall keep in mind the name that God has given and
gives Himself. It was, therefore, a fine custom of
the ancient Jews (and I do not make light of it!)
that they refrained from taking the revealed name of
God—"I am that I am"—upon their lips; but, filled
with awe, they felt that it did not become man to

pronounce God's name and therefore substituted man's name for God—"the Lord." By this reserve they were constantly reminded that God Himself was and is He who reveals to His people the unique and distinctive being that He is. At least one may question whether the unrestrained freedom of speech of Christians about the ultimate and deepest being of God ought more to be commended than the diffidence and restraint of the ancient Jew. The revealed name of God, which one keeps in mind but which actually cannot be spoken by human lips, is not mere sound and breath but an eternal name. It is the landmark set by God between Himself and all creatures visible to men, indicating that He is always God and not a creature. This mark of separation is not changeable and perishable, but, in the words of the text, is a strong tower, holy and terrible; therefore, for us He is the strange, the new, the beyond, the above, never from us, never in us, yet to be feared, loved, praised, and invoked by us.

If you will again ask me: what is the name of God and where and how shall we seek it? I can only reply that we usually do not seek Him, but only find Him; or far rather, only those, who already have found Him, can seek Him. He lets Himself be found—that's it. Where? What else shall I say than what has been said of old: "there where a man sees that he is a sinner, that he must die, that his world passeth away." There God sets bounds to the endlessness of the sinner's sin and death, the transitoriness of his world and says: "I, the Holy One, I, who live and reign in eternity, I, the Creator and Redeemer of this world!" This "I," which is the boundary of man's land, is the name of God. But God Himself must utter this "I"; otherwise it is vain fanaticism.

But how does He speak this "I?" Again I shall say naught but what has been said of old. There is a witness concerning this "I," this revealed name fixed for all of us; though we cannot comprehend that the "I" is spoken. The witness tells us that this "I" has been seen, heard, and handled among God's people and in His only begotten Son; this we are able to hear and to hold for truth. Jesus Christ the boundary of the evil endlessness of man's land! Jesus Christ, who is, in this man's land and for all its inhabitants, the spoken "I"! Jesus Christ the name of God! God Himself must bear testimony to His witness—the testimony of the Holy Spirit in the inner man, so that we can and must hold for truth the outer testimony, the witness of the Scripture. Else it is man's work in man's land like every other work of man. Thus the "name of God" lets itself be found; so it is with the "strong tower," that, according to the Lord's Prayer, stands at the beginning of all praying. It is "strong" because it is wholly built by God himself.

We are told in our text, "the righteous runneth into it." Mark well, running is not an evidence of strength and virtue, not even when one flees to "the name of the Lord." We should like to represent the coming to the heavenly Father in another way: as a soaring up and breaking through, as a battle won and a triumphal entry. But we are not to come in this way; for only as the "righteous *runneth* into it" will

God's name be hallowed. A man who fulfills the first petition will not cut an imposing figure. He is a fugitive: he runs to the strong tower—from which he hears the cry of warning: "Halt! what seekest thou here?"—only because he cannot be at rest anywhere else; because he is pursued and driven from every other place and has no other resort than to seek refuge in the name of the Lord. This is not an uplifting sight. He who "runs" will be called a weakling. Therefore, for example—I say this to the students who are present—theology, in distinction from other sciences, is not a great and honored science, not an advance but a retreat; it is in essence a flight from all human names (also from the human names of God!) to the revealed name of the Lord.

Theology, therefore, does not cut a fine figure. All this must be so. One cannot be, in the words of the text, "the righteous" and at the same time present an imposing spectacle. Here one must make a choice. To "the name of the Lord" we can only "run." He who walks triumphantly goes where he is exalted; only the humble "run." He whom this name draws nigh will find all names given of men, spite of all their worth, to be nothing but sound and breath. A man's confidence in his own understanding and comprehension must be so completely shaken that he cannot keep himself from taking a last impossible step into the darkness in which he and all that he has will be lost forever, unless he believes that through the darkness he will approach the light of God. Believe! That means defeat and flight. How remarkable, how questionable is a man who believes! How great is the danger of conceit, of self-deception through a wish-dream, of a leap which can only be a leap into death! He who believes must drop all these considerations. In this manner and mood one must run to the name of the Lord, not a name given of men, the boundary stone erected by God between man's land and God's land.

How is this to be justified before the eye of man? The "righteous" is the man who has received new eyes to see the *other* in God, His might, His wisdom, His love. Not his way of flight makes a man "righteous"; he is righteous because all other ways are closed to him. Not his running makes him righteous, but the name of the Lord which is the only thing that is left him. Faith is his righteousness; not faith as his work, but faith that lays hold of and subjects him, faith that is a necessity from which he cannot escape. He cannot triumph, cannot be in the right, cannot make claims; for he is a wholly weak, dishonorable, sinful, and unrighteous righteous man. But in such righteousness, through such faith, the first petition: "Hallowed be thy name!" is fulfilled. For when a man "runs" to the name of God and thus gives honor and right to God, not in wisdom but in foolishness, not in power but in weakness, above all not in extreme piety but rather in extreme godlessness, and notwithstanding "runs" thither, lays hold of this name, says "yes," then God's name is known, the name revealed only by Him. In this way faith, for which we must pray, is the true hallowing of the name of God.

It has often been said that our time, with the abolition and dissolution of so many human names, signs and boundaries, is especially favorable for understanding what is meant by running to and believing in the name of the Lord. True, in these years we all feel as if we were sailing hopelessly on a sinking ship and we take it for granted that it cannot be otherwise; so, with one accord, we cry: "Lord, how shall we comfort ourselves? we hope in Thee!" On the contrary this is not the real situation. The indications are that the ship may sink and is sinking; yet an ever increasing number of our contemporaries know how to comfort one another in the cinema or at the football game. Even if we, who are of the better sort, examine ourselves, we shall find that all of us at this time comfort one another, though it may be in a refined, spiritual and devout way. We know how to take courage without God, that we have not lost our confidence in others, in human names, and that much remains for us besides refuge in the name of God. Only let us not imagine that this will ever be otherwise! Things are thus because we are human. The ship may continue to sink for a long time, as deep as in Russia and even deeper—yet with the sinking and on account of it, flight into the strong tower and righteousness through faith will not come. If events and conditions, like these by which we are surrounded, cannot teach us faith, by what else can we be taught to believe? To speak as men, we can only say that we do not learn faith, never will learn faith, neither from ourselves nor under the stress of fate and evil times. Faith comes from God each moment, and when it comes we can say nothing else, astonished and perplexed, but: "I believe, dear Lord, help my unbelief!"

And now, finally, it is said of the "righteous" who runs to the name of the Lord: "He will be exalted." I cannot tell whether he will know himself to be secure. Perhaps he himself is not sure. The chief thing, at any rate, is not what he knows or imagines he knows, but what *is*, not in his own power nor in the power of the "certainty" of his believing, but in the power of the name of the Lord. "He will be exalted": not in vain has he been subdued, humbled, or put to flight. "It shall be that he who calleth on the name of the Lord, will be saved." This is his exaltation that he comes into the light of this promise. The holy and dreadful name of the Lord, revealed to those who run thither—for where else shall they go? He is kind, friendly, nigh to save. The mark of that which is other in God is his distinctive doing and giving; only through revelation, an impartation of God passing all understanding, is it given unto us and do we have even the proof that God has graciously turned and come nigh unto us. The boundary, that separates God's land from man's land, is the boundary, the aim, and the end of unrest, torment, and tears in which we here live and move. He who runs thither, runs well. Ah yes, his faith is the weak, divided, unsatisfactory faith of man, which each moment deserves also to be called unbelief. And yet, on this account, it is true that he has received another faith from God; and in this faith, though groaning under the whole burden of his human nature and all that belongs to it, he has seen from afar (as the publican in the temple) the throne of God. This seeing from afar is the exaltation of the righteous. Ah yes, fear and trembling continue, even the righteousness that we can know only as the righteousness of the sinner. But in this incomprehensible righteousness of the sinner, the other word has its power which apparently is the reverse of that which we hitherto heard: "He who believes, will not flee."

He who once has fled *from* the name of God and then has fled *to* Him; no, he who, on account of the knowledge of himself, must again and again do this, he really needs no more to flee *from* no one and nothing *to* no one and nothing. And if he does it again (and he will do it!), he does not lack in all his uncertainty the most sacred and secret certainty: "I lay me down and sleep in peace; for thou alone, Lord, helpest me, that I dwell in safety." Glory shines out of his shame, strength out of his weakness. Once again: *his* safety, *his* honor, *his* power do not abide for a moment, but: "Only Thou, Lord!" But this is enough. We conclude plainly as we began: This is the exaltation of the righteous, who has run to the name of the Lord, that he is put on the way to pray aright the Lord's Prayer, and to pray further: "Thy kingdom come! Thy will be done! Give us this day our daily bread! And forgive us our debts! And lead us not into temptation!" For who the "Thou" is, to whom with all these petitions he turns, can no longer be wholly hid from him.

THE NEW TIME

God hath set eternity into the heart of man, without which he
could not find out what God does from the beginning to the end.—
Ecclesiastes 3:11.

Perhaps today we understand anew what the Bible
tries to tell us through the word "eternity." At any
rate we are more ready to listen when it speaks of
eternity, than we were in the years and decades before
the war. Eternity is not time—in no sense of the
word. It is neither the infinitely vast sum of all
times, nor is it the so-called new, better time that,
after the passing of all bad times, will finally come
to be. Eternity is eternity; and by that we mean
that it is beyond, hidden from all times, separated
from them by a gulf that (at least from an earthly
point of view) once for all divides eternity and time.
This gulf can never be bridged by progress and development. For faith, which actually carries us across
the abyss, has naught to do with progress and development or with any other upward struggle and
effort of man. Faith comes from God—"God has
set eternity in the heart of man."

Perhaps we understand this saying a little better
today. For we all have come out of a time in which
men have tried, of their own might, to put eternity
into their hearts. But today, through grievous sacrifices, we have been taught, more clearly than ever,
that all these attempts of men have utterly failed.

We do not say that even we will not listen when one speaks to us of the possibilities of progress and development, of the dawning of a new time. But the brightest and best of all times is none the less time; and time is not eternity—no time as such will arise and turn out of the way and course of all time. He who actually waits for eternity, tarries for eternity, tarries and waits, whether he knows it or not, for the end of times. Upon this let us meditate together.

Men speak much today of new times that are about to break in upon us. Gladly, oh so gladly, would we all leave the previous and present order and enter into a world and life of a new order. Gladly would we make a new beginning, as if we were crossing a broad river into a new and better haven. There always is something similar to such a crossing and new beginning. There are clefts in the life of a time as a whole, or of a man, which divide and separate the former from the latter; the old ends, the new begins. But, if we are candid, we must say: "The real, the new, the wholly different life and existence which we actually want and seek is not the new life that begins on the other side of the cleft or with a change of direction." One may begin a new period in life and yet continue to live the old life. Even after conversion we have only apparently crossed the stream to the other bank. In fact those who claim to be converted, separate from the old world, are still living in the same surroundings in which they lived before conversion. In truth, after the deepest experience of a change in life the other shore to which we belong lies still ahead of us. We can only look

toward it with yearning hearts and be prepared for
new turnings and decisions.

The mark of those who actually progress in their
inner life, who have gone through turnings and con-
versions, is that they will say: "We have not gone
very far, we are still a long way from the goal where
inwardly we should be and where one leads a life
that deserves to be called a *new* life." At least the
men of the Bible, who actually have felt something
of a cleavage in their life, have this conviction. Of
those who have given up the ground of their old existence and who have left behind the narrow gate,
nothing is said in our stories of conversion. Among
them there is not one who, to the end of life, has
not been an expectant man, yes, actually become one
by his conversion.

It is so, also, with the times. There are new times
and old times. There are deep clefts. On this side
lies an old, on the other a new, epoch. The French
Revolution was, for example, such a cleft, the last
great one from which we have come. One need only
have read casually the thoughts and words of the
men one hundred and one hundred and fifty years
ago to see how profoundly they felt themselves standing in the dawn of a new age. But is it not true that
today we no longer quite understand the enthusiasm
of that time? We know, however, that the new time
that then dawned was by no means really *the* new
time. It was the new nineteenth century, that now
in its turn lies closed before us as another "old time."
On the contrary, according to our wish and view, the
new time ought just to begin. It is necessary and

wholesome to remember that we are standing in a cleft which divides two times.

At such a moment one is so liable to be wrong. One turns passionately from the old that recedes from us and turns with enthusiasm to the new that is coming toward us. The much abused nineteenth century, out of which we have come, doubtless has its dark spots; its close proves it; but it surely has also much that is good and great. The reproach, that it did not really become the new time of which we dreamt when we stood at its cradle, is justified only when we are assured that the time which is now dawning is actually the new time—the time when salvation and truth will finally be brought to light. But will it be such a time? To ask the question, I think, is to answer it.

What do we mean by all this? Are we to imply that we are to bury all our hopes, to fold our hands and say: "Alas, a new time, another time, there will never be"? No, but rather say: "The really new man, the really new time for which we are waiting and of which the Bible speaks in sublime language, is unspeakably greater than, and wholly different from, anything that we may call new and other." So great and so different is the new man and the new time for which we are waiting, that everything that appears among us as new and different is, in contrast to the truly new, again only the old; and that all changing from something new, which takes place among us, can be understood only as a parable of the change to the truly new. This truly new, really other, time is no more *our* time. It is, in no sense, man's

time; it is God's time. The "time of refreshing
before the face of the Lord."

Because it is wholly God's and not man's time, it
does not come in the coming and going of our time;
God's days and hours are not earthly days and hours.
It is written that upon earth one can know nothing
of them. "The day and hour no one knows." Like
a strange, dark land, God's time lies over against our
time. It is an undiscovered new continent that we
cannot enter, excepting we have left behind us our
time, man's time, the time in which our whole ter-
restrial life runs its course. This time is no more
time; it is eternity. And what else shall we say of
eternity than that we know nothing about it save this:
that in everything it differs wholly from that which
we know here and now.

But now we may be tempted to ask: "Is there such
a thing as this wholly different time? Why do we
speak of this time, which is not time at all, when
we actually know nothing about it?" But when we
ask thus we begin to see that we must change our
question and say: "Is there a time without eternity?"
Whence comes this remarkable insight which enables
us to perceive that all that is seen by us as new is
not the really new, if this really new does not exist?
Why can we not cease pushing restlessly forward, if
there is not another shore over against us which we
have not yet reached and yet must reach? Why
must we forever think of this unattained, other, invisible haven? Why must we always be deprived of
it, always see it ahead of us, always seek it? Why
can we not come to an agreement with ourselves and

with one another that there never will be anything
but insatiable need and unrealized hope; and with this
we shall rest satisfied? Why can we not accustom
ourselves to the thought that there is no God; or, if
there be a God, that He is and will always be far off
and unapproachable? Why is it that something so
remarkably great and full of hope reverberates constantly in the thoughts, concerns and wishes with which
we look upon our lives and the lives of men generally? Can we think even of the shortest step that
can and ought to be taken forward without, at the
same time, if we are actually to succeed, turning to
the All Highest, to the help and blessing of God,
without which nothing can be done? "Without me
ye can do nothing." Why can we not cease to seek
after that "which God does from the beginning to
the end"? Is it perhaps, after all, too true, too great,
too real?

Can we prevent eternity from shining and from
speaking here and there into our time as though it were
pacing beside us, step by step? Is it not *the* perfect,
the wholly other, which, whether we like it or not, in
spite of all the imperfect earthly on this bank of the
stream, reaches into our existence? Do we not see, in
all our doings, that we are brought to the point where
we must say: "I am far from the best"? That which
I actually would, I do not attain. Something wholly
other and new should be reached in my life; and we
must always pause and stand waiting for this new,
other, better, that is beyond the border, if perchance
it may come to us. Our whole life is spent in skirting
this border line, the whole of our time is an expec-

tation of a wholly other time, a waiting for eternity.

And, may I add: "Do we not see that it is just this point in our life, to which we are led again and again, and where we stand at the border, where we can only wait and hope, that is really the vital point from which the deepest impulses and the greatest virtue flow into us?" Is it not clear that the best in our lives is not knowledge and power, but our deep longing for redemption, the shame and unrest in which we must always press forward to something that is different from anything that we are and have. For we live not by the few answers which we know how to give to the questions of our existence, but by the quest for a wholly different answer, for the answer which God alone can give—that we, in the midst of the time of man, must await the Eternity of God; that we, in the midst of all imperfection, will be touched by the divine perfection, and by this we live. "God has set eternity into the heart of man." This indicates need and unrest, but such need and unrest is salvation and blessedness. We must seek after eternity; but it may become clear to us, that this "must" means also a "can"—"Blessed are the poor in spirit."

Thus we are in the midst of man's time and cannot understand it without God's time which is behind it and above it. Ever and anon we are tempted to think that there is no eternity; for what should mortal man wish to know of eternity. Yet out of 'our temporal and mortal state we cannot cease to look toward it. For there is not a moment in time that in its finiteness and limitations does not cry out for eternity.

We are always before it as before the unintelligible, incomprehensible, and super-earthly; but we are, none the less, in the presence of it and must bow and pray before it.

Thus the two shores come together—that of time and that of eternity. We know that they are separated from each other; but no, they are not separated, because God has put eternity into the heart of man. We know that there never is a new, another time in the course of time; and yet we cannot cease to seek for it and wander toward it through time. We know that we are sinful, mortal men; and yet—are we only this? Are we not something wholly different, even children of God? To be sure, it is not yet made manifest what we shall be; but we know that if it shall be manifested, we shall be like Him. Again and again we must say: "World remains world." War, sickness, death will never end; yet, contrary to appearance and experience, we cannot forbear to think of something wholly different—of a world of freedom and of righteousness, of peace and of life. We cannot cease believing that this new, other world it really the true, actual, coming and abiding world, in comparison with which the world that we have before our eyes will be blown away as sand and dust.

Do I say too much? Do I say more than is true? Yes, surely, I say too much, I say more than is true so far as we look at ourselves, think of ourselves, of that which is before our eyes, of the ordinary, small, miserable, commonplace man, whom we all are. He does not *stand* before God, he flees before Him; he does not believe in eternity, he does not live in the fear and adoration of the Lord. And, therefore, seen from his standpoint, the world always remains as it is. But I do not say too much and do not say anything that is not true, when I think of Him in whom this eternal, incomprehensible and true (though contrary to appearance) revelation is given unto us: Christ Jesus. While we are what we are, poor, small, sinning, dying, commonplace people, who each moment forget the eternity which we are approaching, He came and took our forgetfulness of eternity upon Himself and bore it, took it for us upon Himself and carried it for us; for us He thought of God, became for us, through struggling and suffering, obedient unto death, yes unto death on the cross, and by death He broke through into eternal life.

If it is true that God has put eternity into the heart of man; if it is more than a distant wishing and hoping; if it is so true that we can live and die by it, then it is true only in Jesus Christ. In Him the opposite shores come together, in Him that which is divided becomes united, in Him time and eternity meet. In Him God, who is hidden from us and of whom we of ourselves can know nothing, is revealed as the Father.

Hence everything depends upon this, that Jesus Christ speaks to us men who pass on with the fleeting times. There are men and times to whom Jesus Christ becomes manifest. They are not yet new times and new men in the final sense; but they are the times and the men that, in the midst of the old time and of the old condition, point and aim toward the really new time and the really new men who hear the word of the eternal love of the Father, the word of the forgiveness of sins, and know the one thing besides which there is nothing else. There are times and men that have to do with eternity, because they have learnt to look upon Him who has brought to light eternity in the midst of time. Life for such men does not flow smooth and easy. He, who has received eternity into his heart, must seek to understand "what God does from the beginning to the end." That means unrest, conflict, and pilgrimage. But there is rest in this unrest, there is victory in this struggle; this pilgrimage has a goal and an end. For God has set eternity into the heart of man, and how could God leave those without an answer who at His behest are seeking Him?

If such a time ever dawns—and why should it not dawn? Let it bring what it will in other respects, it will be a new time (yet with all reserve be it said!), a year of salvation and refreshing, a year in which peace and truth and righteousness will come to light, even though it be a time of heaviness. Let us pray God that He send us such a time and make us men of such a sort. If we earnestly pray for it, the new time has come through such praying; for how could we earnestly beseech Him, if He had not already heard us, had He not already set eternity into our hearts through His Spirit?

THE SMALL MOMENT

For a small moment have I forsaken thee; but with great mercies will I gather thee. In overflowing wrath I hid my face from thee for a moment; but with everlasting lovingkindness will I have mercy on thee, saith Jehovah thy Redeemer. For this is as the waters of Noah unto me; for as I have sworn that the waters of Noah shall no more go over the earth, so have I sworn that I will not be wroth with thee nor rebuke thee. For the mountains may depart, and the hills be removed; but my lovingkindness shall not depart from thee, neither shall my covenant of peace be removed, saith Jehovah that hath mercy on thee.—*Isaiah 54:7-10.*

Our text speaks of a "small moment." But it is the moment of wrath, when God has forsaken us and hid His face from us; while the waters of Noah go over the earth, the mountains depart, and the hills are removed. In a "small moment" Adam sinned and in "a small moment" Christ died on the cross. But how great was and is the darkness of these small moments. Measured by the endless ages of the mountains, the sea, and the stars, my life, also, is but a "small moment." But when I consider that the riddle of my life is the moment of my guilt and punishment, it seems to me the endless times are no longer than this "small moment." The dark, grievous years, through which the nations of the earth are now going, will be regarded in the future as "a small moment," of which one may speak in the shortest words; a curious picture from the distant past in which few will be interested. But what then will appear as a mere drop, our unrighteous deeds and sufferings, our woe and helplessness, is, in this "small moment" of the present, a great ocean, for it is *our wrong, our woe, our distress.* Sometime there will be for each of us a "small moment" when we die, die as our fathers did. The narrow gap behind us will quickly be closed up and the small track which we have made will soon be obliterated. But the small moment will determine whether we shall go from reality into nothingness or from nothingness into reality. All our earlier decisions will be questioned, and, by a knife's edge, it will be decided whether our way has led into eternal life or into eternal death. And this will be most difficult—in no case can we ourselves give the answer; neither by what we wish, nor by what we know, nor by what we are. *Dies irae, dies illa* (day of wrath, that day); who, O Lord, can stand in thy presence?

What is meant by a "small moment," when the smallest moment through the weight of its content outweighs thousands of years, when it is at hand, not in the past, not in the future, but in the present. Should not the moment, of which the prophet speaks, be just as long as time? Or will there be a moment in time, of which, when it has come, we can speak with the same dreadful seriousness as the prophet speaks of the "small moment," and which will turn it into a really weighty, great, unending moment? Yes, it is a "small moment," says the word of God. But that it is small does not seem true to men—one cannot merely say so. When it is said, it is either one of those cheap consolations with which men try to comfort one another or it is true, mighty, comforting, redemptive as the spoken, revealed, unbelievable word of God, which one can only believe.

A "moment of wrath," the prophet calls it. At any rate he does not think of comforting us as men seek to comfort one another. He does not try to make easy what becomes easy only when it is taken to be altogether difficult. He tells us that the door of our prison is bolted on the outside and can be opened only from the outside. In answer to the question: Why this "moment," so "small" and yet so great, is so mysterious? he says what one scarcely dare say after him: "Because God is angry, because he has forsaken us, because he has hid his face from us." That is what is meant by this "moment."

Or do *we* understand it better? O yes, at any rate, we may understand it better. We need much grace and truth before we really will accept the word of the Bible concerning the wrath of God. No more and no less is needed than that which was first told us: "My lovingkindness shall not depart from thee, neither shall my covenant of peace be removed." Whence could we know what time is, if we did not know what eternity is? Whence would we know that, without God, we are lost, if we would not be saved through God? In Jesus Christ we know what eternity is, that we are saved through God. But before we know this and since we constantly forget it, we simply cannot bear to hear of the wrath of God; we oppose it with innumerable restrictions, mitigations, and open or secret protests. You may have looked

deep, yea very deep, into the goodness and the bad-
ness of man; you are not ready to grant that the
last word that may be said by us, from our point of
view, is that man is under wrath, indeed under the
wrath of God. Perhaps you are a severely humiliated
and, through the discipline of life, a broken man;
but something within you rises in protest when you
are told that God is, for you and all of us, really
and truly a hidden God.

The honor of God may lie close to your heart and
you gladly will grant that His thoughts are higher
than our thoughts; but for the sake of the very honor
of God, as you imagine, you will deny that His
thoughts are so much higher than our thoughts as to
compel us to concede that for "a small moment he
has forsaken us." If there is a God, you will say:
"All this must be taken as figurative language." But
how do you know this? What do you call "God"?
Is He what you try to think for yourself of God and
what you can think of Him—or is He the One who
has revealed Himself and whom men can only believe?
He, who believes in the revealed God, will not quarrel
about His hiddenness. You say: "I live!" You are
able to lay hold of God in the world of reality or as
the author of your corporal, psychic, spiritual, religious being. True, you live, but you live no other
than a life subject to death from the crown of your
head to the sole of your foot. What do you know
of aught beyond? What do you know of the presence of God in your present life? But, you will say,
in my conscience I have come to terms with my God.
I reply: "Can you come to accord, in your conscience,

with God about anything else than this: that you are under judgment?"

You complain: "How disturbing, how intolerable, how unsatisfactory is the picture of our condition, if things are thus!" And you remind yourself of Jesus Christ. Men say that through His coming the world has become another world and that we are no longer under the law of the Old Testament. But would not Jesus pray today as He prayed then: "My God, my God, why hast thou forsaken me!" And did He do this only that we might be spared the necessity of facing the truth of human life, which is the same yesterday and today? Or may we turn away from this truth because it is so disturbing and unsatisfying? And then you reply: "But God cannot always be angry, nor can he wholly have forsaken us!" Now you are really close to what the prophet says. For he says explicitly: "A small moment have I forsaken thee! For a short time have I hid my face from thee!" But listen closely! He speaks of that which remains when nothing else remains for us. He speaks of the God whom *he* has found and who has found *him*. When he says: "not always, not altogether!" he does not wish thereby to justify and to save either himself or the world; he knows that he cannot do that; he knows that the "moment" is the moment of the wrath of God. Why do you defend yourself against this? Is not, perhaps, the very defense itself, which we put up with more or less ground against the word of God's wrath, proof of the truth of this word? May it not have been just this that Adam was the man who made paradise impossible for himself and was driven out into a world upon which God's wrath rests, into a world in which the mountains always depart and the hills are always moved—this creature that will have everything; that will be moral, good, pious; but that will not acknowledge that in him there is nothing to save and to justify, so that with his own knowledge of good and evil he can only die?

Is the shadow in which we walk perhaps so dark because all of us are bearing our own torches with so much ardor and refuse to have them taken from us? Is perchance the need which man suffers, nothing else than man himself who wants to judge instead of permitting himself to be judged? Is it perhaps so difficult for us to hear and heed and believe the words of the most blessed promise, with which the prophet would point us beyond the "small moment" of wrath, because we stand in the midst of this "small moment," as sure as we are human beings whether we would or not, and yet we are always stirred to revolt and rebellion against the truth, against the meaning of this "moment"? O that for a second only we could see ourselves from without (as we see others). How as upright citizens, as cultured men, as Christians, or simply as men we always defend ourselves, defend ourselves against the fact that we are under the wrath of God. If we could hear the arguments that we put forth to show that it cannot be so bad with us; if we could see and hear how out of these arguments and of this attitude with which we deny God what belongs to Him, all the guilt and with it all the punishment which we suffer have come from the beginning of the world—then with one accord we would say Yes to that which we dispute. Yes, God *is angry* with us, has hid his face from us, has forsaken us, has let us follow our heart's desires. How else could we be as we are? Just because we fight against it, because we are building up our whole life upon the will to do as though we stood in normal relation and fellowship with God, we prove how true that is which we fight against.

And when we no longer fight and lay down arms, we acknowledge and confess how it stands with God and us. I have said already this cannot happen unless we have heard what is spoken through the prophet: "Hear ye! But with great mercy will I gather thee! But with everlasting lovingkindness will I have mercy on thee! But my lovingkindness shall not depart from thee! neither shall the covenant of peace be removed." Take heed that by repeating three times the awful "But!" he says this wholly other? And parenthetically he adds, as if God permitted him to share his counsel: "I have sworn that I will not be wroth with thee nor rebuke thee!" And for the sake of the second he spoke the first. Only because he speaks that glorious word, does he speak this dreadful word. Only where *this* light is can *that* shadow fall. *That* may be the way, *this* is the goal. And the way is here for the sake of the goal, not the reverse. *That* may be called knowledge but *this* the *truth;* and the truth is before knowledge; and when the truth is here, knowledge ceases. Or, *that* the truth of man, *this* the truth of God; and *this* is greater, infinitely greater, than the truth of man, and only by beginning with *it* can *that* be known. Behold, now the prophet says that which hitherto we have missed; what we thought we had to add by deceitfully limiting or supplementing. Does it not become clear to us how much richer, more powerful, and more believable, the threefold "but" of the prophet sounds than the little "and yet!" which we keep ready for our justification and deliverance? Do we not keenly feel the difference between that which on our lips is only a pious wish that will never be fulfilled, and that which on his lips is a promise that bears its fulfilment with it? He received them at that moment when all their pious and impious wishes became dumb. Not *therefore*—but *then* "spoke the Lord." What is the content of this promise?

Again one may ask himself whether one can and may seriously repeat after him what he has said here. But the Bible is open, let us read it to the end. True, the prophet says God will not always be angry, nor has he wholly forsaken us. True, God reveals himself, rending the veil of his secrecy just there where it seems to be most impervious. True, God is in the center of our life, just there, where, through death, is confirmed what our life in truth is. No, God is not angry forever; He is angry so long as time lasts, but His grace is eternal. And if it is the disagreeable human pride in which God's wrath takes form, punishing us with that with which we sin, it is true also that this pride is not eternal, that it lasts only as long as time; eternal is the other—the forgiveness which destroys sin, though we still must bear its penalty; eternal is the truth that we are God's dear and humble children. And, understand it well, there is no time that is without eternity, no condemning human truth without a comforting divine truth, no earthly goalless way without the light of the heavenly goal. We are not what we appear to be, that is, what we have made and are ever making of ourselves in our rebellion and revolt. We are not what we must acknowledge and confess ourselves to be, far removed from God, separated from God, laden with the divine curse. How could we acknowledge ourselves as such, if we were not already the children of grace and mercy?

Our acknowledging and our confessing are indeed true to that which we are at the moment; grace, that triumphs in our acknowledgment and confession, is eternal. And while it triumphs, the moment is to the "small moment" as an island in the endless ocean. And now the mountains may depart and the hills be removed, yea, the "moment" may be death and hell itself, it is still only the "moment." "My lovingkindness shall not depart from thee, neither shall my covenant of peace be removed." But, remember, this is not a truth like other truths. One cannot affirm or defend it or formulate it into a system. With each breath we would be deprived of the right and the ability to say this, if God had not said it. One can hear it only as God's promise. As a discovery and conclusion of man, it is mere folly. The prophet does not let us doubt that it is only true because God does and will do it: "I will gather thee, I will have mercy on thee, I will not be angry with thee." Take this "I" away, and you will take everything away! Let it be understood then that *we* do not do this, *we* do not know this, we do not have this. God does and knows and has this, and we await it as our heavenly inheritance.

To wait for Him in hope and to be happy, because the Spirit confirms in our hearts what the Word says: "I will . . . saith the Lord!"—that is our portion. For the moment continues, and does not cease to be the moment of wrath. And so we also will not cease to be (without the Spirit and the Word which are God's) children of the Old Testament, by nature children of wrath. The answer to the second great word, that the prophet speaks, can only be faith. And faith that is not empty-handed is not faith.

But can we indeed believe? Is not everything only an artificial human comfort with which we deceive ourselves? What shall I say? The Christian Church must learn again to proclaim the word of God's grace and to listen to it as to God's word. Otherwise it cannot be believed. Without this we hang and hover half way between as those who are apparently dead: not really condemned and not really pardoned, not really abandoned to the wrath of God and not really happy in hope, all by halves, all weak, all only "as if," all only figuratively and with reservation.

Perhaps this is the greatest calamity of our time, that such preaching and hearing of the word of grace, as the word of God, has been taken from us and has not yet been restored to us. And yet we hunger and thirst for reality, for the reality of revelation, without which faith, even though it removes mountains, has no reality to speak of; it is only our little faith. The prophet says: "Thus saith the Lord, thy

Redeemer, the Merciful One." This is reality. Christ in his witnesses is reality for which we hunger and thirst. We may doubt their witness and we do so continually; but we can also believe it, overcome our "no" through its "yes." God be praised, "who according to his great mercy, begat us again to a living hope by the resurrection of Jesus Christ from the dead!" He who will conquer us is the Spirit in whom we pray: "Our help and our beginning is in the name of the Lord who hath made heaven and earth."

THE ETERNAL LIGHT

The sun shall be no more thy light by day; neither for brightness shall the moon give light unto thee: but Jehovah will be unto thee an everlasting light, and thy God thy glory. Thy sun shall no more go down, neither shall thy moon withdraw itself; for Jehovah will be thine everlasting light, and the days of thy mourning shall be ended.—*Isaiah 60:19-20.*

"The Lord will be thy everlasting light!" This is, like the content of the whole Bible, an announcement, a promise. Nothing more, but nothing less.

"Behold I stand at the door and knock!" A strong large hand reaches out after us. What does it want of us? What will become of us in its grip? That is none of our business. We need only know that we are in this hand. He, who knows this, understands the Bible, the heart of the Bible—Jesus Christ. One may live without knowing this, for Jesus Christ does not thrust himself upon anyone. We must again and again remind ourselves that we have forgotten this fact. We may call to Him: "Come, Lord Jesus, be our guest!" but He will not become once for all a member of any household. The announcement is and always will be a question addressed to each of us. For Jesus Christ is and always will be the living word of God; and his thoughts are not our thoughts and our ways are not his ways. We may or may not hear; Jesus Christ speaks to those who have ears to hear.

"The Lord will be thy everlasting light!" How

shall we take this? The words of the text speak a two-fold truth—twofold at least for our ears. First: All lights, the greatest and most brilliant, even the sun and the moon, must lose their splendor and radiance, for another incomparable light will take their place. "I am the Lord!" and: "Thou shalt have no other gods beside me." But let it be remembered that the sun of this light will never set and the moon of this light will not lose its brightness. The days of thy sorrow will have an end. The great enemy, who seeks to rob us of all things, is also the great friend and helper who seeks to give us all things. O that in one word we might speak and hear this contradiction! Here it is actually spoken in a single sentence: "the extinction of all lights and the rising of the one true light, God's taking and giving, judging and pardoning, casting into hell and exalting into heaven, killing and making alive, law and gospel." Hear the one without the other and you hear only the word of man and not the word of God. Hear both in one and one in both and you hear God's word, living, powerful, and sharper than a two-edged sword. But so far human lips have not spoken it and human ears have not heard it as one word. No sooner do we speak and hear it than it divides itself upon our lips and in our ears; it becomes an enigma and a question.

Why must this be? So that each moment God's word may be for us God's own word that must be revealed and believed. Precisely this is necessary, that only with human lips we pronounce and with human ears we hear the contradiction—God's wrath and God's mercy, God's dominion and God's help, God's majesty and God's love, God's law and God's gospel. This enigma in the external words of God must ever again overwhelm us and convince us, witness to us that God's goodness and faithfulness are new every morning, lead us to repentance, raise us up, and so prepare us to let God actually speak and to listen to Him. Were we to ignore the external word with its contradiction and enigma and speak outright with our lips and hear with our ears what God himself says, we perchance would become too haughty. Then we might want again to be like God and for that God could not speak unto us in truth. God speaks to us only when he Himself can speak to us and when we must believe in Him. For this He uses the external word—its darkness and its contradiction.

Behold, by this we all live, that God speaks with us, even He Himself, and tells us that we are His and that His hand has reached out after us. In the end it matters little whether we hear this more from the one side or from the other, whether we hear the first part of the announcement that all lights which shine for us must become extinct so that the everlasting light may lighten us; or hear the second part, that this one light will take for us the place of all others and that then the days of sorrow will end; whether we know ourselves to be judged through God's grace or pardoned by His judgment, whether our helper becomes our Lord or the Lord becomes our helper, whether our heart and conscience are wounded through God's love or healed through God's wrath. If we only will hear and heed the word of God: "I am that I am," and the promise: "I will be your God, ye shall be my people." God and the whole truth of God is in this promise; and, therefore, in it is all comfort, the highest hope, the final victory—even for us who are comfortless, hopeless, defeated. We live by that which Jesus speaks out of the heart of the Bible into the heart of our hearts: "You have not chosen me but I have chosen you." When and how He speaks this—whether in anger or in goodness, whether to our terror or to our rapture, whether we receive it as judgment or as grace; for all that, wherever he speaks it, there is freedom, even though we are sinners and dying men—freedom to live as God's children, always again another day, the next day; what more do we want?—to live, to bear, to endure, to work and not to despair, to make our lives a sacrifice. Here the great never-ending shadow of eternity has fallen upon us and humbled us; and here, just for this reason, we have the great uplifting outlook upon the new heaven and the new earth.

Thus we live by the word of God, just as it comes to us in the letter, a word dark and full of contradictions; as it is constantly revealed to us by God Himself and we are always able to believe it. If there is any one, who does not yet live by it, he awaits the time when he will live by it; and perhaps the difference between the two is not as great as we think. It is quite impossible that there is anyone who does not wait to live by it. For we, as sinful and mortal men, are inseparably bound up with that God who leads from life in death into life. Some one has said: "There is no heart or conscience that is not bent by God to find its master in Jesus of Nazareth."

"The Lord will be thy everlasting light!" O, it is indeed true that we are in dreadful shallows and hear this promise only from afar. How have we come into this state? How is it possible that for so many days and hours we are comfortless, hopeless, defeated without being called to a consideration of the divine "nevertheless"? Why is it that our life in its farthest reaches is not under the healing shadow of eternity but in the shadow of a stupefying godlessness, though we are by no means atheists but so-called believing Christians? Where is the clear light of the eternal day of Jesus Christ, by which all our days will become radiant, at least in a small degree?

I shall mention first a minor matter as in part responsible. We allow ourselves, all too often and too easily, to be entangled in situations in which God cannot speak to us and reveal His word to us; and we cannot believe Him because, without knowing it, we have turned our backs to Him. For example, we defile our conscience by a little harshness, laziness, insincerity, ambition, or the like. Perhaps such conduct may be perfectly harmonized with Christianity; perchance we may be able to give good religious reasons to prove that we must be just as we are—but we cannot square our conduct with the word of God. The word, in consequence, avenges itself because we no longer can hear it and we are left alone. It may be that, in an unprofitable way, we boast how good or wise or pious we are; yea, we set ourselves on a "high horse" and tell people that we have got something from God. How easily one is beguiled to do this; as for example, when one thinks that he must "bear testimony," as it is called in Christian circles—a fruit-less and a dangerous procedure. You ought never give testimony about yourself, but about God if you really feel that you are fitted to bear witness. If you are not and are only a prophet of yourself, be not astounded if the open door between you and God has blown shut long before you observed it.

It may be, indeed it not only *may* be, but it actually happens each day, that we think ourselves in the right against another and all the while forget that God alone has the right to be in the right and that, there-fore, we dare not speak and act as if we were in the right. Men should be able to tell, by a certain diffi-dence in us, that we know that even when we are right we are in the wrong. Only then can God speak to us. If we do not understand this, then at once we are, as it were, in a dark room and no longer know the way out or in.

I shall mention a second cause that strikes deeper and has more weight. Christianity, as a whole, has forgotten for a long time that men can live only by the eternal light of God. It has forgotten that we can only *serve* this light and cannot be its owner or its master. With its view of the world and of life, with its churchly tradition, with all its alliances, which, in the course of time, it has made with the powers of the world, Christianity has placed itself before the light. And now it says: "Behold, this is the eternal light," and is amazed and angered, because the darkness in the world is so great, that men turn in such large numbers from the word of God. Are we quite sure that they turn away from *God* when they turn from *us* and from that which *we* represent? Are we quite sure that what we, with hasty decision, call the gospel of Jesus Christ is the gospel? Are we quite sure that a victory of a so-called Christian view of the world would be a victory of God? Are we quite sure that a prosperous church is evidence of the progress and coming of the kingdom of God? Whence do we know all this? It seems to me only when this questioning, this doubt of the soundness of our own Christliness, burns in our hearts, when our confidence is wholly and exclusively placed in God— then only can we actually serve the eternal light. If we bind ourselves to our own refuge, even if it is the Christian refuge, we will cover this light and are perhaps more godless than those whom we call by this name. The power of God at all times has been mighty only in the weak.

The third cause of which I shall speak is the most common and the most weighty. We are so deep in the abyss, so far from living actually in the power of the promise given to us, because so often and so persistently we have refused to recognize that the God, who seeks to speak His living word to us, is the *living God*—the God who goes with us on the way, to be sure an unusual and steep way, a way upon which we may become dizzy, yet for that very reason a way that leads forwards and upwards. Our supposed ways, upon which we go forward, naturally and without giddiness, are on this account no ways at all or only such ways as lead us around in a circle on a level space. Here we come once again to the contradiction in our text: "The sun shall no more shine for thee by day, and the brightness of the moon shall not give thee light, but the Lord will be thy everlasting light and thy God will be thy glory." And then we are told that we shall have this light for a sun and a moon whose light will never be extinct; and the days of our sorrow shall have an end. Accordingly, a shining of all kinds of lights, then an extinction of these lights, to be followed by the shining of the one eternal light. From life unto death and from death unto life. That is the steepness and cause of dizziness of the way of God, which again and again we face with so little understanding.

The shining lights, that will become extinct, are those that were lighted by God Himself on the fourth day of creation, the lights of which we are told, as of all the works of creation: "And God saw that it was good." We do not go with even and easy steps out of creation straightway into redemption. God himself, according to the text, sets over against the lights created by him, his light, the eternal light, as a second and new light before which the old lights must pass away. He remains free and above His creature, over against His creation and its order. That is the aliveness of God which speaks to us in His word. We have reason, indeed, to be astounded that God is God in such an unheard of way. We err, however, when we close our eyes to the fact that it is He, that His word delivers us inwardly not only from our sins, not only from ourselves, but also from that which He has created and created good. His word wants to bind us to Him, to the Creator; and on this account it must loose, I do not say break, but loose the bonds that bind us to his creation. We must know that we live not for the sake of our own life; not for our family, not for our children, not for our calling, not for our nation, not even for our church.

No one has the right of himself to put out these lights; nor has anyone the right to confound them with the eternal light of God. No one has the right to break the natural order of things; and no one has the right to read from them the will of God as if it were written in nature. The Creator Himself will tell us what His will is; and no creature can speak for him. As sure as we must die, so sure must we be prepared inwardly to let each of the created lights go out. Is it not true that we resist this preparedness! It appears strange to us that the Creator should stand above the creature. We are afraid of that which God Himself may tell us! "I turned from thee and loved the created light." On this account we cannot actually hear the promise that we shall live by the will of God. God cannot speak with us as the living God, as the one God, who will not yield His honor to another; and therefore it is so dark about us. That is the weightiest obstacle in our path—in the path of all of us.

Yet we must not allow this obstacle to stand in our way. There is neither depth nor distance in which God Himself is not nigh unto us, where we cannot hear His word. Jesus Christ stands above sin and the world. He is the forgiveness of sins and the victory that hath overcome the world. Who will separate us from the love of God which is in Christ Jesus?

The words of our text were first spoken to the people of Israel, evidently to the exiles in Babylon; to say the least, at a time when their misery was great. If we read the story we shall see that they were hedged about by words of comfort. We also seek comfort but rarely the true, abiding, eternal comfort: "Comfort us and we shall be comforted." How can we say this seriously without the longing, without the will, to forsake the leaking cisterns and to seek again the springs of living water?

REPENTANCE

Come unto me all ye that labor and are heavy laden.—Matthew 11:28.

Jesus calls us: "Come unto me!" Whence comes the call and whither are we called? The place where Jesus stands is nearer to us than any other place. It is perhaps for that very reason the farthest away and the least known to us. It may be that we do not see the woods for the trees. Jesus stands in the center of our lives, in the center of this world of reality, in the center indeed. What benefit to us are all the experiences of life and the knowledge of the world if we never know and enter into the center of them? It is a simple matter to find the place, easy to walk in it, if we know ourselves; that is, if we really know ourselves and not merely examine ourselves; take ourselves seriously, love or even hate ourselves. Who knows himself? And so the place where Jesus stands is everywhere and nowhere. We see Him always and yet never. Everyone knows about Him and yet no one knows Him.

Jesus calls us: "Come unto me!" He seeks to tell us what is true. He desires to speak truth to us. He wants to talk God to us. He, who lets himself be told, repents. Repentance is turning about to that which is nearest and which we always overlook; to the center of life which we always miss; to the simplest which is still too high and hard for us.

67

God is our Nearest. God is our Center. God is
the Simple. God is—this is so natural, so plain, so
self-evident, that all else seems more natural to us.
God is—this is so clear, so manifest, that all else is
more obvious to us. God is—this is so important
that all else seems more important. Just as the fact
of our life is a mystery to us; just as we forget the
ground on which we stand, the air in which we breathe;
just as in counting we no longer think of the numeral
"one" on which all counting is based. As if the first
had been given, the foundation laid, the beginning
made. But has it really been made? Is our life so
natural, so plain, of such import, as it must be if it
has its origin in God? Is our security really more
than fancy and pretense? How great must the darkness in the world become to remind us that we were
too quick to presume that we were like God; that we
have lost and must find again the beginning; that we
must turn about so that our life may become natural,
plain, and worthful in God? That we live, move,
and have our being in God is, indeed, not a platitude;
it is a great and painful discovery which is to be con-
summated only with fear and trembling.

God is hidden from us. Therefore Jesus is a dis-
turbance in our life and His call to repentance is as a
stone rolled in our path. God is—this word, spoken
by Him, is something incomprehensibly new in the
midst of all that which is natural to us; a mystery
in the midst of all that which is otherwise plain to
us; something hostile, alone important over against
all affairs of weight. Hostile because he wishes
really to give us that which ignorantly we think we

already have. He wishes to open it for us—for this, first of all, much must be pushed aside. He wishes to give it to us—for this, we must have first of all, empty hands. He wishes to remind us of it—for this, first of all, we must learn to forget. Jesus shatters us so that He may set us on a firm foundation. He judges us so that He may make us just. He robs us so that He may enrich us. He slays us so that He may make us alive. In no other way can that, which is, be told us. In no other way can God be spoken to us. In no other way can help be given us. Enter in through the narrow gate!

Jesus calls us: "Come unto me!" Other voices also call us: "Come unto me!" The voice of the church, for example. Today she calls us to the Confederation's service of thanksgiving, repentance, and prayer. The word "Confederation" reminds us of home and fatherland and of many things that are dear to us, weighty and precious. But still greater are the words "thanksgiving," "repentance," and "prayer." These words are also in the Bible. A certain similarity between them and the words of Jesus can easily be discerned. So much the more must our ears be sensitized that we may distinguish the call of Jesus from other calls in the world. More than 1900 years ago the men of the synagogue literally said almost the same thing as Jesus. Yet it was not the same, but directly the opposite. When the church says something, it is always an open question, and perhaps more than that, whether she does not say the direct opposite of what Jesus says, even when she speaks his own words. At all events it may be asked whether the word "God," spoken and heard in the church, has the least thing to do with God Himself. Perhaps the church—she and no other—has betrayed God all too often; betrayed Him to the needs and humours of man; to the spirit of the times; also quite readily to mammon; and not last, to the different fatherlands, to Switzerland, Germany, or England. Is God in the church the unheard of *new* that Jesus wished to tell us; and not rather that which is known of old, heard so often that men hear it no more? Is He the mystery: He, that dwells in light which no man can approach; and not rather something about which it is easy to chatter and which can be readily understood? Is He really the only One of consequence and not merely one among many worthful persons and things, an idol beside other idols? Does the church indeed dare to witness, in clear and unmistakable terms, how matters stand—that God is hid from us and must be sought *in* fear and trembling? If she dare not, then she cannot, in the way Jesus did, call men to thanksgiving, repentance, and prayer. If she dare not push aside, then she cannot open. If she dare not empty the hands of men, then she cannot give them anything. If she dare not say *No*, then she cannot say *Yes*. If she has forgotten the cross of Jesus, the way from life to death, how can she presume to know anything of his resurrection, of the way from death to life?

Why wonder then that her call: "Come unto me!" sounds hollow and untrustworthy? "The hands are the hands of Esau but the voice is the voice of Jacob." Her call has a different meaning from that of Jesus;

because, with all her speaking of God and Christ, she does not direct man into the depth where man, through Christ in God, ends and begins. She directs him rather to heights of ecstasy and to presumably Christian ways of righteousness. Her call has another effect than the call of Jesus; for though she assures and commends, she does not know and show; though she judges and condemns, she does not speak and work the right; though she stirs up some, she moves none. Her call is something different from the call of Jesus because it is a call in this world and out of this world, and not a call out of another world; because it lacks Jesus' wisdom of death and his zeal of eternity, which alone can make it an actually redeeming attack upon this world. I must say all this just because I am a preacher, a servant of the church, and just because today is the day of prayer, the occasion most loved by the church.

The call of Jesus resounds despite the church. But the church is a great, perhaps the greatest, hindrance to repentance. If we wish to hear the call of Jesus, then we must hear it despite the church. Forget that today is the day of prayer! Forget that we are in a church! Forget that a minister stands before you! True coins can be told from counterfeit by the ring. O, that we might learn to tell the sound of the call of Jesus from its imitations.

Jesus calls us: "Come unto me!" *Who is Jesus?* We know him best by those whom he calls to himself. By the brightness into which we then enter, we know the light by which we are lighted. Come unto me all ye! so he says at the beginning. Jesus concerns all. Jesus is here for all. He is broad and free enough to invite all to Himself, to regard all as belonging to Himself. He has confidence in His right, and above all else, in His might to draw all men unto Himself. He also is sure enough of Himself to need have no fear that He will lose what is appointed for Him when He manifests Himself and gives Himself to all. By this we know the specific purpose for which He has been sent. It can be nothing else but God. God alone concerns all men. God only is free to call all men. To this end God alone has and gives power and authority. God alone does not lose Himself when He is God for all men.

Here we see the difference between Jesus and other great men, other aims, movements, devices, even the best and most necessary. Goethe and Gottfried Keller are not for all men, not even Jeremiah Gotthelf or Dostoyevsky. Too bad, we may say, but so it is. One cannot expect that all men would be able to think seriously about God and life. Nor can one encourage all men to remain through life implicitly believing Sunday school scholars. The church, unfortunately, is not for all men; but, to be sure, neither is the mourner's bench or the Salvation Army.

One cannot require of all men that they become total abstainers or socialists; neither can one ask that all men become "duty-conscious citizens." One cannot demand of all men that they be "happy, always happy, happy every day"; nor can one demand of all men that in their walk and conversation they manifest fully the seriousness of life. Unfortunately one cannot, with the hope of a favorable response, make

even the simplest moral demands upon all men; for
example, the demand that one's property should be
assessed justly. Thousands upon thousands have never
heeded it, not even with the inner ear; to say nothing
that they have ever obeyed it or will ever obey it according to human standards. Millions of men, in
these latter years, have learned to break without a
thought the commandment, "Thou shalt not kill."
To them blood has no value; and by the standard of
reverence for human life they are no longer to be
tested. The more seriously we take the demands of
moral living the more we come to realize, for example, what are the requirements of truthfulness, consideration, tact, tenderness, and love which we owe one
another, of purity of heart and thought; so much the
more must we recognize, to our sorrow, how the number of those who will take these requisites seriously
decreases; so much the more will we be frightened
at the innumerable host of men who are hopelessly
shut out; if they are judged by these standards how
at last scarcely one, yea, not one, Paul said, remains
within. At this point we see the difference between
Jesus and other masters.

In reality He is not in a class with them. Jesus
concerns all of us. Jesus attacks the entrenched positions of men not on the front, nor where they stand
in armor, hardened in their great sin and guilt, the
one more coarse, the other more refined; He does not
lead the assault with accusations, instructions, and ad-
jurations, not with a strategic movement, effort, or
concept, not with thoughts, ideas, and demands, not
morally, and above all not with the familiar sermons

of the day of prayer. He attacks men from the rear, at the point where they got into their sin and guilt and where one may still have free access to them. He attacks them from the side of God—God, whom they have lost but who has not lost them. He attacks them with forgiveness. Jesus wants nothing from men. He wants them only for God. He is for all men. All men have need of Him. Jesus at the outset excludes no one, not even in the most refined sense. He tells all men that they are included in God's love, that God counts them as His, and that they may count themselves as God's, despite their sins, despite their guilt—all men, without exception, all men without condition. The word forgiveness, when He speaks it, is the free access to all men. The word forgiveness, if they hear it from Him, is actual deliverance for all men—for the proficient and the foolish, for the cultured and the uncultured, for the converted and the unconverted, for the prisoners and the preachers in the pulpit on the day of prayer.

Jesus has only one complaint against all of us: that we have gone away from God! And only one promise for all of us: that God is faithful! This all men can understand. This all men can accept without belittling themselves and without exalting themselves. Here is the key to all the prisons in which we languish. Here the whole issue is raised. Yes, Jesus is free enough and strong enough to ask us all to come to Him. He is, also, so sure of his God that he betrays and yields nothing when he calls us all to come as we are. Precisely in these words, "Come ye all unto me!" He reveals himself as the one He is, the Son of God, the Risen One. He tells us that which, only from the standpoint of God, can be said about all of us. He alone may say it. All of us need forgiveness, and forgiveness is at hand. He who lets this be told him repents. "Come unto me all ye that labor and are heavy laden!"

Who is Jesus? we ask ourselves once more. He who calls the laboring and the heavy laden to Himself. After all, not everyone? Yes, truly, everyone, for the words "labor and heavy laden" define the word "all." These very words show us on what side Jesus lays hold of the world to claim it for God. Jesus does not see us as we again and again would like to see ourselves; not in our fitness, not in our zeal, not in our earnestness, not in our believing, not as "warriors in the army of light," in the words of a famous novel, and not as "God's co-laborers," something which so many would like to be today. He sees us as laboring and heavy laden. He does not depreciate the good that we think, purpose, and do, surely not! but He does not praise it; He does not give it any special value; He is silent about it. He assumes that we know what is good, that we will do what we know, that we do not overvalue what we are, live and do; but that we ourselves would gladly cover it up. He is interested in our labors and in our burdens. He is interested not in our answers but in our questions, not in our security but in our restlessness, not in our finding but in our seeking. He passes the healthy and turns to the sick, goes, quietly and resolutely, past all kinds of righteous persons and turns to the publicans. He asks our young people not about their reports from school, not about their industry in the mill, not about their good repute, not even whether their parents and pastors are satisfied with them. He asks them about the remarkable dissatisfaction and longing, which disturbs every young person and which is not to be silenced by work or idleness, by obedience or license. He asks them about that doleful yearning which is so great and often so dangerous because there is no ground or name for it.

Jesus asks our wives not about the correctness of their housekeeping and not about the excellence of their qualifications as wives and mothers, but about their fatigue, spiritual destitution, and helplessness because they do not know how to accommodate themselves to the lot of womanhood—which they, most of all, would like to escape. He asks us men not about our character, not about our services, not about our activity as professional people and citizens, but about our secret shame, about the wounds of egotism in our conscience, about the open or hidden tragedy of the struggle of our passions with our ideals of righteousness. He asks the socialists not about the nobility of their theory and not about results—be they ever so evident—but about the final questions of social life of which they have yet hardly thought, about the questions into which the most upright socialist cannot go farther without putting himself in the wrong. And He certainly does not ask the citizens about the points where they are right as against the Bolsheviki—where it is childishly easy to be right; but about the other points, where they know that Bolshevism uncovers only a disease, of which even they, yes, just they, suffer,

and for which today a cure is sought by them in vain.
And so, also, Jesus asks our pious people not about
the state of their conversion and sanctification—for
these are Pharisaical questions—but about their inward part from which the unredeemed soul cries out:
"I believe, dear Lord help my unbelief!"

For Jesus the notable thing about us is never that
in which we are right, but that in which, though with
much right, we are wrong. He takes account only
of this—that we know that we labor and are heavy
laden or that we are in some other state. He takes
it for granted that we really are in this condition and
that this, in all cases, is the only noteworthy thing
about us. He comes into our lives when the only
thing that remains to be said about us is that which
can be said by God: *"forgiven!"* Because we labor
and are heavy laden we belong to the *"all"* to whom
his invitation is given. That, and nothing else, is for
us the window open towards Jerusalem. That, and
nothing else, is the side of us on which we are bound
to Jesus and through him to God. Blessed are the
poor in spirit! Blessed are they that mourn! Blessed
are they that hunger and thirst after righteousness!
Only when we labor and are heavy laden do we know
Him—Him, who is not the improver, but the redeemer, of the world; Him, who restores the lost first
estate. He can begin to speak and act only where
in the end we must be silent and stop; where God
alone can give the only answer that is left for us. His
yes springs forth from the deepest and bitterest *no*
of man in this world. His life breaks forth through
death that is upon the earth. He says, *Forward!*

after he has called a *Halt!* by his death on the cross,
to mankind and to all that is human. He is not superior, powerful, wise, not even pious. Behold! He
is the Lamb of God which bears the sins of the world.
He does that *to* us, which starting with God and God
alone, can be done *for* us; He puts himself beyond
our good as well as beyond our evil, and confines Himself to the difficult question which remains when one
takes account of both together—*He forgives us.* He
confirms our only hope: the resurrection of the dead,
the passing of the old man, the new creation. He,
who has eyes to see, repents.

"Come unto me!" What does Jesus want of us?
He wants nothing of us but that we come. He does
not want *ours* but *us.* If we come as we are, all is
well. For this is the new and all-important thing, the
mystery that confronts us in Christ. Our coming consists in this, that we permit Jesus to tell us that we
labor and are heavy laden. On this account it is so
hard for us to come. For this we delay again and
again. It is this throughout Christendom that keeps
people from Jesus. To come to him means to labor
and to be heavy laden. If the issue today were to
proclaim, at the direction of the church, so-called
thoughts suitable for the day of prayer about our na-
tional condition, to hear them and in some measure
to take them to heart, then truly we would come easily
and quickly. If it were merely a matter of converting
oneself for the first or second time, then, also, we
would come. We would come with gladness, if Jesus
were to teach us a way by which one even here on earth
could climb into heaven, as, for example, among the

anthroposophists in Dornach—or a method by which one could set up heaven upon earth as among the "Siedler" in Germany. We would say yes, if Jesus were to demand of us that we align ourselves with the I.B.S.A.—"earnest Bible students" and fathom the "dear God's" plan for the future; or let ourselves be taught by a jovial American how to become a happy and contented man in the easiest and simplest way. Any kind of upward move, attack, advance, upbuilding strikes us favorably.

But when Jesus speaks, this is not the issue; it is rather to be still, to retreat, and to tear down. On this account it is so hard for us really to come to Him, to labor and be heavy laden and nothing but that. Mark well! here one can only *believe*. Believe, that God gives grace to the humble. Believe, that His power in the weak is mighty. Believe, that in forgiveness we have eternal life. Believe, that it is worthwhile to sell all our pearls for the sake of the pearl of great price. Believe, that Jesus is victor. It is hard for us to believe. Let us freely grant that it is harder than all that is high, great, complicated. Faith is not for every man. Much already has been gained when we recognize this. Faith begins with the insight that we have little faith. Finding begins with the pain of long futile seeking. Coming to Jesus begins with the knowledge that something difficult is asked of us. It is they who labor and are heavy laden who come to God through repentance.

MAKE ME PURE OF HEART

Blessed are the pure in heart for they shall see God.—*Matthew* *5:8*.

Where is the trouble? For there is trouble some-where and it is high time—it is the eleventh and twelfth hour—that help should come. But we have not yet discovered where the trouble is and therefore we cannot give help. We live in the midst of daily increasing distress and perplexity, in a time which has all the symptoms of serious, yes, critical illness; and we stand by as helpless as physicians at the bedside of a patient stricken with a perplexing disease whose cause, despite all their searching, they cannot find. We know perhaps from personal experience the dread-ful feeling of depression that steals over us when we see the dire distress of someone whom we love and must stand by helpless, knowing that we cannot give relief.

Such is our condition today; and we are affected by the despondency that comes with it. Cloudlike it hangs more or less over everyone of us. The un-controllable distress of the unemployed, the collapse of our industrial life, and the spiritual confusion are a guaranty that we shall not soon free ourselves from this sense of heaviness. There is no lack of physicians who stand by the bed of the patient, examine his wounds, and write prescriptions. Almost every day a new doctor appears on the scene with another remedy.

Oh, the number of discourses we have to hear, the
number of books we have to read—each discussing
the crisis of our time.   One can scarcely enter a church
today without hearing something about it; and how
many movements and tendencies there are which in one
way or another are concerned with it!

There are those who laud apparently simple plans
of bettering the world; there are others who, like
the anthroposophists, commend more complicated
ways of salvation; there are still others who would
solve the problem—in the industrial order—by a re-
form of the monetary system.   There are those who
see the root of all evil in the prevailing method of
educating the youth; they call for a revolution of
our pedagogy.   There are not a few who hope for
better things through a revival of life in our churches.

It is possible, it is indeed desirable, that all of
us in one way or another take part in these endeavors
to help—some here, others there; perhaps in the front
rank as resolute advocates and directors of some such
movement, or perhaps in the background as observant
spectators who share the needs and hopes of the time.
But it is none the less inevitable, that, sooner or
later, we shall be disappointed and disillusioned when
we are forced to see that all the arts of the physician
do not cure the disease; that all attempts, begun oft-
times with great expectations, either entirely fail after
a short time or at least dissipate themselves without
results into the broad expanses of our age.   They
do not unfold or blossom but wither slowly as a plant
whose roots are worm-eaten.   This is true also of individuals.   Many high-minded persons with pure mo-

tives and champions of all that is good and true, venture into the darkness of the times; so many flaming outbreaks of new spirit, perchance, among the youth of a city or region; but the fire does not keep on burning, it does not break through, it does not spread farther. One feels more and more as if a mysterious barrier were thrust before us, as if we stood before a locked door which must first of all be opened from within if our endeavors to help are not to remain idle and meaningless gestures.

Perhaps it is a good omen that we are in this condition; perhaps it was necessary for things to come to this pass, so that when we are in this mood we really shall be closer to the truth and to an effective remedy than before—when we were still hoping to muddle through with the aid of all our many endeavors and devices. Perhaps we had to be made to see just this—that through these efforts we could not succeed. Perhaps all the many and wearisome exertions and efforts which we put forth are the last sure proof of our illness; as for example, in severe sickness the fever rises before the crisis; perhaps in the very distress of all these struggles and efforts something very simple, great, and healing for us must, and finally will, break through; a deep, clear, all-embracing knowledge of that which alone helps.

I am convinced that this is the meaning of the distress and affliction of our day; that we are ever moving nearer to that knowledge; and the higher the distress rises the closer will we come to the point where the knowledge—which is likewise our help—is to be found; so near that it may break through any moment like the sun through a layer of mist. I say break through, for this clearness, this knowledge, this salvation, lies, as it were, behind a wall; and, at first, it is not the truth and the help itself to which we draw nearer and nearer but this wall behind which they lie concealed.

We need not wonder then at the mounting distress, the increasing afflictions, and the barriers which arise. Our personal experiences are similar; on every occasion of trouble, when we received help, it was not by the ills becoming lighter and lighter until finally help appeared, as if it was a matter of course; but, on the contrary, conditions became harder and harder and then, when they were at their hardest, help came. The Bible at all events sees things in this light. "Immediately after the affliction of those days," so Jesus begins the passage in which he speaks of the everlasting help which shall make an end of all the sorrow of time and of the world; help, salvation, and deliverance really are the final end; but days full of affliction, days full of fear will precede this last end. Such was the experience of Jesus. Before the light of Easter stood the cross and the journey to Jerusalem. The place where all things change is not a height, not even a plain, but an abyss. And the greater the changes the greater the depth from which they arise. Just as if help could come only after we are face to face with a last impregnable door, when we must pass through a last scorching heat in the face of which, with no other alternative, we become wholly ready, wholly open, wholly free for help.

The help, which really helps us, is clear, great, and

simple. It confronts us like a dark peaceful mountain ridge in the evening sky. "I will lift up mine eyes unto the hills from whence cometh my help." God helps—this is the only true help. To it we must become accessible. We must reach the point where the simple statement of the Psalmist is so true for us that we will stake our lives upon it. But are we now free, open, and sufficiently prepared for God's help? We are bound and unprepared because we kept from being free and ready. It seems to us to be too simple; and we are still too much distracted, too little gripped and penetrated by the seriousness of our condition to commend ourselves wholly to God as the only efficient helper of our lives. We are still too spiritually rich, too wise, too gifted, not to desire any other knowledge than that *God helps*. We are still not poor enough, not humble enough to permit this assurance to enrich and exalt us.

Perhaps we should be ready to listen if some sort of profound, difficult solution, which would require all our strength, were offered us. On the contrary, something is promised us that is not at all difficult; something about which we can say nothing more, to which we can add nothing, before which we can only be silent; something that may be compared to the sunrise that ends the night without effort of ours. *God helps*—this is the simple assurance. "If thou heal me Lord, I shall be whole." This is the help that appears to us far too plain. "We spin webs of air, practice many arts, and are moved farther from the goal." *God helps*—this announcement shuts off all our discussions, makes all our movements superfluous, breaks up all our commissions and assemblies. It requires obedience; not enthusiasm. *God helps*—this commands silence, ends all attempts to help ourselves rather than to permit God to help us. By it, as Luther says, the head is taken from all our self-reliant will and deed. *God helps*—therefore we must get out of our complicated ways; come from behind the walls and towers of our notions and counsels; dismount from the high horse of our own viewpoints and convictions. *God helps*—this means that no thought of our brain, no counsel born of our wisdom, on the whole no device, no act, no theory, no practice can help— God alone helps. *God helps*—but this in turn must not become advice which we give one another, a thought upon which we may light. *God helps*—humanly speaking this is meaningless because it reaches beyond all that is human. *God helps*—one can only understand this when one's eyes, far above all petition and reason, are opened for that which helps by Him who helps.

But for this one really must stand before the wall where there is nothing more that can help. Gladly would we permit ourselves to be helped in all our suffering and need, but again helped only by something human, by help which we can understand, which comes from us, and which is in accord with us. But just this cannot be. This is the wall behind which help is hidden. It requires a final purification, a final renunciation, a last straight-forwardness, before we can see the ultimate, the eternal, that which God is and does. Purification and uprightness are necessary so that we may see how completely we are captive and give up all efforts to help ourselves. As darkness, as dying, it comes over us; and we must go through it; but right behind the darkness, aye, in the midst of death, we see that which we could not see before. We see life, truth, help—we see God. "Blessed are the pure in heart for they shall see God."

"Blessed are the pure in heart." Our impurity does not consist in this, that we are sinners, that we have committed faults, that we have weaknesses and passions. These will never entirely cease; and if we shall wait for them to cease, as many do today, we shall wait in vain. Our uncleanness consists in this, that we, in our shortcomings and follies, will not permit ourselves to be helped by Him who alone can free, heal, and deliver; in short, who can forgive. Either, we, on the whole, do not take seriously the dangers of our sins and follies. We pass over them lightly. It matters not much whether we shall again defile ourselves, whether we shall fall again; for we know, indeed how to comfort ourselves. Or, perhaps, we take them seriously and wage the battle as stubbornly and resolutely as is in our power. These are the two possibilities, which as a rule are open to us and between which we vacillate. But neither in the first nor the second instance do we do that which really can help us; we do not call on God.

Ah, yes, we call upon Him, indeed, as our partner in the covenant and as our co-laborer, who shall fight with us in our battles. But that is not at all calling upon God. One does not call upon God as co-laborer and partner; one calls upon Him as the King who has all power, from Whom all decisions come, Who com-

mands and Whom one obeys. But for this something
is needful, an inner victory, the deep insight that we
are helped neither by passing lightly over our misery
and sin nor by oneself by a reliant will to battle with
them. We must realize that nothing other remains
for us than the exclusive third possibility: *forgive-*
ness, so great, mysterious, simple and for that very
reason so difficult for us to accept.

It is easy to repeat the word "forgiveness," or "help
of God," because it is the language of religion. But
it is difficult and it requires courage to resolve to live
no longer in self deception; to take it really seriously and to deal with it as with the simplest fact:
we are forgiven; Lord God, thou art our refuge in
all generations. And yet we live by it; and to find
the way through life means nothing more than to be
a man who hears and heeds the words: God liveth
and God helpeth. If we were to live in this way,
salvation and truth would come to light amongst us.
But who is able to do this? Who does it? That one
is able to do this and that he does it, does not go
without saying. Here then we stand before the
barred door. Oh that we were really standing before it, then we would not have to wait long! He
who perceives, he who knows, he who is pervaded
with, this fact: I should do something which I really
cannot do, something which must be given me or I
shall forever remain helpless, he is already going
through; to him the door has already opened. For
to know this means to be pure in heart; means to
have cast out all deceitfulness; and where ye stand
with this conviction, says Jesus, there God already

has opened the door from within. Blessed, blessed, are the pure in heart!

"They shall see God." No doubt Jesus added this because He was facing a time when man tried to see God in many ways. There were countless attempts, through stirring up distinctive emotions and experiences, through sacred rites and services, through submersion and exaltation, to obtain a vision of God. Such attempts, also, are not wanting in our day. Indeed we need not look for them only in the Catholic Church. But we ought to guard ourselves against them! We shall not see God in these ways. The publican, who in the depth of his despair smote his breast, beheld Him; Job, also, saw Him, when he could no longer help himself and therefore bowed down before the inscrutable God. We shall see Him when we become wholly bereft; learn to face the perplexing problems of our lives and of our time; go down to the bottom, and no longer permit ourselves to be comforted, but know only the one thing to do, namely, really to call upon God. But we must be on our guard lest the uprightness of the pure in heart be turned into man's doing, a way of salvation, a remedy, an advantage, an ability. It is really only distress, only dilemma, only a need for help into which one sinks deeper and deeper, when one becomes thoroughly pure of heart. That this need becomes the supreme virtue; that just the afflicted, the weary, and the heavy laden are called blessed; that the publicans and Job come out of their sins and misery justified; that the blind see, the lame walk, the deaf hear, and the dead rise up, this is a miracle; this comes from

God; this is effected through God's word. *We* do not say, but *He* says: "Blessed are the pure in heart for they shall see God." He says it and what he says must be true, namely, that at the very place where we see only our affliction and our sins, only misery and death, there and just there we shall see God. This assurance we can only hear, we can only believe, we can only wonder at, when it is told us again and again.

BE NOT ANXIOUS!

Therefore I say unto you, Be not anxious for your life, what ye shall eat, or what ye shall drink; nor yet for your body, what ye shall put on. Is not the life more than the food, and the body than the raiment? Behold the birds of the heavens, that they sow not, neither do they reap, nor gather into barns; and your heavenly Father feedeth them. Are not ye of much more value than they? And which of you by being anxious can add one cubit unto the measure of his life? And why are ye anxious concerning raiment? Consider the lilies of the field, how they grow; they toil not, neither do they spin: yet I say unto you, that even Solomon in all his glory was not arrayed like one of these. But if God doth so clothe the grass of the field, which today is, and tomorrow is cast into the oven, shall he not much more clothe you, O ye of little faith? Be not therefore anxious, saying, What shall we eat? or, What shall we drink? or, Wherewithal shall we be clothed? For after all these things do the Gentiles seek; for your heavenly Father knoweth that ye have need of all these things. But seek ye first his kingdom, and his righteousness; and all these things shall be added unto you. Be not therefore anxious for the morrow: for the morrow will be anxious for itself. Sufficient unto the day is the evil thereof. —*Matt. 6:25-34.*

In all our anxieties Jesus calls unto us: "Be not anxious!" No other word so precisely describes our actual condition. We can never find a place upon earth where we are not beset with anxious care and where Jesus is not able to reach us with this admonition. Jesus could not utter a word that so concerns all of us, that so commands our attention, as the word "anxiety." If He would raise a question in which we are all interested, it can be no other than the question of existence, the question of the stomach: What shall we eat and drink, wherewithal shall we be clothed?

This may seem to us humiliating and shameful; for we should like so much to be spiritually minded men and women, hovering high above material things, yet only so far that we may continue to eat and drink our fill. There are deeper, more spiritual, loftier questions than the question of what will be served at table today or tomorrow; but there is no question that is more urgent. The so-called questions about God, man, and the world, *Weltanschauungsfrage*,— for example—may give us much to think about; whether man has a free will or not, whether God can be thought and how, may profoundly engage our attention; but no one will say that he cannot live two days longer, if he does not answer these questions. We are quite certain, however, that we cannot live in peace two days without knowing whether and whence we have the things by which we live. There are today so many agitations throughout the world and the nations are so restless, because this elemental question is not solved for innumerable people.

We shall do well, not lightly and proudly to ignore anxiety for food and drink, as if it were a small matter. Jesus did not so treat it. And we need not be ashamed if these less spiritual, ordinary kitchen questions seriously engage our attention. There are those among us who are deeply, very deeply, in need and burdened with thought for the morrow; on this account they are not to regard themselves as inferior persons. At the point where one is anxious, one stands

nearer to Jesus than anywhere else. To the afflicted
and troubled He says: "Be not anxious!" and the
more we are afflicted and troubled, so much the more
do we belong to those with whom Jesus speaks and
to whom He gives this admonition.

"Be not anxious!" Jesus, to be sure, could not
have spoken a more enigmatical word than this. Or
is there for those who are worrying, anything harder
to understand and for this reason more offensive than
this exhortation: "Be not anxious!" What does He
wish to say? What does He mean by it?—What can
one reply to it? Is this word by itself clear and plain
enough? Or is there in it something to be explained,
to be clarified? Is there perhaps behind our desire
for a clearer explanation of that which Jesus could
have meant, the easily understandable wish that something less offensive, less unattainable, might be read
out of His words than what He actually says? Such
an interpretation would not be a clarifying but a darkening of the word of Jesus. We must hear it as it
sounds. We must take it as it stands. I know that
this is dreadfully difficult. As with each word of
Jesus, so with this, it is nothing less than a miracle
when we permit it to tell us what it is intended to
say to us. But who gives us the right to deal with
it in any other way? Jesus wants nothing else but
that we take these words as they are. He seeks only
one thing and that is to say to us: "Be not anxious!"
and that we permit Him to say it to us. If He can
actually say it as He means it, and we allow it to be
actually said to us, then He has attained his purpose,
then has happened what must happen. He seeks to

win power over us with these words as with all his words. He wills that we believe Him, that we obey Him, as soldiers obey their leaders. That is the aim of his speaking with us.

"Be not anxious!"—Jesus simply says this without giving a reason for it. For his allusion to the lily and the bird is not a reason. Therefore His word is all the more perplexing. How are we to go about living as a flower blooms, as a bird sings and flies? So self-evident, so responsive to the innermost law of life, so unquestioningly simple, as if it could not be otherwise? To be sure it would be marvellous, if something of the necessity and freedom were to come to us, which we observe, on the outside even before our window, pervading the life of creation, the life of the beasts and plants, and working in everything! But how shall men, agitated and torn like we are, come to this! How can one command us, saying: "Be not anxious!" . . . "see the birds of the air" . . . "behold the lilies of the field!" . . . We are commanded, if this is to be taken as a command. At all events, it is a word that is spoken with high authority. This is really the difficulty and the offense of it. It sounds, indeed, so simple that even a child can understand it, and yet it is by no means so simple that one really can understand it like a child. For this implies that we are to understand it as a word of the Father, with which we are not to play fast and loose, as a word that is authoritative even though it is to us wholly incomprehensible. That weighty word: "I am the Lord thy God!" which introduces the Ten Commandments of the Old Covenant and gives them truth and power, that same word confronts us when Jesus speaks to us and on that account has authority. The word "Be not anxious!" finds its truth and strength in the word introducing the Decalogue. He, who would understand the word of Jesus without it, will not now or ever understand it. This word is as a hand extended to us of which we, blind in the midst of our anxieties, can take hold, may take hold, if we have the courage to do so. This extended and incomprehensible hand of God is, in the main, the whole content of this, as of every word of Jesus.

It is not natural, of course, for one to grasp this hand. It is easier, or so much easier, to be anxious as men are anxious, than to look upon lilies and birds and not be anxious. Again it is to be said: this is fully understood only by the afflicted and the oppressed, who themselves are in the midst of anxieties. He, who has come through more or less anxiety, also may speak of not worrying; but since he does not know aught of anxiety that involves the whole life, he knows nothing of the venture of not worrying about all the things that give us anxiety. He mistakes his going, by his own strength, through moderate worriment for the "Be not anxious!" of Jesus. He is like the man who, in his own way, trusts in God; but who at heart is glad to have in addition a reserve of gold upon which in case of need he may depend. So long as a man has not learnt the deceitfulness of all reserves, he is not yet in the trial of fire into which the word of Jesus is spoken and in which alone it can unfold the fulness of its truth.

It would be something wholly different if Jesus

would promise that He will save us from the fiery trial, that He will remove for us the things that give us anxious care, once for all take away the need that rises up before us like an unscalable wall of rock, take away, forever remove, what lays hold of our lives. But here one finds nothing of this. On the contrary: "Each day has its troubles." A miracle must happen each day if we are to pass through it sound and whole. But in the midst of this trouble, in the midst of this unspiritual, banal, unescapable question: "What shall we eat? Wherewithal shall we be clothed?" in the midst of all this one only is told: "Be not anxious!" In the face of a hundred worriments that arise in the various relations of life, we are here challenged, not to be anxious. And indeed without any reason except on the ground of faith. For the reason that *He* says it, that *He* is behind it, that it is *His* word that comes to us.

What is meant by the declaration: Jesus stands here? Is He, indeed, such a man that, at His word, we can venture not to be anxious? Is He not of all trouble-laden men the most trouble-laden? The sight of Him may increase rather than diminish our cares. Is it not through His fate that we see how dark the world is, how cold and loveless, what sort of devils men may be, how burdensome life is, what sin is, and how bitter is death? Is there anything that provokes more anxious care than the end which Jesus suffered? And yet He, even He, says to us: "Be not anxious!"—Yes, He says it, He! He tells us that we are the children of God and that therefore nothing is left for us than with unbounded trust to permit God to care for us. And because He says it, we can accept it. Because He speaks to us from such immeasurable depths of trouble, we cannot take it otherwise than the word of God. His words can no longer be man's word, man's counsel. We cannot take His word as well-meant human comfort, such as, for example, we give one another: "It is not so bad as you think! Do not worry! It will come out all right!"

For where He stands, it does not become better; on the contrary it always becomes worse; here the cross and death break in. He did not say: "Be not anxious"! and at the same time think only of a human way of facing and overcoming trouble. He thought really and truly of God, of God's counsel and God's help, and of nothing else. "God will preserve thee wonderfully in all need and sorrow"— that is meant here. And, therefore, Jesus did not prove his word. What is true in God and because of God, cannot be established by us. It is a miracle, incomprehensible mercy, that passes all understanding. And, therefore, Jesus can present it only as something unthinkable: "Be not anxious"! All that we can do is to *believe* that we must not worry. If we had human reasons for this belief, if we could take it in a different way from that in which children take the word of a father, then it would no more be the Father's word, the word of God which it is; but a mere word of man like other words are. We can live and die only by God's own word, not by the words of man.

"Be not anxious"! Now only do we understand

the final meaning of this word, understand wholly what it promises and what it does not promise. It does not promise a sudden transporting of ourselves into a world in which nothing troubles us; we remain in the world in which we are, but in the midst of the burden of care and anxiety we shall have the incomprehensible freedom from worry in spite of this burden. This is promised us. Perhaps it may appear a thing of little account to us; perchance we should rather be reminded, each day, each hour, of God's help. But can this be a small matter for us? Is it not the greatest thing of all—to be directed to God? Is it not the greatest of all things that we, who are burdened with all the infirmities of life, encompassed by danger, want, and death, may live as those who each day are wonderfully preserved by God? And, therefore, we live as the lilies of the field, as the birds of the air, in the midst of this dreadful world; though in all trouble yet without care, though in all bondage yet free. We may always escape, escape completely, that which worries us. But even the desire to flee from that which gives us anxiety and the wishing away that which is disagreeable, even this Jesus calls worry! and just this we are to stop doing because it profits us nothing. We are to leave off because we can never escape that which troubles us, as long as we are men such as we are, men of the time, men of sin, men that sometime must die. As long as we worry, we shut our eyes to the stern facts of life and our helplessness over against them.

Anxious care commonly counts as prudence. But it is at the root the most foolish thing that we can do, because it rests upon the unspeakably short-sighted opinion, that one can escape, by dint of his own strength and skill, by his wit and wisdom, the universal fate. "For after all these things do the Gentiles seek," says Jesus. But there is nothing to be expected of this way of thinking, to suppose that one of himself can surmount his fate. "You cannot," says Jesus, "add a cubit to your stature," though you try ever so hard. What will your foolish cunning and worry help you? Can you even tell what tomorrow will be? Can you have your life or the life of your children in hand for a day or even for an hour? No, all your worry is at bottom in vain. But do you, on this account, need to be afraid? No, in the midst of all that fear will do, you need not fear. Because at that very point you are in God's hands. Have we really not yet come so far that we can see how it is with us, how it is with our life and with God? Are we not yet deep enough in the cares of life to see who is caring for us?

One may put it thus: As long as we worry we do not live in the present. We live in a wishful way in the future. He who worries says to himself: "Tomorrow it will be better! Sometime my children will be better off than I! In ten years we shall see! When once I have found my calling!" Strange hopes and wishes are all these! Strange hopes of men for coming events! Strange dreams of something that in time will come to be! Why should your children prosper more than you? Why do you think you will have it easier in ten years? Why do you expect to find peace sooner in another station than that in which you now are? All these are attempts to escape. You are not willing to stand fast and face the moment that is at hand and demands something from you. You want to evade the burdensome, serious, and great things that confront you, the task that this very hour, this day, is your task. But "deserters will be strangled!" If today you will not stick to your task, how can you stand fast in the future? With all these hopes, in reality you give up hope, the hope for yourself, for the present, for today. "Be not anxious for the morrow"! says Jesus expressly. The moment is weighty. Today decides who you are and what you can do; today, not tomorrow.

In the kingdom of God there are no other tasks than those of the present. Today you must look difficult problems straight in the eye; the rearing of your children, it will not be easier tomorrow. Today you must be the husband of your wife, the wife of your husband. If today you will not seek the way to each other and with each other, how will you find it tomorrow? Today you must strive to find the right way of life; nothing is gained by postponing the analysis. "Be not anxious for the morrow"! means as much as to say: "Take the present moment seriously! Know today, in the face of your cares, that you cannot at all care for yourselves, that your life is heavy and dark, and is today as it will be in ten years! That there is only One here, who is Master of Himself; Who alone, therefore, can actually care for you: God! That for you only one thing is left: to seek Him, His kingdom and will, "and all these things shall be added unto you."

What would become of our lives if we were to take seriously the admonition: "Be not anxious for the morrow." Oh that we would begin to abandon our wish-and-dream-lands and live in the present! Then our cry to God at once would become serious, sincere, and constant! how God in a short time could then deliver us! We should still be, yes, with our eyes open, in the midst of the misery and sorrow of existence; but we should be wonderfully preserved by the word of Him who has overcome the world. We should still be pilgrims through the night; but there would be security in our steps, a solid path beneath our feet, the goal before our eyes.

We are all far from that way upon which one ceases to be anxious in the midst of anxieties. By our own effort we cannot attain such a state of mind. Whenever a man walks on this way, he did not put himself upon it; God put him there. One thing, however, we can do: make the most of this knowledge. We are directed to God. All our worries are to teach us this. The moment that we do not try to escape them, we stand before Him and we can do naught else than to pray to Him that He give us the freedom which passeth all understanding, to cast all our cares upon Him. He will do it. He wants to call us upon this wonderful way and lead us through the midst of everything that gives us anxiety. It is God's word when Jesus Christ says: "Be not anxious!"

JESUS AND NICODEMUS

Now there was a man of the Pharisees, named Nicodemus, a ruler of the Jews: the same came unto him by night, and said to him, Rabbi, we know that thou art a teacher come from God; for no one can do these signs that thou doest, except God be with him. Jesus answered and said unto him, Verily, verily, I say unto thee, Except one be born anew, he cannot see the kingdom of God. Nicodemus saith unto him, How can a man be born when he is old? can he enter a second time into his mother's womb, and be born? Jesus answered, Verily, verily, I say unto thee, Except one be born of water and the Spirit, he cannot enter into the kingdom of God. That which is born of the flesh is flesh; and that which is born of the Spirit is spirit. Marvel not that I said unto thee, Ye must be born anew. The wind bloweth where it will, and thou hearest the voice thereof, but knowest not whence it cometh, and whither it goeth: so is every one that is born of the Spirit. Nicodemus answered and said unto him, How can these things be? Jesus answered and said unto him, Art thou the teacher of Israel, and understandest not these things? —*John 3:1-10.*

The conversation between Jesus and Nicodemus, of which we have become witnesses, is so difficult to explain because it takes such an unheard-of turn. We, too, conduct such conversations with each other; and also preferably by night, as it happened in this instance. Our conversations are marked also by wide difference of views and by the enormous range of the subject under consideration. Sometime in the course of the arguments and the counter-arguments, we approach each other as from a far distance. At no time does the distance between us become more clear than when we talk about God. At first we do not understand one another at all, then we come a little closer together; and, in the end, we are glad when we have come near enough to salute one another at long range, as ships at sea far apart pass one another, or as neighbors, beside a wide river, can make themselves at least measurably understood by shouting and waving hands from bank to bank without actually coming together. Never is there more of a barrier between us, separating us as a high mountain, than when we talk about God; at best we come just near enough to each other for each one, from his location, to see the steep sides of the mountain. Then we say to one another: "You see God in one way, I see Him in another." We rejoice that, to this extent, we have come together. Each one leaves the other with his own views on his side. And this we call tolerance; and we are right proud of it.

The conversation of Jesus with Nicodemus takes a wholly different course; it begins just at the point where our conversations end. Nicodemus, indeed, is innocent of it. He most assuredly has no other intention than to lead a cautious, judicious, tolerant, religious conversation as from one bank of a stream to the other. "Rabbi, we know, that thou art a teacher come from God." But he had scarcely opened his mouth when the Teacher stopped and silenced him, saying: "Verily, verily, I say unto thee, Except one be born anew, he cannot see the kingdom of God." All the cards of Nicodemus were struck from his hand. All his charted positions were unrolled before the battle began. He finds himself face to face with

something new and incomprehensible, something that
he cannot fathom. "Nicodemus saith to him: How
can a man be born again when he is old?" There is
to be no carefully moderated talk from shore to shore,
in which each will maintain his own opinions. Nicodemus suddenly found himself in the middle of the
stream. The ground was taken from under his feet.
He could not take a position of his own nor engage
in a genuine exchange of opinions. The time for
tolerance was past; a choice had to be made—"Either-
or"; he was at a point where he had to fight for his
life. "Jesus answered: Verily, verily, I say unto
you, Except one be born of water and the Spirit, he
cannot enter into the kingdom of God." Nicodemus
stammered: "How can these things be?" Jesus answered: "Art thou the teacher of Israel and understandest not these things?" Nicodemus was check-
mated by three moves.

Let us consider this conversation more in detail.
We all have reason to take Nicodemus quite seriously
although he succumbs so quickly. We are like him
perhaps far more than we think. He was, indeed, a
Jew but he stood as a Jew with his Judaism about
where we stand with our Christianity. "Rabbi, we
know that thou art a teacher come from God; for
no one can do these signs that thou doest, except God
be with him." This was his confession. Nicodemus
wished to say, translated into our language: "You
are a religious person, whom I cannot pass by. Strong,
decisive impulses proceed from you. Scarcely anyone
provokes me to think as you do; one feels that something vital is in you that may become significant for

all time and for the whole world. I should like to talk with you. It will be worth much to me to obtain your opinion on many issues that agitate me. I have many things to ask you because I see that you have many serious and profound things to tell me." This is probably what was in the mind and heart of Nicodemus when he came into the presence of Jesus and greeted him as "a teacher come from God." Why could not Jesus be content with his manner of approach? Must he not give him full credit for it? Do the words of Nicodemus in the presence of Jesus differ widely from what we think and say of Jesus? Should we not be glad when our "Masters" and "Rulers" of the people venture to go as far with their confessions as did the Jew Nicodemus with his? We agree among ourselves that Jesus has been a leader in religious things, that it is worth while to take cognizance of that which he did and willed to do, that he ranks, by comparison, higher than the other religious leaders of humanity; that we do well to let the light, that radiates from his words, fall upon our ways and views. That is the average opinion. That is the substance of our Christianity. On these points, perchance, Nicodemus was in accord with us.

He, however, did not content himself with holding this opinion about Jesus; he went further and drew inferences from it. He was a serious inquirer and desired to enter into conversation with Jesus whom he honored and from whom he expected help—into such a conversation as one holds from bank to bank, from mount to mount, such as the spiritually moved and awakened souls among us repeatedly strive to

open and from which they expect further emotions
and impulses as they go on their way. He had real
questions, earnest burning questions; and now he
wished for once to hear what answer Jesus had to
give to his questions. He was of a reflective mood
and suffered acutely enough, under the thick darkness
of life, to be attracted powerfully by the light which
he beheld in Jesus.

We know from the gospels some of the questions
that at the time disturbed the more serious souls and
that on occasions were submitted to Jesus. For example, a tower fell and buried eighteen men under
its ruins. The question was raised: "What is to be
thought of God's rule of the world, when he permits
such things? Were these eighteen men more sinful
than other men, were they sinners above the others
who escaped with their lives?" The Romans occupy
the Holy Land and take customs and assessments. "Is
it right that one should pay taxes to them? If one
submits to these exactions will he not become a traitor
to the righteous and holy cause of the Jewish people?"
We must take these questions seriously. We may
well say that now we are not further on than men
were then. For we ourselves have similar questions:
"Can a man believe in God and at the same time be
a scientific thinker? Can one listen to God and at
the same time take part in politics? Can a man be
a Christian and at the same time be a Judge?" To
speak concisely, Christianity and modern thought,
Christianity and politics, Christianity and business.
Lately I have seen a whole list of such questions that
were to be discussed in a week's course of Christian

addresses. Laden with serious questions like these, Nicodemus must have come to Jesus and begun his conversation: "Rabbi, we know that thou art a teacher come from God."

Jesus answered: "Verily I say unto thee, Except one be born anew he cannot see the kingdom of God." What kind of an answer is this! That means nothing else than that Jesus denies, even with his first words, that Nicodemus has any ability to understand him. Jesus says to him: "You want to speak with me, want to let the light of the kingdom of God fall through me upon your questions? Do you think this is so simple? Do you really know what you want? Do you have eyes for this light? It may be possible that I cannot show it to you, because in the main you cannot see it. Let me tell you: When one is not begotten of the Spirit, born anew, he cannot see the kingdom of God. Think for yourself whether you are really meeting the requirements for understanding me and my words. Then come back with your questions, if you still wish to put them in this way." This is Jesus' answer.

But is this an answer? Nicodemus must have felt as if suddenly a flashing sword was swung over him while he sat there with harmless and friendly intent. He came by night to Jesus, not indeed because he feared to come by day, but because for such conversations, in which the most personal, the deepest, and the tenderest matters are dealt with, the night is the most propitious time. At any rate he desired to enter, under the cover of darkness, into a delicate, refined, personal conversation. And now Jesus gives him a jolt and throws him out of this mood. He must have felt dazzled, startled, disconcerted, even as one in the dark is suddenly struck by the light from a refractor. For he met something in Jesus so wholly different from what he expected, an unheard of lack of regard, something sharp, clear, bright as day.

And is it not true that again we are on the side of Nicodemus; we do not at all understand that Jesus can receive this inquiring man in this manner. We may be astonished, as appears so often in John's Gospel, with how little tenderness and refinement and respect Jesus conducts His conversations. We should have expected that He would have rejoiced in the visit of so prominent a man who was on the point of becoming a disciple, and that with tenderness and simplicity He would have spoken upon the things that lay upon His heart, as one gently touches a wound. So we expect to be treated by a true curate of souls. Instead of this, He wounds him. Instead of meeting Him half way, He cut off his words before he had really begun to speak. Instead of answering his question, He put to him an enormously difficult new question. Instead of showing him a way, He leads him to a wall where all ways end. "Except one be born anew, he cannot see the kingdom of God." But how can a man be born when he is old?

If we think upon it, we shall understand why Jesus and the conversations with Him were so much feared in the camp of the Pharisees and the Scribes. They felt something in His words with which they would sooner not meddle, like certain dangerous currents into which one is irrecoverably drawn, like a sharp

sword under which one comes to stand and which
slashes all the clever and tolerant religious conversations, or like a checkmate which overtakes one after
the first move. Yes, we also share their feeling that
there is something sharp, cutting, inflexible, true in
the words of Jesus, when we listen to these conversations in the Gospels. Away with you, we are told, if
you will not venture actually to strike out into the
deep! Away with you, if you are not sincere and
true to the end! Away with all those who at heart
wish only to have their own opinions confirmed by me!
I am not here to deal indulgently with the religious
views and opinions of men, that in the end they may
let me also keep my religious opinions. Such conversations have no sense. They are trifling; and, therefore, I break them off before they have begun. Upon
this way one gets no further; therefore it is cut off
at the beginning!

But, where this way ends, there the true way begins. When there is an end of trifling, seriousness
begins. When the hodgepodge of questions is silenced, the only question, about which conversation is
profitable, is taken up. Come hither, not you who
are devout, important, convinced, not you with your
religious questions and opinions—"come unto me all
ye that labor and are heavy laden and I will give you
rest"! Perhaps, after all Jesus' way of dealing with
Nicodemus is not so severe and sharp! It may be
filled to the brim with mercy—his apparent unmerci-
fulness! It may, in the end, be nothing else than
the Savior's love seeking the lost, his stern and repellent bearing! "Marvel not that I said unto thee,

Ye must be born anew." It is after all an answer, the answer which Jesus gave to Nicodemus; and perhaps, perhaps, he has ears to hear it!

Jesus did not wish to enter into conversation with Nicodemus. He could not do it. For upon the basis upon which all these religious questions are conducted, one never comes to a definite goal; because from this basis one cannot catch sight of God. Jesus saw Nicodemus standing, as it were, under a roof that kept him from looking toward heaven. He could not show him heaven at all, as long as he was under the roof, even though he would have taken endless pains. Therefore he did the only thing that he could do. He tried from the first to take him away from the roof and lead him under the open heavens, to place him upon wholly new ground. So it was intended,— this merciless saying—"Except one be born anew . . ." He gave him a sharp jolt; but it was necessary. Even as it may become necessary to awaken one out of a dangerous dream. Nicodemus was dreaming. He did not see at all what was involved when the conversation was to be about God. He thought only of *his* questions, *his* needs, *his* concerns. He wished, even though in a refined and deep sense, to confirm his own opinion on the authority of Jesus.

But Jesus would not permit Himself to be used in this way. As long as one stands under the roof, one only dreams of God. But Jesus came to drag men out of all their dreaming of religious ideas, their feelings, and conversations and to put them before the supreme reality—God. He cannot answer our questions for us. They are dreamer's questions. They come while

we are dozing. They arise at a distance from God.
They are evidences that, notwithstanding all our piety
and prudence and religious zeal and subtleties, we are
still sticking under the roof, where one cannot see the
heavens. We must not expect that, regardless of
where we are standing, these questions will allow
themselves to be solved. We must come forth from
under the roof, then the questions will cease. We
must awaken to God. We must have eyes for God's
concerns, then our concerns will shrink for us. We
must recognize that God wants us for him, then we
shall not think so much about always getting something from Him. He must enter into the center of
our life, then much that today troubles us and op-
presses us will of itself come to the brim, overflow
and run away.

But even for this we must be born anew. We will
not ask: "How can this be, how may I bring it to
pass?" Else we shall give proof again, that of all
this we have understood nothing. Nicodemus had to
learn and we must learn with him, that our religious
opinions, views, feelings, and experiences, matter nothing. All this is "flesh." And "the flesh profiteth
nothing." The Spirit alone availeth. "That which
is born of the Spirit, that is spirit." The Spirit, however, is not at hand. The Spirit is a part of life out
of the other world, out of eternity. "The Spirit
bloweth, where it will." We stand before God when
we say "Spirit"; we are and remain cast upon him,
upon him alone. We live by his grace. He gives us
what we cannot give ourselves—access to him. We
can come to God only through God himself. He is

the new man who knows that he comes *to* Him because he comes *from* Him. That is the mystery in the life of Jesus. Therefore He gave men no recipe about ways and means of coming to God, as all the other religious "Masters" do. But He was Himself the new man born of God and lived wholly by God's incomprehensible strength. We may continue to converse ingeniously about these things; we may spin again our religious dreams about Jesus. It has been done repeatedly in Christianity. It may happen, also, that by God's grace we will awake and understand Jesus Christ as he wills to be understood. With Him there is no room for religious dreams; no ways are prescribed how we, without God, can come to God. But He said of Himself: "I am the Way! He that hath ears to hear let him hear"!

FIRE UPON THE EARTH!

I am come to kindle fire upon the earth and what would I desire more than that it should already burn.—Luke 12:49.

What shall I say about the fire which Jesus came to kindle? Above all, that this fire does not yet burn upon the earth, as little today as then when he cried out in a deep desire, half-prophetically, half-entreatingly, "what would I desire more than that it should already burn." It has never burned anywhere. I do not know of any place in the past or present to which I might point and say, "See there, in that person, in that achievement, the fire burns which Jesus kindled; there you can see it with your own eyes and touch it with your own hands." I know what is stated in the hymn which we sang a while ago, " 'tis burning now with brightest flame, now here, now there, in East and West!" I will not argue with the author of this hymn; poets often may say more than other people. But let us look at life to see what it is; look at the Bible to see what it is. And as we do, we shall see that we have no claim to the somewhat keen assumption that here and there the fire is burning and with a clear flame.

Oh yes, there is much *smoke* upon the earth, smoke of fervid, urgent love for God and man; smoke of quiet, sincere faith; smoke of anxious, unshakable hope; smoke of profound, progressive ideas, ideas so exhaustive that they reach that beyond which one cannot think; smoke of noble, courageous zeal for the good; smoke of universal movements for the betterment and re-creation of temporal circumstances. Who would dare to ignore this rising smoke, especially in our day in which the hope and the good will and the earnest search of men for something new reveals itself as the deepest nature of man. Where there is smoke there surely is a glow, always and always the glow that Jesus has started. But smoke is not fire, even if there is ever so much smoke. We dare not become too easily satisfied about that which Jesus expects. Jesus was not so easily satisfied either, in what he desired to bring and give to us.

Some people are frightened at the sight of rising smoke. They become deeply disquieted when there are plain indications and action of a power that can disturb and interrupt the entire course of life. To them we must say: "Yes, you are right in being frightened, but in time it will grow much worse. Something entirely different is yet to come. Beware of that day, when not only smoke, but, out of the latent glow that you now surmise, bright flames will break forth." There are other people who are happy when they become aware of the rising smoke. They welcome the indications and the activities, at least those which they understand; they are overjoyed by the faithful light which is being diffused into the darkness of this life by these indications and activities; they would like to see more of it. To these we must also say: "You are justified in your rejoicing, but in time it will become much better. Something entirely different is in the coming. Rejoice, rejoice, concerning that day, when the bright flames will break forth out of the latent glow which you now surmise." Thus the word of Jesus about the fire is today, as then, a threat for some and a promise for others: "What would I desire more than that it should already burn!" For all, however, this points to the fact that that which is real, essential, true, which Jesus wishes to give and to bring us, is not here as yet. The glow has been started, but the fire is not burning as yet. The Advent Season is life for us, for some a time of fear, for others a time of hope, for all a time of expectation. And yet, when we think it over quietly, we must always admit that fear and hope are strangely mingled in us all.

First, we want to hear something about the glow that was in Jesus' heart. Indeed who can find words to talk about it? It is remarkable to observe how people were at sea when faced with Jesus in His lifetime; how the glow that was in Him, even then could not come to a flame. "He is a prophet," said some; "He leads the people astray," others thought. "He is the Holy One of God!" they said on the one hand; "He is a glutton and a winebibber, the associate of publicans and sinners," on the other hand. "Blessed is the womb that bare thee," some are saying, and others answer, "He hath Beelzebub. By the prince of demons casteth he out the demons." "He preaches with authority," thus some praised him; "He is beside himself," thus others reviled him. Judging from these conflicting opinions, we can see plainly that the people met something in Jesus with which they did not know what to do, something that did not fit in with their habits and conceptions. One could look at it this way and that, as something glorious beyond measure, or as something really vicious, in fact frightful, and we will simply admit that to this day it is about the same with us. When we look into this glow, our eyes overflow with tears. We can say all sorts of things about what Jesus was and what he wanted, and we ministers and other people, too, are fairly well skilled in talking about it, but, if we are honest, we must admit at the same time that we really do not know just what we are saying. Either what Jesus says and wants simply has no place in our world, or our entire world has no place beside that which Jesus is and wants.

Now just think about this one thing, *the forgiveness of sins*, about the way Jesus regarded mankind. What a remarkable vision, or rather insight, that was into all that is really important in our world! It certainly is important for us, whether a man is good or bad, Christian or unchristian, whether we can commend his speech and actions, or, whether we must criticize and reject them. For Jesus, however, that is decidedly unimportant. He overlooks all that, or rather, He sees through it all as though it were glass. He sees through the man himself, the man just as he is, nothing added. What seems important to us, is to Him something added. He sees him and puts this question to him: Do you see what you are, and what your plight is? That is, before God! Do you see that you are entirely dependent upon God, but also judged by God? Do you see how God has taken you up, that you are nothing before God, that between

God and you there can be only a plain No? Do you
see that you are also sustained in the good hands of
God, and how near God is to you in the very fact
that you are entirely dependent upon him for grace
and disfavor? Do you see that in your life you are
facing a wall, that you cannot go any farther? Up
there, however, upon the wall your way continues and
it is no longer your way. For the wall that you are
facing and the way it continues, is God. God is the
halt! and the forward! Do you see that? Do you
see that God is your father and you are his child? In
the face of this question all else comes to an end for
us. Things may go well as long as we do not understand the end. We may possibly think that not by any
means does everything end here. But when we do
understand the question: Do you see that you have
been forgiven, regardless of what you are, Pharisee, or publican, pious or ungodly, good or bad—do
you see that you have been forgiven? that is the beginning, the real, the essential thing in your life.
Then everything comes to a final end for us. Then
sinners must rise up from out of the depth, and, irrespective of their sin, they belong to God. Then the
righteous must come down from their height, and,
irrespective of their righteousness, they belong to God.
Then all comes to a final end. Then all that counts
with us will cease to be valid. All that counts then
is God. But what shall we make of this? If our
world is really valid, then God is not valid in this
fashion. If God *is* valid in this fashion, then our
world is not. That is the alternative! What shall we
choose? As Jesus considered men, they can be regarded

only from the standpoint of God. What Jesus wants is evidently possible only with God.

Now what shall we say to this? It is plain that before this glow (that is in Jesus) we must close our eyes. There is nothing we can do with it. We can only become thoroughly confused. Whoever can speak about this with smooth, intelligible words, whoever can listen unperturbed to this, only shows that he has not yet understood what it is all about. It is the glow of the divine power, the divine love, the divine Spirit, the divine grace and mercy, that is radiant. It is in reality the impossible, something which eye has not seen, and ear has not heard, and which has not entered into the heart of man. And yet this glow is there, at least at the brink of our world, there, where we cease to comprehend, at the boundary line of humanity. Plainly we feel the warmth, the light, the radiance that emanate therefrom, we see the smoke that rises from thence, the indications that Jesus, what He is and wants, is living, regardless as to the position we may take thereto. Our life takes its course, our world as well. But back of and above all of this is forgiveness, always the way in which Jesus looked at people, the urgent enlightenment that we are all sinners, the message full of promise that God verily wants to be our God. It is like a great question mark and exclamation point after all that we are and have. No, the fire is not burning as yet; for that little bit of love, faith, zeal and good will in the world can certainly not be called a "burning." But is it not enough that this glow is kindled in Jesus, so that we do not forget we are always unintentionally coming

too close to it? Is it not enough that our entire life
is lived in the reflection of the glow of this divine
truth? How could we endure it, how great would be
our terror and our exultation, if it should really burn?

Indeed, in that case we would lack words and
ideas to say what it would be like if not only smoke
but fire would break forth out of this glow. Jesus
used this strong word consciously: I am come to kindle
fire. Whatever gets into the fire is not only changed,
but it is transmuted in a manner unheard of, into
something different from what it was. Wood ceases
to be wood when in the fire; it becomes ashes and
gas, light and warmth. Jesus meant to say: such trans-
mutation, such radical change is what I bring and
give. Just so he purposely used that other strong
word: I am not come to bring peace, but a sword, the
sword that brings death, that is, not just a change and
an improvement in this existence with which we are
acquainted, but a transition from this existence to an
entirely unfamiliar one. Let us think for a moment
that that which Jesus is and that which he wants, this
Immanuel! God with us! is true; that it is not simply in the Bible, and spoken by a minister in the
pulpit, but that it is simply true. What then? Clearly,
then, something new, something different begins, something as different from all that now is, as ashes, gas,
light and warmth are different from wood, death from
life.

God with us! That is too strong a contradiction,
not only over against our sins and sufferings but also
against the nature of our existence even down to the
very deepest depths of its roots. God with us! That

conflicts too much, not only with our unrighteousness, but more yet, with our righteousness; not only with the atrocities of history, but more yet with history's supposed progress and achievements; not only with the misery on earth, but more yet, with the supposed happiness and satisfaction on earth. God with us! That subjects our total human nature to a judgment, to a No, that will leave nothing left of us, and will bow us under a grace, a Yes, that we cannot comprehend. God with us! That is not only a better man, but a *new* man; not only a beautiful world, but an *other* world; not only a higher life, but an *eternal* life. God with us! That is redemption, but real, all-embracing, serious, and therefore, radical redemption. That is the fire of which Jesus spoke, the fire that wants to come forth out of the glow that He started. Hence the impossibility for us to look right into the glow; hence our helplessness in the presence of Jesus, now as then. Hence the earthquake, the disquietude, the confusion which inevitably arises, when the word of reconciliation is really preached and heard. Hence the alternative (either-or) with which we are inevitably confronted when we understand what is at stake, when we come too close to the glow in Jesus.

From Jesus' announcement—God with us!—to the realization of this announcement; from the glow to the fire; from ourselves to redemption there is a transition, entirely unheard of, a dying, alongside of which that which we usually call dying is only a semblance, just play, notwithstanding all the seriousness of dying; a world-judgment alongside of which the destruction of the world which can come at some time, is insignificant. We stand here before an abyss over which there is no bridge. For Jesus' death actually stands between here and there, His death upon the cross. The word about the fire that is not yet burning has a continuation, namely: But I have a baptism to be baptized with; and how am I straitened till it be accomplished! It will always be surprising and remarkable that Jesus had to go this way, the way of death so soon after so short a period of activity, and that He had to fix his eye upon this end from the very first. It is as though He had had to say for all times and to all mankind with the surrender of His life: Wait for redemption, for the victory of the divine truth, for the fulfilment of "God with us"; do not expect anything of your own activities, of the progress that you achieve, of the structure that you can erect. Redemption is not a work that you can do, not a way that you can travel, not a power that you can use. Redemption comes, and comes from an altogether different side, it comes really and in truth from God Himself. It comes from thence where you are at your extremity, where you are and have nothing any more, and from thence where you are lost. There God will glorify himself through you. There resurrection and life are waiting.

Therefore, Jesus' fire does not yet burn upon earth. Between it and the glow that has been started is the cross, is death, the end of all things. To the Jews an offence (stumbling block), to the Greeks foolishness, to them, however, that have been saved, a divine power. A divine power, yes, because it is the open way. But who has already walked this way? Who does not need to walk this way again and again? Who can be said to have already passed the cross and to be standing on the other side in the resurrection? Who does not take offence here? Who does not shake his head? Who would not turn about with Peter and go another way? Who dares leave it all to God?

Now if we would like to ask what we should do, the only answer would be that perhaps this very question ought to be able to die. For, as long as we ask this question, we really show that our longing for Jesus' fire, for redemption, for the resurrection, is not very great as yet. Evidently we still have expedients and a way out so that we can contrive without Jesus' fire. "Behold I make all things new" has evidently not penetrated to our very marrow. We could ask ourselves why this is so with us, why we can go along in such ease, when we are really confronted with an alternative (either-or). Why is it that we still think what *we do* or *do not do* is so important, whereas in reality we are dependent upon *God* and live in Him? When these questions awake in us, we become shocked, unsteady, undermined people. Then we realize that we must die, not at the end of our days, but today. We then become people who not only wait, but know what they are waiting for, people who are waiting upon God. We then become people who are standing, so to speak, in the shadow of the Cross and looking forward to Easter. Then our lifetime becomes consciously an Advent season. Perhaps that is what we can do, and nothing more is needed then than a certain honesty and watchfulness (soberness), a sense of what it all depends upon.

This much is certain: if we are silent before God, we shall hear the message that continually sounds from the other side over to ours and which could continually be heard on our side: "Behold, I bring you good tidings of great joy which shall be to all people."

JESUS AND JUDAS

Then one of the twelve, who was called Judas Iscariot, went unto the chief priests, and said, What are ye willing to give me, and I will deliver him unto you? And they weighed unto him thirty pieces of silver. And from that time he sought opportunity to deliver him unto them.—*Matthew 26:14-16.*

"Man is something that must be overcome." In these words of Frederick Nietzsche one could gather up the whole truth about our existence which Jesus uttered and which he, while he lived a man among men, brought to light. Certainly Jesus did not come solely to proclaim this truth. He did not come to announce the ruin of mankind. He came to reveal God and to save men. But even so, only He can reveal God who has thrown down and conquered man. For our humanity itself is the wall of partition which separates us from God, the layer of fog which must first be penetrated before God's light can clearly shine again. To be saved? Man can be saved only by God through man's complete ruin. That is why the Cross stands in the center of the life of Jesus. At the cross is where God was revealed and where we were saved, for there man and all that is human was conquered, sacrificed, given unto death. The new, the saved man, the man who stands beyond the Cross, the man of the resurrection is different, wholly and absolutely different, and more than the "old man" merely improved. There is no bridge of progress or evolution from the old into the really new life. The Cross, death, stand between the two. The old human must disappear in the face of the divine new. Between the two stands the truth that "man is something that must be overcome."

"Man is something that must be overcome." Man! No only the bad, the godless, the unbelieving, the immoral man, but man in every form, man as such, man as he is, irrespective of his evils, or of his noble, helpful, good characteristics and high aspirations; righteous and unrighteous, godless and pious man. There is a place within us which is situated beyond all these differences, beyond good and evil, beyond piety and impiety. In this place, at the deepest, the most hidden, the most inward part in us, an ultimate bastille, so to speak, an unconquerable citadel, a mighty fortress lifts its walls. That is the throne of the original human in us. In this fortress we are ourselves, without any good or evil additions here we are alone with ourselves. Behind this wall, in this fortress, dwells our "I." Thence it goes forth, to it it retreats. There it hides itself, there it sighs and suffers, there it defies and triumphs. This wall must be shaken, this fortified city must be overcome, must be stormed and broken down. Before that, man is not conquered. Many battles are fought out in our lives, but the final, the decisive crisis is not in these conflicts, even though they may wage fiercely. That final conflict results only when the fight for the inner citadel takes place. All others are preliminary skirmishes in the van, not the skirmish before the real inner position.

Forefield fighting is the method by which we ordi-

narily fight evil. All of us have a lot of evil about
us. Sometimes it rises up in awful power. I think
of physical suffering or the greed for money. It takes
possession of the length and breadth of our lives and
breaks forth either unbridled, or in mere bad conduct, in our thought, speech and behavior. We protect
ourselves against evil. We battle against it. Perhaps we succeed in controlling it or suppressing it until
the dam breaks and it emerges anew! And so the
battle wages without success, back and forth. For, is
it not true that the evil in us will not permit itself
to be overthrown, annihilated or decisively defeated?
It always rises up again, it always returns. For evil
would long ago have been defeated and destroyed,
it would have been easy to be through with it, if, yes,
if, it did not always have a strong place to flee to in
that fortress, if it did not receive its power of opposition from that "I" of man behind that wall so deep
within us. That is why it never is completely driven
from the field. What would money be, or sensuality,
alcohol, or the sword of might, if *man* would no
longer ally himself with them, if he would not secretly consent to them? For it is only out of this
alliance with man, only out of this demoniacal yes
of man that these powers do suck their life-blood and
their life-sap. If this inner retreat should collapse,
then evil would be powerless. Therefore "Man is
something that must be overcome," if evil is to be overcome.

And it is no different with the good for which all
of us wish to fight. We all have so much good about
us, so many selfless motives, so much loveliness, child-

likeness, joyousness. But why do men generally feel
so little of it? Why does it not penetrate through?
Why does it not radiate victoriously from us? Why
is not good king of the world? For this reason—because it possesses only the forefield. It does not possess the central, inner place. *There,* in the inner place,
something else, the defiant, crafty "I" of man
reigns, which has not yet fully surrendered itself,
which still remains for itself, which still wants to be
something by itself, not fully good nor fully bad. As
long as this "I" sits in this fortress, all this busy chas-
ing and running after the good is futile. This fortress must be stormed, this human place must finally
surrender, must allow itself to be overcome. Before
that happens, the good will never be king on earth.

Here is the key to the enigmatical and disturbing
fact that in spite of all the sincerity and zeal expressed
by Christian believers, there does not issue from our
Christendom, our faith, our religion, the decisive
power there ought. Or are we not aware of the evident weakness and impotence of our faith and of
church-life? We repeatedly assure ourselves that we
have God, we stand in the power of his Spirit, we
boast about our salvation. But—"these Christians
must show to me that they are redeemed before I
will believe in their Redeemer," shouts Frederick
Nietzsche, who spoke that remarkably profound word
about the conquest of man. And there are others who
side with him, even convinced Christian disciples
such as the great Dane, Kierkegaard, and utter similar
statements. And we must admit their truth. We, too,
feel it is true that a certain ultimate, mighty, secret

line of defense in man is as yet unbroken. It is not even broken within that realm we call Christianity. All our churches and chapels without exception are situated outside the zone of this inner fortress, even outside this last bastille, behind which the "I" of man has his last and strongest position; they are still in the forefield. And that is the reason why practically all that is thought, spoken or heard about God and his redemption within the churches and chapels, earnest and zealous as it may seem, is always so remarkably impotent.

That is why our Christianity is not taken seriously. The world knows well enough that our Christianity as a whole does not take hold of this central place of man in earnest. It knows that even the lives of convinced Christians without exception do not root up and conquer the "I" of man. It knows that we Christians, while we contribute much, yes, the most, yes, we give and offer even the last thing we have, yet that last thing we will not give—ourselves—not *all* of us. For that reason the world does not fear us very much at present. One condition we persist in laying down, perhaps unwittingly, even to God, even in our praying and pious living—and this condition is ourselves, we, the human, our "I." We will not let ourselves be conquered. On the contrary, we assert ourselves! We defend ourselves. We appear to be strong. Whatever *we* think, do and say, should be attended to. Only one misfortune could happen to us in our estimation, and that would be that we, the human, the man, should weaken, become afraid or fall. With tooth and nail we defend ourselves against such a pass.

That is the central thought which rules us. We fear and avoid the evil, not because it is evil but because it might endanger *us;* and should we allow ourselves to be enmeshed in it too deeply, through its fettering powers, it might make our *human* life precarious. Likewise, we consent to the good, not because it is good but because it assists *us* in the establishment and the fortification of the "I." "A good conscience is a peaceful pillow." Yes, and more, we seek God, not for *His* sake, but for our own sakes; we seek Him, because *we* are strengthened by Him, comforted, and hope to be saved. We seek Him, so that *we* might *use Him* for a mighty retreat for ourselves.

That is our religion. That is our morality, our ethics. Practically all our disciplines of thought make this their premise. In it the heathen-worldly and churchly-christian philosophies of life are interchangeable and similar. The mode of expression may not be the same but the goal, the purpose is the same; man, the human, who will not allow himself to be conquered; man who seeks himself and desires to assert himself. Here is the point at which all differences, whether of classes or religions, must stand back in favor of the one, common reflection and tendency. And in that place stands Judas Iscariot, who betrayed the Lord. He is different from all others only in that he is *conscious* of standing at this point; he knows what he is doing and he is holding this place and defending it against the one, the only One who does not stand in this place, but who, on the contrary, seeks to take possession of it. He stands over against this

One, this *only* One, who does not want to be the sort
of man who asserts himself, but rather, that sort of
man who surrenders himself, that man who dies, that
man who sacrifices himself, the wounded, the suffering, the one despised by all, the broken, humbled,
crucified Man.

For that is Jesus. That is the decisive thing about
Him. He desires this, and this alone—to strike
against and to collapse this inner wall and citadel of
man. He was not concerned about the things in the
forefield, whether good or bad. He began where we
leave off. He opened and fought His way through,
beyond those things which we think important, beyond our minor battles and play-struggles to the battle
against the innermost and the ultimate.

It has often struck us how little weight Jesus put
upon the differences in men, whether they were moral
or immoral, pious or worldly. Undoubtedly He saw
these differences better than we, but He looked beyond
them as though He saw the enemy with whom He
had basically to deal, the enemy who stood behind
these other little enemies with which we often engage. He saw the good and the virtuous in good people and He did not lightly regard it. But at the same
time He saw that behind all these goodly virtues there
arose this absolutely unbroken line of defense which
continually hinders the good from gaining a complete victory. And He, indeed, saw the darkness and
the unrighteousness of the ungodly and worldly and
He certainly did not call them good. But at the
same time He saw, behind all their evils and ungodliness, the last stronghold which made it indeed pos-

sible for their evil and ungodliness to continue to maintain itself. And above all, He saw that this last inner stronghold is most unbroken in the pious and believing people whose piety serves to establish more firmly the defiant, crafty "I" of man. Continually Jesus realized that this inner position must be stormed. God must be captain of this strong bulwark of man. Everything else is futile. And so Jesus never took any part in the attempts to make the world better, or in the attempts to make good triumph over evil, or to bring about the destruction of evil which is often undertaken without touching this last ultimate premise, without overcoming men, without making God first of all absolute and only king.

Jesus made short shrift of all the ideals and religious and patriotic endeavors of His time. He quickly passes by the whole forefield of life. But He had one point to which He hurried and that was the last wall beyond which it is impossible to go without attacking man himself. This is what Jesus attempted to do. He possessed the profound insight that man must be overcome. A sacrifice must be made; no, not just *a* sacrifice, but *the* sacrifice, the sacrifice of man. And he made it Himself. He forfeited everything, everything wherein He was humanly great, good, virtuous, everything which men could have understood and admired and imitated without needing to acknowledge or make this last sacrifice, which was of the utmost importance to Him. He allowed Himself to be humiliated, He gave Himself wholly to the end that once for all there might be a place in this world of humanity where God might come into His complete glory.

It was not an easy path. In this way it was shown just how strong the inner position is. He had to experience what it meant for one of His own, who could have understood what it was all about, to betray Him to death. How resistant man is, especially when he realizes that his last strong bastille must be crashed in—a bastille which is so cruel, cold, calculating, crafty, defiant, cynical. It might be well for us not to turn away too quickly from Judas, with a feeling of abhorrence. He is nearer to us than we imagine. He did nothing else than to hold this last, inner position of man against God in a critical moment and with obstinacy. He profoundly perceived that with Jesus and himself it was either He or "I," and he decided for the "I." But in the night when Jesus sat with his own, not one of the disciples was entirely certain whether he might not decide for this he or "I." Anxiously they inquired of one another, "Lord, is it I?" This should give us food for thought. We call ourselves Christians, but we do not seem to understand clearly what sort of a decision that demands. It is not at all certain that we would remain Christians, if the time should come when we hear the call before our own wall and door: "Man, you must surrender yourself, you must allow yourself to be overcome!" For us there can be no absolute certainty that we would not in such an instance defend *ourselves* to the utmost with every means and strategy.

Another thing. To conquer man and all that is human means that even the last gable in the attic must be surrendered in which man sought protection and hiding. It means the renunciation of those arms and weapons with which we ordinarily, in human fashion, have cut our way through the world by fair means or foul. It means that we hand over as spoils all these moral and religious advantages to which we continually love to appeal in support of ourselves. It means that we shall no longer prop ourselves, defend ourselves; no longer shall we assert ourselves upon such a respectable, indulgent, or refined basis. It means that we shall not make any demands upon God nor in the favorite modern fashion, attempt to prove the righteousness of God by those emergencies in the course of the world that seem to favor *us* and bring *us* joy. It means to realize that the righteousness of God means that no man is righteous before Him, that no human can expect any special patronage or special consideration from Him. And this is the case precisely because men always weaken the good and strengthen the evil, especially when they seek to establish the good and to fight against the evil.

Therefore, the man who has allowed himself to be overcome is one who makes no demands, has no surety, no rampart upon which he can depend, no wall behind which he can defend himself; he is driven out of every human position, without any human support, into an exposed spot in the midst of the profound circumstances and enigmas of life; he is hounded about, disturbed, stormed, shaken, humbled, the opposite of an assured man who has an answer for every question. Indeed, this is the man who has allowed himself to be overcome. The nearest simi-

larity and picture of such a man is the suffering and
benumbed Job, the publican in the temple, the prodigal son, the thief on the cross.   This besieged, abased,
and shaken man is the one well pleasing unto God.
For he is the man who no longer asserts himself, the
man who sees himself in the wrong in the face of
God, himself and life, and he stands before his judge
like a debtor awaiting his judgment.   If the word of
pardon follows his waiting, it appears to him as a
deed of inconceivable liberality and mercy towards
him.   When a man stands thus before God, then he
is again giving God the glory.   The "I" is overcome.
Then all is placed in the impenetrable will of God.
There is where Jesus stood.   He was this One, humbled, defeated, sacrificed man.   For he desired nothing but that the "I" of man should be overcome and
that all things should be placed in God's hands.

To this place Judas would not accompany Jesus.
For, did it not mean that he would lose all ground
beneath his feet and plunge into a chasm?   Man
defends himself against this plight as he would against
an unheard of demand which contradicts reason.   Jesus
may tread that way, but I shall not.   Rather shall I
set myself upon the side of darkness which will master
this defenseless man, than that I shall allow myself
to be unarmed.   I shall not let myself be crowded
out into the forefield, where He is, where I must surrender myself and where I shall face nothing but
death.   I shall not engage in combat with that mysterious God who demands my surrender.   I should
rather turn to the company of betrayers of the old
faith, to the Pharisees and Scribes.   There, at least, I

can grasp hold of something as tangible and secure
as thirty pieces of silver. That is Judas. That is
man as he stands immediately in front of the place
where the human must and will be humbled—the
human who imagines he can defend himself with the
defiance and the vigor of one who fights for his life.
To feel the hand which waves powerfully over us
and all our positions, and yet not to let it have its
way, not at any price! That is Judas, that is man,
the man as such, the human who must be overcome,
the human for whose sake Jesus endured death.

The betrayal by Judas proved to be a terrible illusion. Judas wanted to defend the secure foundation
under his feet, but he did not see that where this
very foundation is completely given up, *there only*
man really stands upon firm foundation. He saw
that Jesus really brings about the destruction of
man, but he did not perceive that this destruction becomes man's salvation. He heard the demand to resign all and to surrender life, but he heard it with the
fearful ears of the "old man" who will not and cannot understand that "whosoever loses his life saves
it." He had high hopes, great resolves, but down
deep he was a coward like all betrayers. He lacked
the great resolve, that final high hope which is necessary if man would throw himself into the hands of
God only. He saw the Cross only, only the blood
which must needs be shed; he saw the No only, only
the suffering, the great enemy death. He did not
see the resurrection, the victory; he did not see the
Yes, the life, the reconciliation, the kingdom, the
power, and the glory of God which illuminate us at

just that place where all our little lights are extinguished. It was quickly, terribly, and clearly indicated in Judas, how precarious is the strength of man's
foundation when he softens the reality of the Cross,
when he would rather reckon with the so-called realities of life than to plunge into the night and reckon
with God alone.

Judas' attempts did not escape the mighty shake-up
of his own fall which he had hoped to avoid. He
had to become a witness to the fact that Jesus is right,
when He holds that a man is something which must
be overcome. God is much too real, too great, that
a man can hope to hide from Him and dwell in his
own security. God surrounds him upon all sides. He
drives us into a corner so that He may force us to
meet Him. Jesus has made every position of man
quite easy to storm by means of his death and resurrection, so that it is impossible to hold it by deliberate defense.

> All things pass, God alone stands without vacillation.
> His thoughts, word and will have eternal foundation.

There comes a time, sooner or later, when this truth
shall be evident. Sometime an hour of terrible up-
heaval and ruin will come to us. This no one can
escape. Against it no betrayal can avail. The only
question is whether we shall, like Judas, defend *ourselves* against it to the utmost, only to have to encounter
it finally with despair. Or, perhaps, the Cross has
given us a presumption that this terrible, this impossible way, this way into very death which all of us
must travel, is perhaps *a way*, yes, *the way*, which

leads beyond death; a presumption that precisely *there* where everything about us comes to an end, there, on the other side, all things really begin; a presumption that if we but endure to the end, even out of the end, the judgment, the ruin, there might break forth the victory, the redemption. The question is whether we see some of the imperceptible light of the resurrection in which the Cross (as Rembrandt has painted it) stands. Oh, that we might see it, so that in the midst of our fears we would not fear, that we might dare to say "Yes,"—even against ourselves, to God. For that is the reason why Jesus endured death.

GOOD FRIDAY

Fear thou not! I am the first and the last and the living one. I was dead and behold, I am alive from everlasting to everlasting and have the keys of hell and death.—*Revelation 1:17-18*.

Fear thou not! Will we really hear, understand and accept this? The life of Jesus was the one tremendous proclamation: Fear thou not! And the death of Jesus again embraced in clearer, stronger, more penetrating fashion than any of His words and deeds which His life preached and proclaimed, Fear thou not! You should not fear because you need not. Your fear rests upon an error, an illusion. You imagine you must be fearful. But that presumption is a fallacy. You must not fear, for there is no sufficient or necessary foundation for it. You are free to be and dare to be fearless. For that reason you should be fearless. For whoever has freedom should use it and not refuse it. Will we permit this to be told us today, as the living One speaks to us His mighty word out of His death and transports us from our error into freedom?

Why do we fear? Does a child that lies in the arms of its mother need to fear, surrounded by her providing love which long before has thought of everything that is good and necessary for it? No, certainly not. But it may be that its body is racked by a terrific, delirious fever, it does not know where it is and it is "seeing things." Therefore it fears,

although it does not need to. That may be our case.
We fear because we do not know where we are. We
see many things we cannot understand, in the face
of which we feel insecure. Whence have we come,
and whither do we go? What is this little life of
ours between the cradle and the coffin, lived in the
stream of the centuries? For what purpose are these
great stormy afflictions of love and hate and greed in
which the life of mankind is tossed, about which we
shudder and from which we cannot flee? For what
end are these high thoughts of man about truth,
righteousness, freedom and progress which seem to
make life so blessed because they are so lofty, and
yet make life so miserable because they are too high
for us, because we know from our experience that our
ripening fruit falls before the night of Spring has
barely passed? How aghast we stand before the mon-
strous enigma of time, a time like our own which holds
so many questions, so much judgment, so many demands in her bosom; a time which we scarcely understand, let alone know how we should prepare for
what it will bring us. How shall we appear when
that is born which today wants to emerge, whether
good or ill? Will we be too late, will we have missed
the right moment or situation, as we have always done
in the past? Oh, who shall tell us what we are as
we flounder in the sea of uncertainty which surrounds
us? Is there around about us nothing but ghosts and
menacing shadows? Can we do anything but fear
and plaintively acknowledge that we do not know
the way in or out? (whence or whither?)

But there is in the midst of the inscrutable things—

these delirious dreams about forms and ghosts of our lot—Jesus, the crucified. Yes, in the midst of them. He, too, is a problem, an enigma. He, too, is surrounded and embraced by the incomprehensible fate of mankind. He, too, is pressed by the negativity of our existence which has such miserably small territory staked out for it. He, too, is a sacrifice of these incomprehensible and inescapable human afflictions. He, too, is in this twilight of good and evil, for he loved the good and because of the good he was rejected and condemned. He hated the evil, but to the men who were evil he was an ally and a comrade. He, too, lived in the twilight of a time of transition (turning point), a decisive moment, in the uncertainty whether a better day might emerge or even a deeper, darker night. Is it not the enigma of enigmas that Christ had to die on the cross? Is there a worse darkness in the night in which we walk than that darkness about the cross on Golgotha? Is there a stronger reason why we should fear than this fact that Jesus of Nazareth came to an end on the cross?

But this fact has another word to speak to us. He, too, is in the midst of our misery! Yes, He, too! "My God, my God, why hast thou forsaken me?" We know this question, do we not? He, too, was pressed, thronged by all sorts of ghosts which press about us. He, too, was in our state of restlessness. He, too, did not know the way out. He, too, did not know whence He came and whither He went in this world. He, too, was in fear and trembling upon a way where at every step the impenetrable darkness beclouded Him. We are not alone; He, too, is there.

Is there an uncertainty, a question, a doubt in you that is not also in Christ? He, too, is with us in death, but the *living one* in the midst of death. In His uncertainty there is certainty, assurance in His doubt, an answer in His question. There is knowledge in His boundless fear which He shares with us, a knowledge that our times rest finally upon the eternality of God, knowledge that good and evil, the righteousness of the high priests and the unrighteousness of the thief on the cross are united in the grace of God, knowledge that the mystery of the future is the mystery of God and for that reason it is a blessed mystery. In that He does not know who He is as He is beclouded by the incomprehensibility of human existence; there is one thing He does know and that is that He is in the hands of God, into which He has freely given Himself, obedient unto death. God's hand led Him into this terrible depth, God's hand sustains Him, and in God's hand He rests—*there,* where *we* dwell, in this whole perplexity and confusion—in the hands of God!

Notice that this is what the fact of the Cross seeks to tell us—it means to walk life's way upon that foundation with *God,* not to evade restlessness with *God,* to become perplexed, erring, uncertain with *God,* to doubt and question with *God!* Behold, *there* light will come, in the most lightless place of our darkness. *There* room and freedom will be found for fearlessness, where we had most reason to fear. *There* the child opens its eyes to discover itself in the arms of the mother, looks its mother in the eyes and knows that its dreams were mere dreams, for the love of the mother is *the* real, that it was there from the

beginning and will be there at the last. *There* the
strong foundation will become perceptible, the foundation which dispels all ground for fear, because of which
we will not need to fear. There the words "I am
the first and the last" are proclaimed. Christ dares
to express in the name of God, something which only
God dares to speak. He obeys God, therefore He
reveals God. He is God's first and last thought. He
is God's love which encompassed heaven and earth.
He is the meaning of man's existence, the meaning of
the world. And we see Him as the One who is with
us and dwells in our midst. We see the heavens
opened above us, the heaven we have forsaken and to
which we are again treking. It is our errors and impulses, misused powers of God, which have lost our
Lord and yet not completely lost Him. The grasping, understanding and perception of the possibilities
within the mystery of our times, the power to assent
to all that is divine in them which seeks to emerge—
how impossible it seems when we look upon ourselves,
but how simple, how easy, how near at hand it is if we
look upon Him who is the first and the last. Why
do we not know what we are and where we are? Why
should not the imperceptible become perceptible?
Why should we not learn to take sure steps in the
dark if the First and the Last is in every case *with* us
and in our midst? Should not our eyes have been
opened because He closed His on the cross? Does
not a divine light lie upon the whole world, a light
that continually battles with the darkness, but a light,
a bright light, since the darkness was so immensely
great? Was the fortress, which lay before us so threat-

eningly, pounced upon and possessed from the rear
by Him who is with us in our need and struggle,
yet who is so different from us? Were not all things,
both heavenly and earthly, made to cohere in order
and harmony through Him? "In the world ye have
tribulation, but fear not, I have overcome the world!"
We must fear no more.

"I am he that was dead, behold I am alive from
everlasting to everlasting." For a moment let us re-
consider. We must present to our minds the way
and the method of God in Christ, if we can, as a great
descension and a great ascension. "I was dead"—that
is the descension. We are fearful because we live in
the midst of death. Death is disintegration, disorder,
dissolution. So our lives appear. Here are affliction, fate, the natural order, unrighteousness, the good
and the evil, the mysterious movements of our times.
Here within us is anxiety of soul, everything is chaotic,
dissolved as death itself. In the night of this death
Christ is with us. He does not stand above us upon
a pedestal, as a righteous one over against an unrighteous, a fortunate against an unfortunate, a contented against one discontented. He enters with us,
enters deeper into life than any of us, as one over
whose life is written the placard: Death! There is
no station of our lives which He has not passed. He
is the confidant of the heathen, the friend of sinners,
the comrade of the poor, the brother of the sick, the
companion of the dead. There is no depth to which
we may descend, no difficulty into which we may
chance, no twilight in which we may stand, no struggle
we may endure, no failure we may encounter, where

we may not say: at that point Christ groaned and struggled with God in shame and loneliness and depth of soul-humiliation. Only when we delude ourselves about the majesty of death about which we groan, only when we suppose that we are secure, righteous, errorless and strong, then we must realize that Jesus Christ did not stand in such a position. We must not thus deceive ourselves. Life will see to it that a time will come when we will stand at some point on the way of life where Jesus will pass by us, at a point of the way which leads down into the depths of hell. "Blessed are those who are poor in spirit!" Those who mourn! The meek! Those who hunger and thirst after righteousness! Theirs is the Kingdom of heaven! Christ has descended and preached to the spirits in prison and hath preached the Gospel to the dead.

"Behold I am alive forevermore!" That is the ascension. Because He descended he does not make Himself commonplace. He did not sin in that He became a companion to the publican and sinner. He was *in* death, but death was not in *Him*, because He carried life into the midst of death. For that reason He cannot remain in death. He brought into the disintegration of our lives that which disintegrates disintegration. He who was bound to God now binds that which was separated. He brings the Creator to His creation again, and causes the dried-up canals to be filled, the blind to see, the deaf to hear, the lame to walk, the lepers to become clean, the dead to rise! *Now* it may simply be affirmed that mankind *is* in the power of God. Now we can reckon with that fact and we may point men to it and claim them for it. One can now proceed from the premise: every man can be helped. The deeper down he may be the surer it is that Christ passes by him and desires to take him along. One may now start from the position that there are no God-forsaken people. Not because of the virtues of men, or *their* progress, but because of the love of God in Christ which has touched the God-forsaken as well—"I have the keys of death and of hell." Christ did not fully become like unto us humans to indicate to us how poor we are, to let the penetrating light of heaven fall upon our chains, to proclaim to us that we are sinners and nothing but sinners. His blood does not cry unto heaven for rectification and vengeance as the blood of Abel. His blood shouts about mercy. The keys of death and hell which He took upon Himself are forgiveness, forgiveness and, again, forgiveness. He does not bring to an end, He brings a new beginning. He does not bring judgment, but overflowing grace. He does not cast out, He takes to Himself. He does not trample us deeper down, He leads us out. In His ascension He is not alone; rather He leads those with Him whom He has found, the children of grace and of God whom He sought in death and in hell. It is a triumphant march of the victor accompanied by many, many freemen.

And should we fear now? We must not fear if our eyes are opened and we realize that the blood which was shed on Good Friday speaks *for us* and never against us through all eternity. We must not fear when we are gripped by the prying lever of God which has been placed deep in the roots of our human burdens. When we hear the voice of Christ as the voice of God and accept it, thankfully answer with the words which we have made our own: It is finished! Yea, Amen, truly, let the whole world praise the Lord!

JESUS IS VICTOR

EASTER

And you did he make alive, when ye were dead through your trespasses and sins, wherein ye once walked according to the course of this world . . . But God, being rich in mercy, for his great love wherewith he loved us, even when we were dead through our trespasses, made us alive together with Christ and raised us up with him and made us to sit in the heavenly places in Christ Jesus.— Ephesians 2:1-2, 4-6.

What is Easter? The Bible answers: resurrection, resurrection of Jesus from the dead; and that means: the living God, forgiveness of sins, the empty tomb, conquered death—in a word, Jesus is victor. But really, are these answers? Answers which we understand, with which we may do something. Are these clear, plain, understandable words, from which light streams forth? Are they not rather hard to understand, hazy words which follow one another, which only involve us in deeper enigmas? May we not say to ourselves, "We have had enough of these old questions, these enigmas of life which daily puzzle us? We do not care to deal with these old, nor with these newer, greater questions. Life is hard and dismal. We have little enough light; and we come to church that we may receive more light in order that the little light we have may not be made dimmer, or be stolen from us."

Perhaps we are deep in doubt. We do not under-

stand life and we do not understand ourselves. We
are afraid of life. There are so many dark shadows
around us that we can scarcely find the way. After
all, is there really a way out? Does life have a meaning? And along comes Easter and says, "God, the
living God, exists. God lives. God triumphs." "Yes,
that is *the* question," you reply. "It is with this
question that I struggle. *That* is which I do not
understand, and no assumption of the Bible or of a
preacher helps me over my difficulties. The darkness becomes extremely black just when you speak
about that. Just then the question starts to burn as
a freshly inflicted wound. The living God—if only
I could grasp and understand that! If that would
only speak to me!"

Or it may be you are not a brooding person. Your
situation is quite different. You are an active, or, at
least, an ambitious, striving, progressive person. But
you chafe beneath your failures and weaknesses, and
with all your progress they still cleave to you. Perhaps you have lived for years under the curse of a
moral trespass. And no one knows why you secretly
slip back into your old faults and feel so ashamed of
yourself. Perhaps others know it, they can see it on
you. Anyway, it is a curse, an imprisonment in which
you are held. You know: "There is a worm eating
away at the roots of my life and it disturbs whatever
might grow out of these roots." And you do not
know how to be done with it. You—your better self
—are bound with chains to another, a baser I, which
you must detest, and yet you cannot slough it off,
because it belongs to you. You miserable person,

who shall deliver you from the body of this death! And here comes Easter and says: "Forgiveness of sins! Broken chains! If God is for us, who can be against us!" "Yes," you sigh, "how wonderful it would be, but it is just my burden, my misery, that I do not experience *anything* like that. This shout of joy cannot well up out of my own experience any more after all these countless failures which I have endured. Let shout who will, but rejoicing is not for me. On the contrary, forgiveness means freedom, and I first discover what chains and fences really are when we speak of freedom."

Or, finally: We must die. The untold dark moment will come for us all, when the end comes, at the place where this world sinks away and where we have to bid farewell to the realities of this life with all of its lights and shades. Where do we go then? What will be left of us? From our position we can answer nothing. As far as our human thinking and living is concerned, that is the last word. A gravemound, a few frail flowers, that is all that is left. O enigma of dying, O enigma of life, which faces us at the exit of life. And yet, again Easter comes and speaks the unheard of word about the conquest of death, the empty grave; and this word is for us the most unheard of, and the hardest to believe. Who can understand it: where all ends, there all really begins. Are we not tempted to say: "O, cease this talk, we have done once-for-all with this terrible enigma of dying. You are ripping open the old wounds anew when you speak of it!"

The final summing up of all this which is told us

at Easter is: Jesus is victor! Jesus—is it not He who was born in humblest lowliness, who died on the cross crying the cry of a derelict of God, He who forgave sins but who collapsed under the burden of sin, He, the humble, smitten by His fate; and of all those laden with grief, is He not the most burdened man of Nazareth? And He is to be *victor?*

Yes, it is always a difficult, a dark truth, a word that scarcely can be tolerated by our ears—that word "resurrection." That is to say, it is not necessarily hazy. What it really means is clear—too clear, plain —only too plain. It means what it says: something mighty, crystal-clear, complete. It signifies: That is the world, that is life with its imprisonments and tragedies of sorrow and of sin, life with its doubts and unanswered questions, life with its grave-mounds and crosses for the dead, a unique enigma, so immense that all answers are silent before it. Nothing, absolutely nothing, can one do who is in this fate, sin and death, with its thousandfold festering need; nothing can one do to stop it; everything is too insignificant to fill up this vacuum. Admit it; it negates everything; there is no way out! There might be the possibility of a miracle happening—no, not *a* miracle, but *the* miracle, the miracle of *God*—God's incomprehensible, saving intervention and mercy, the all-inclusive renewal that leads from death to life that comes from Him, God's creation-word, God's life-word—and that means resurrection from the dead! Resurrection, not progress, not evolution, not enlightenment, but what the word means, namely, a call from heaven to us: "Rise up! You are dead, but I will give you life."

That is what is proclaimed here, and it is the only way that the world can be saved. Take away this summons, and make something else of it, something smaller, less than the absolute whole, less than the absolute ultimate, or less than the absolutely powerful, and you have taken away all, the unique, the last hope there is for us on earth.

Perhaps, we still allow the word "resurrection" to *please* us very well. Yes, we reach out our eager hands towards it. Who is there that does not eagerly desire the promise of freedom, life and hope for the future! But that which disturbs us and which we will not endure, which we scarcely or absolutely will not and cannot admit, is the divine encroachment which all this presupposes, and that is our distress, the awfulness of our chains, the imprisonment which we suffer, from which there is no escape. We will gladly let anyone tell us about the love of God; we rejoice when it is ardently proclaimed to us. But do we not see that all this is meaningless patter, if we are not at the same time shocked as by a crash of lightning with a sense of the depth of our lost condition to which the love of God had to stoop? We do not like to see that we are deeply imprisoned, and that it is true, so irrefutably true, that we can not, absolutely can not, in any way help ourselves; that it is true, we are a people who live in the shadow and darkness of death; that this is true, and is proclaimed to us in, with and under the word "resurrection"—Oh, that is for us the bitter, unacceptable and unendurable truth which stirs us to rebellion. That is the darkness in the clear word "resurrection." Oh, yes, we gladly allow it to be proclaimed to us, *but* that the victory in *no* sense grows or issues *from us*, that it is *God's* victory, and that this victory is contrary to our wishes, and comes as a result of our impotent helplessness— is what we do not care to hear at all. "Ye were dead in your sins and trespasses, in which ye walked according to the course of this world. But God, who is rich in mercy, has made us alive with Christ." If only we could take the words, "God has made us alive" by themselves, without that word "but" which precedes it, and which so emphatically refers to our "being dead in our sins"! Nevertheless, it is true that wherever that crystal-clear word "resurrection" shall resound and be heard and understood, the prior word must be resounded and heard and perceived, which is—"Death." It must be seen and understood that in the midst of life, even in blooming and healthy life, there is a yawning chasm, a deep pit that can not be filled by any art or power of man. Only one word is sufficient to cover this chasm, to fill this pit, and that is the word: "Jesus is victor!"—the word "resurrection." First of all, one must see and realize that all the paths of life upon which we walk are the same, now or at any later time, in that they all lead to the same edge of the precipice, over which there is no bridge man can build in any case, but which in incomprehensible fashion has been made manifest in the resurrection of Jesus Christ from the dead. Who would partake in this resurrection, must first have seen this chasm, have discovered this pit.

And life is not easy; on the contrary, it becomes dead in earnest and difficult wherever this word "resurrection" resounds, because this word is serious. It throws clear light upon our existence and in the clarity of it we see how dark our existence is. It proclaims true freedom to us and lets us painfully discover our prison chains. It tells us that the one and only and last refuge is God. But it tells us that only because it tells us that all our positions on life's battlefield are lost and that we must vacate them. Against this fact we defend ourselves. We do not tolerate this assessment and pronouncement upon our lives, which inheres in the resurrection proclamation. For that reason we deny the resurrection, or we, at least, minimize it. We alter it. We seek to minimize this maximum word. We seek to bedim that illuminating light that falls upon our existence. We denature that truth of its unconditional, wonderful, divine essence. We alter it into something human.

And then, in our preaching on Easter day, we say something about the rejuvenation of nature, or the romantic re-appearing of the blossoms, or the revival of the frozen torpid meadows. We interpret the message that Jesus is victor, not in its literal sense, but we interpret it as a symbol or a human idea. In that case the message tells us that the world is not so bad off. After each and all evils there naturally follows something good. One must not lose his courage! Only hope! And should it be that we stand beside graves and we talk about the resurrection, we should not think of it as a literal resurrection, but rather as a continuation of life in a spiritual sense, in a limbo-like, mystic beyond, or, perhaps, in the memory of those loved ones who survive, or in those acts and deeds which the deceased one left behind. We may seek to be satisfied with this sort of a resurrection. We may get along very well for some time with the comfort that death is not so terrible. One must just not lose his courage! We may succeed for a long time with the romantic reappearing of the blossoms and the rejuvenation of spring, and thus forget the bitterness of present reality. It may be that even as we stand beside the graves of loved ones, we might find contentment in the thought of a spiritual continuation of this life. But the remarkable thing about it is that the real truth of the resurrection seems to be too strong for us, because it will not suffer itself to be hidden or concealed in these harmless clothes. It always breaks forth, through all these romantic dreams about re-appearing blossoms and the comforts which men offer each other, whereby we have concealed it; it rises up and shouts at us, asking us: "Do you really think that is all I have to say to you? Do you really believe that is why Jesus came to earth, why He agonized and suffered, why He was crucified and rose again on the third day, to become merely a symbol for the truth—which really is no truth—that eventually everything will be all right?"

And it is remarkable that this resurrection truth has a companion, namely life itself. Life itself stands up and, grasping us, asks? "Do you really think that by this easy and convenient way you can solve me? Do you not yet understand what I am all about? Do not the riddles of your existence, your sins and your futile battles against it, your death, which you are daily approaching, do not these things give you enough to think about that you imagine you can come through all these dark things without an absolutely mighty, absolutely true, an absolutely ultimate word of victory that is the vital core of life? This mighty, true word of victory is resurrection! Is all this still obscure to you? Ah, this *word* is certainly not dark, it is your *life* that is dark. The world is dark because mankind is imprisoned." But we will not admit it. And as long as we will not admit it, the word "resurrection" will be a difficult word, a rock of offense, hard and offensive, because it is so sincere and because we can not honestly face it without having to admit that life is difficult, that the world is dark, that death is not child's play, and that we are not done with our sins. No cultural education, no art, no evolutionary development helps me beyond my sins. I must receive assistance from the ground up. Then the steep walls of our security are broken to bits and we are forced to become humble, poor, pleading. Thus we are driven more and more to surrender and give up all that we have, surrender and give up those things which we formerly used to protect and defend and hold to ourselves against the voice of the resurrection's truth which spoke to us so mightily out of the facts of life. Thus we edge over very close to the place where we can hear the great "but" which immediately follows, "But God who is rich in mercy, because of his great love wherewith he loved us even when we were dead through our trespasses, made us alive together with Christ."

"*But God!*"—Yes, *there* resurrection is proclaimed. *There* eventuates a new emancipating beginning in the very midst of human transiency. There a new door opens, when all other exits are barricaded. There a new page is turned, the old is past, turned over and laid back. "But God, who is rich in mercy"—a tremendous, new and unexpected possibility opens to us after all possibilities are exhausted; a great, radiant freedom bursts forth after you harbored no more hope that you could escape the imprisonment of your character and your circumstances, your troubles and your burdens. "But God!" Perhaps you have not yet reckoned in earnest with that phrase. But you must now reckon with it and with nothing else. Perhaps you will now remark: "I cannot understand it, I do not sense it, I have not yet experienced it. It does not harmonize with my experience. I am not pious, not religiously inclined. In short, I do not have any rational ground to trust myself to it." But I might reply: "Do you not understand that the resurrection is a goal for which there is no rational ground which requires no reason, to which no human support, human knowledge or human experience can be brought to prove or make it true? It is not a question as to whether *you* can *grasp* it or not, whether there is some supporting proof of it; but the main question is whether you have that freedom which is without ground or support, without knowledge, proof or experience in the midst of your impasse, darkness and the afflictions of your life and death."

Do you have that freedom to breathe and be happy about this 'but God'? That is the primary question. Are you free enough to let your life come to such a point, where without your assistance 'even though you are dead in your sins' this is true: 'but God, who is rich in mercy . . .' Yes, truer than your sin, truer than all your experiences and your thoughts, truer than all your doubts and afflictions, truer than death, graves and hell. This freedom God will gladly give you, this freedom to breathe in His atmosphere, even though you have a thousand griefs; this freedom to rise from the dead in the victorious power of Christ, even though you are a sinner and a mortal. This is the Easter message.

This is the Easter Gospel. Why do we not believe it? Why do we always strive against this mighty "but God, who is rich in mercy . . ."? Why do we not crash through the imprisoning wall of our thought-life which keeps us from the great resuscitation which can become our possession? Why is not this Gospel preached from every pulpit? Why is it not heard in all our human constraints, upon all deathbeds and at the side of all graves? Why do we not really know that all have been made alive through the mercy of God? And even when we do know it, why is it not *the one* and *only* truth against which there is not anything of importance to invalidate it, because it pierces everything, suspends everything and renews everything? These questions are synonymous with the question: Why do we still think that we can live our life without God, even for one hour? Have we not yet sunk deep enough to see how little progress we can make alone? Yes, that is the enigma of all enigmas about which a great, single, tragic wonderment reigns in heaven— the fact that man thinks he can live and die in his own strength. On the one hand we find life with all its need and its enigmas, and on the other is God with all the lights and powers of the heavenly world, and in the midst is man in whom both seek to unite, whose existence shall become the stage upon which God desires to meet the needs of man, a stage of the resurrection, for that is resurrection.   But man will not surrender his life to it; he rebels, he does not understand and will not believe, he hides himself even in the resurrection!

Yet all we can say is to repeat, "But God, who is rich in mercy . . ."; God will have done with this enigma, the enigma of our unbelief. He has already done with it. For the resurrection is not simply *one* word, *one* idea, *a* program. Resurrection is *fact*. Resurrection has happened. The contradiction is broken. The life of man has already become the stage of the divine triumphant mercy. Jesus Christ has risen from the dead. Let us ask God that He may conquer us through His word.

HE HIMSELF

Now if Christ be preached that he rose from the dead, how say some among you that there is no resurrection from the dead? But if there be no resurrection from the dead, then is Christ not risen. And if Christ be not risen, then is our preaching vain, and your faith also vain.—I Corinthians 15:12-14.

The Chinese philosopher Lao Tse once compared man's thoughts with a wagon wheel. In this parable he said that the twelve spokes converge at the hub of the wheel, but at the place where they converge there is a hole, an empty place. And the usefulness of the wheel is dependent upon the hole. For in it is placed the axle, around which the wheel rotates. Of what use is the wheel if the hole were missing? What would we think of a wagonmaker who, perhaps in his hasty zeal tried to do his best, forgot to make a place for the hole and attempted to fill it up with his own work. Lao Tse wants to tell us that *our* thoughts are not the ultimate. They point to something else, something that is more than they, greater and quite different. Our thoughts arrive at a point, especially when they are true worthy thoughts, where they themselves cease and something quite different from mere thoughts begins or ought to begin. We love to speak of this "something different" to which our thoughts point as "the life." And we rightly test the worth of our thoughts by the criterion: do they really lead to "life" or are they of any value to "life" or not? We never consider thoughts good or valuable that are alien or antagonistic to life.

Even Christian thoughts about God, the world and man, if they are true thoughts, have an empty hole in the midst of them. At that place they stop short, or they begin, as you please. There they seem to converge into something very simple, even though they may have been ever so complex before. There they become a finger which points to something that they themselves are not, something that is greater, different, more than any thought or conception of man. At that place life, *the* reality, occupies the place of all thoughts, namely the essence itself to which all thoughts fundamentally point, that of which they seek to speak, that of which they are but reflections and mirrors. Let me be more concrete: There is where all thoughts converge, *there* all our Christian thoughts and words cease to be, there they really begin, just *there* where He himself, God, is—*not as a thought* but rather in *His essence,* in His truth, in His complete reality. As truly as a wheel has a hole in its center through which the axle is placed, so truly our thoughts and words about God and Jesus Christ (who are the same thing) must have a hole through which He Himself can come and meet us; otherwise our thoughts and words have no value. We also hope and desire to make our words and thoughts something more and different, something very great, yes, even greater, so much greater than mere words and thoughts. We grasp after Him Himself, after the living God. That is what is meant by the words that are written upon our pulpits, for preacher as well as for worshiper, in unmistakable clarity: "The Kingdom of God is not in words *but* in power!"

Do we give this truth enough consideration and do we realize its far-reaching implications? The dangerous thing about our thinking and our speaking is that we always forget it so easily. We should test every sermon that we hear or read (or preach), every Christian thought, all our pious words and, not least, our wordless feelings by this. Do they lead to that end and to that beginning where they become a finger which points beyond to the One who in reality is meant, but who is more than all our thoughts and words about Him can express, to God, the living One? Are we really serious about Him, about Himself, with whom we have to do, or are *our* pious *thoughts* and fervent *words* about Him more valuable than *He Himself?* Simply put: Is there in *our* thoughts and words a free place through which God Himself can come to meet us? Are we aware of a reverence, a humility, a respect before God? The Bible has one peculiar expression for words which fulfil these qualifications, words which are not of themselves sufficient and which point beyond themselves, words which seek to place us directly before God's presence. Such words are called: witnessing. It may be that we might come to some conclusions altogether different as regards our Christian thoughts, our Christian sermons, our Christian books, if we were to question about the *witness* that inheres in them, or that does not exist in them. For instance, there may be sermons that are brilliant, inspired, spiritual and resonant with piety, and yet they do not witness; on the contrary, it is pos-

sible to listen to simple, perhaps stammering and halt-
ing words issuing from homely lips about which we
immediately feel that in them there is witness.

Perhaps this will offer an explanation to the serious
fact which we are constantly facing: that there is so
little healing power, so little truth and help issuing
from all our Christian thinking, preaching, hearing
and praying. We do not lack zeal, or earnestness, or
orthodoxy of belief, or good will, but we lack in
witnesses and witnessing power. We should always
consider with greatest concern (even if it is only in a
casual conversation or when we are alone with ourselves) that a free space is left through which God
Himself can come to us. But instead of doing that, we
have to confess that generally our Christian thinking
and speaking is such that in place of free space where
that which is more than a human word and more than
a human thought should be, in the place where God
Himself and His Word and creativity should be, we
attempt to place something *human*, a *human* word; a
human thought is allowed to occupy the place and
assume great space. We might say that instead of
giving witness, it is prevailingly an attempt to get
along with a *human* word and thought without *witnessing*, to neglect that unseen and unspeakable Word
of the living God. We take *God's* honor and su-
premacy unto ourselves. We make His eternal, *living*
Word superfluous, because we put in its place our weak
word of man. We speak of God, but we speak of
Him in such a way that no one notices that the one
we speak about is *really God*. We speak about Him
in such a way that He cannot reveal *Himself through*

our words. To speak in the parable of Lao Tse, we
make the axle superfluous because *we* fill in the hole
at the center of the wheel.

I do not say that is always and universally the
case in our Christianity. I do not say that there is
no more witnessing. Thank God, there still is, in
words and places we scarcely imagine. But there is
very much less than we imagine. And it would be
a good thing if we would come to a point of realization and anxiety about it. But what has all this to
do with the resurrection of Jesus from the dead, of
which our text speaks? Do we not see that this is
the essence, the content of the word "resurrection"?
"Resurrection" is the word that, of all words in the
Bible, wants to tell us in the strongest and most unambiguous way: God is not *a thought*, God is not *a
word*, God is not a *feeling*. God is *the* Great *One*, the
True One, the Real and Living One, who waits to
meet us precisely at that point where *our thoughts*
about him end. The resurrection of Jesus from the
dead is the goal in the New Testament, which throws
a stumbling block in our path. "Halt!" it says. "You
are now standing before something you cannot comprehend, because He who comes forth and acts out of
the resurrection of Jesus from the dead is more than
you can think; you stand not only before the origin
of your thinking, but before your total life, you stand
before God Himself. That One who was dead should
rise from the dead is something impossible, incomprehensible and unprovable. This impossible, incomprehensible and unprovable is now proclaimed. You
have all sorts of ideas and views about God, but

now you see that God is greater, different, more powerful and more real than we had ever dared to think. From now on as you speak of God, or reckon with God, you must keep this impossible, incomprehensible in view; you must know that in your thoughts about God you confront One we can never exhaustively fathom with our thoughts. Only then are your thoughts correctly thought out, true and living thoughts." If we have forgotten who God is, resurrection will proclaim it to us, it will tell us what He is, what He wills, what He can do and continually does, and what an awful thing it is for us to dare to think about this God! If we have really understood the word "resurrection," is it possible to forget the Word of God, dare we allow Him to become something of indifferent unconcern, something nonessential?

It is this and nothing else that Jesus proclaimed throughout His whole life. It is said of Him that He preached with authority and not as a theologian. That is what differentiates Him from all that has been thought and spoken about God in the Judaistic Church before Him and in the Christian Church after Him. As none other, His word was filled with witness through and through. In all of His words and deeds He led men to that place where their hearing and seeing capacities, as such, were lost, to the place where either with rapturous joy or fear they stood before something incomprehensible, great and eternal, something which broke into their world, something which was in, with, and under His speaking and doing. He carried them into a deep uncertainty about everything old, so that He might let them reckon with something

absolutely new. There was no coercion, for real witnessing works best in the fullest freedom. Men might
think of Him as they would, but there was one thing
they all saw, namely, He reckoned with *God*, and
that means with an existence, with a power, with a
reality which is different from everything they had
seen in the world and in life. Something flashed
forth from Him, as it were, from a new world, an
absolutely other life. That is what made Him so
awful to men, for we read again and again in the Gospels that they were amazed at Him. They could not
endure the fact that He forced a vacuous hole into
all their old habitual thoughts and habits and that He
glorified God so intensely, making Him not a human
thought, a mere humanly-created God, but the living
God. They killed Him on the cross, but just *there*
that broke forth in great freedom and power which
always was breaking forth in every word and deed
of Jesus. *There the* truth was really manifested which
cannot be called a new human thought about God,
which was extinguished when its messenger died.
There was Easter. There he, God Himself, stood
before the eyes of those timorous disciples—He in
all reality, the living One, who broke forth out of
death, the resurrected One.

The "resurrection" has become the Biblical word
which expresses in the strongest and most unambiguous way who Jesus is and what throughout His life,
in word and deed, He really sought to express. Strike
out this word with all that it means, and we are striking from Jesus what He really was. From this view-
point we can understand why this word occupies the

central point of importance in the New Testament,
why it is the word that contains in itself what the
whole of Christianity really is. It is evident that
very early this word became an offense against which
we human beings rebel. As our text relates, there
must have been people in the first Christian congregation for whom this word was too strong, who would
gladly have stricken it out. But Paul says plainly,
"then everything is vain." Then Christianity becomes
as other religions, a pretty system of thought, an opportunity whereby one may cultivate *his* spirit. *But,*
then it no longer can be that which it wants to be.
"If Christ is not raised, then is our preaching vain,
our faith is vain also;" Paul wishes to say that if Christ
is not raised, that there certainly will continue to be
talk about God. God will still be thought about, there
will still be religious emotions and religious intuitions
in men, *but* as long as it is *only that,* as long as there is
nothing more, God is still obscured. The various lights
and powers of the world of God do not help us any
as long as they are merely described and thought about
and seen and promised from *afar.* These lights and
powers must come themselves in reality. That is the
novelty about, that is the mystery of, primitive Christianity over against all other religions. It does not
consist in some sort of a wisdom of *this* world, some
sort of a religious mystery cult or new-fangled worship
—the other religions of the world may even surpass
Christianity in these—but, rather, it consists in this,
"He Himself." That is why Paul fastens onto this
word: Jesus lives! He is raised, He is truly risen, not
only does His spirit continue to live somewhere beyond

death; "He Himself," the whole Jesus has come forth from the dead as the new man of God. If that fails, then the whole of Christianity fails.

Jesus lives! Let us think about the way we regard the ordinary course of our life; about the way in which our life is lived, through fortunes or sorrows, and how thereby we progress piecemeal in the power of thought and judgment; about those impossible barriers which we all sooner or later ram against. But inevitably there comes a time when we all ram against them. There is none so fortunate as to master life completely. There are iron facts which we simply cannot evade: sickness, fateful occurrences, sin, death—who will ever be done with these! How remarkable it is that life seems to be so constituted that sooner or later we inevitably stand before these facts, before these limits of our wills and activities, often in shocking, unheralded crises. And yet over against this stands the proclamation, the witness: Jesus lives! Do we not see how near this is to us? How His resurrection is the turning point of our destiny? Do we not realize what a shock our world-outlook receives *if it is true* that Jesus lives? That means that there are possibilities which we never thought of before. Jesus lives! That means that our thoughts have come to an end; they break off and through that crevice something awfully new, different, wants to break into our lives as a flood of water through a breach in a dam so as to fundamentally alter it. Jesus lives! That means that we become uncertain about everything which we thought stood firm, which seemed valid and which, in our estimation, stood unchangeable. We detect happenings that are far beyond all our thinking and imagining. We feel the foundation quake upon which we stand, the foundation of nature as we *thought* we understood it heretofore, the foundation of history as we previously understood it, the foundation of man's destiny with all of its foregrounds and backgrounds. What is nature, what is history, what is destiny, if it is true that Jesus rose from the dead on the third day? What *do* we really know about ourselves, about the world, if such happenings really take place in heaven and earth, about which the wisdom of our schools scarcely dreams? Whoever enters into this uncertainty, into this doubt about everything that before seemed so unshakable, whoever ventures out to this frontier where everything ends and something altogether different commences, he stands where Christianity begins. Yes, Christianity is an unheard-of demand, this resurrection from the dead; but if it is true that Jesus lives, how can we get around this demand? Jesus lives—that lifts the world off its hinges. "If Christ is preached that he arose from the dead, how say some of you that there is no resurrection of the dead, that the resurrection from the dead is nothing?"

Perhaps our whole impotence and perplexity, which confronts us again and again in the complex problems of life, really rests upon the fact that we so seldom, so little, or perhaps never, press through to this end and this beginning. The end consists in that it becomes unmistakably clear to us that what *we* are, what *we* overlook, what *we* do, is *not everything;* it is not the *final* thing. Jesus lives! That is the finality. But this finality is at the same time the beginning, the first thing. For it reveals God to us; it places us before *God;* it declares God to us; it asks us: Do you wish to go on and on reckoning solely with the well-known powers and capacities of your life, with that which comes out of yourself and what is readily accessible? Are you never going to reckon with what you do not know and what you are not, but what God is and can do? Or does God already belong to those many things which are all too familiar, all too ready at hand and all too easily understood?

Then your God is not God Himself, but an idol. Jesus lives! The impossible is possible, the incomprehensible is revealed. At the place where there is no way out, there *is* victory and redemption. That is God. Be quiet before this God! Is it not this quietness before God, quietness in the face of what He says, and quietness because He speaks and acts that must lead us out of our perplexity and the narrows of our life? To be quiet before God, before that God who woke Jesus from the dead, means to thoroughly doubt whether things will remain as they are, and to absolutely wait for the mighty transformation and renewal upon that God who meets everything, even through pain, yes the suffering of death. It means that we must become patient, and to become patient means to acknowledge that there is an end, not a *human* finality, but *the* divine finality to all grief. It means to have a sense of the totality and the perfection of God which is the solution of every riddle and burden. It means that we do not halt any longer at the halved and imperfect, the provisional and fragmentary which we perceive all around us, but to press forward with vigor to the highest mountain peaks, the final truths, the divine solution. To be quiet before God means, for instance, not to be quiet before money, before cares, before the powers of earthly circumstances, before men's theories and theologies, nor before death itself; to be quiet means to possess the knowledge regarding that hole which is found everywhere, through which He Himself, the living One, desires to come into our world. We will paint no pictures of the future, but it is certain that we could have a future if men among us would be quiet before God.

Yet one more thing. If we understand this we will cease to think thus: I cannot do anything for the introduction of a new world and life into the world; I am too small, too helpless, I stand in too tiny a niche for any help or salvation and truth to radiate from me. It is certainly not necessary that a man should stand in a prominent position to mean something for the world in the name of God. Why should one not allow himself to be led to that finality and that beginning and there learn to be quiet before God! Life is the same everywhere and God is the same everywhere. A child, a servant girl, a factory girl, a confirmant, as they learn how to be quiet before God are of as much worth as a minister of state who does likewise. As far as the resurrection is concerned it is not a matter of *who* you are, what you think or are able to do, but it is a matter of *God*, He Himself, and what He is, what He can think and is able to do. It is nothing else than a matter of whether we are willing to give Him place, He who can and will help beyond our pleading and our understanding. Jesus never made any distinction between the great and the small. When He laid His hand upon a child and as He died on the cross, both times, it meant the same thing! God must step into the centrum, God must become great in the life of man —God, God Himself, God alone. If in our little troubles which our own life or the lives of other men provide for us, and with which we have to deal; if in our heavy burdens which our larger responsibilities provide for us and which rest upon our shoulders; if in them we would only think of God, call upon God, become quiet before God, become quiet before *Him*, Him *Himself*, the terribly great might lie latent even in the small or even the infinitely small.

Is not the truth we must learn very simple and very close to us? Why is it that this which is close and simple is so hard to understand and so remote? Why is it that time and again we do not understand this "He Himself," in which the whole of Christianity is encompassed? Is it not possible that we should awake and be done with this resistance to God, that God might select us to become His witnesses? Watchman what of the night—is it not nearly past?

COME, CREATOR SPIRIT!

And they were all filled with the Holy Spirit and began to preach with other tongues as the Spirit gave them expression . . . They were all amazed, marveled and began to say among themselves: Behold, are not all these that preach Galileans? How does it come that we each hear in the language wherein we were born? Parthians and Medes and Elamites, and those that dwell in Mesopotamia and Judea and Cappadocia, Pontus and Asia, Phrygia and Pamphylia, Egypt and in the remote Lybia near Cyrene and sojourners of Rome, Jews and proselytes, Cretes and Arabians, we hear them speaking in our own tongues the mighty words of God.—*Acts 2:4, 7-11.*

Undoubtedly in our reading of the Pentecostal event, we have wondered how all those strangers who had streamed into Jerusalem, the Parthians, the Medes and the Elamites and those who dwelt in Mesopotamia and in Judea and Cappadocia, Pontus and Asia, Rome and Egypt, how all these heard the Apostles in their own tongues, so as to understand the great deeds of God about which the Apostles witnessed. We have wondered about it, and perhaps rejoiced over it, as we would over a great promise. For we feel remarkably near, or somehow related, to these strangers, as though they were flesh of our flesh and bone of our bone, feeling ourselves even nearer to them than to the Apostles. Just as they came from afar, so do we. We were not present when Jesus lived, taught and wrought, died and rose again. We are separated from

Him by centuries, we speak a totally different language, we have totally different insights and outlooks. What has a person of today in common with that age, with that generation?

What is told us about Jesus is certainly beautiful, but still it is so distant, so distant. Again and again we discover anew that there is a terrible chasm which yawns between the now and here, and the then and there. And shall this chasm be bridged, this difference dissolved and be no more? Shall human beings who are separated from Him through time and space hear Him speak as though He were present, out of the mouth of His witnesses? Is there no space nor time separating them from Him and His time? Did He become their contemporary? Is the old distinction between Jew and Greek, Persian, Mede or Elamite, invalid; is there no more such a thing as estrangement or alienation?

This is what the story of Pentecost tells us. Now if we pleased, we might look upon this story as a beautiful tale born out of literary emotion. But if we have ears to hear we shall hear more than a pretty tale. Here is real knowledge, deep ultimate insights into that existence which Jesus is. What is told us here is that Jesus not only was, but that He is, and will be. He does not exist here or there in a certain place; for Him there is not only a "once" and a "then," but he is yesterday, today and the same in all eternity; in a word, Jesus is "standing in the midst." That is what is told us here. He "stands in the midst" means that what He says is not only a historical utterance of truth which has validity for, and was understood in, a certain time, but here—and wonderful to say—the eternal appeared in the casual, the Godly has appeared in the human. He "stands in the midst," and that means that around Him the world stands still as a circle around its central point. And just as every point on the circle is equidistant from the centrum, just so it is no farther to Him today than it was in times past.

Not without reason is there engraved on our communion table, "Take, eat, this is my body broken for you, my blood which is shed for you for the forgiveness of your sins." That is as true today as it was a thousand years ago, and it will be as true a thousand years from now as it is today. He stands as the centrum. This story wishes to tell us nothing else. It tells us that on Pentecost, when He was spoken about, all understood. When speech really tells about Jesus, then there is not a single person who, when asked to understand, could not understand. Of what significance are the differences of language and culture as compared with this one, great redeeming Word which He came to tell us! That He stands in the midst means: these thousandfold distinctions of world and life outlooks sink away in His presence. We are often concerned how we may present Jesus to the differing ages and stages of life, so that men may understand Him. How should we preach to the cultured? to laboring men? to youth? How much more important it is to consider whether it is really *Jesus* who is proclaimed and whom we would have draw near us. If we actually gripped the centrum, where He stands, with our speech, if it were really He of whom we spoke, would we need to trouble ourselves about these differences of age and social station? As the circumference of the circle is around the center, so all the ages and stages are placed around Him. Or as a grenade crashes through the structure of the house from the top to the bottom, so the Word of God which Jesus brings, crashes through the structure of life in which we humans dwell, from the pinnacle to the deepest basement.

There is no floor nor wall that is too thick for Him. There are no fundamental psychological, racial or social distinctions which confront Him as an unscalable barrier. Would that the Church might not be so timid when she speaks of Him, especially in the face of human foolishness and misunderstanding which are so often put in His path! If only she had a holy fear to really speak of *Him* and of no other! That is Pentecost. That is what Pentecost proclaims—this one thing: that Jesus is the centrum, and that history with all its generations stands still in His presence and that all distinctions dissolve before Him.

Now, of course, *that* Pentecost in Jerusalem, that past event had, and still has, something of an advantage. Even this, that particular Pentecost became an actual reality! There *were* people who had ears that heard, eyes that saw, people who were permitted to perceive, and, because they perceived, they were able to express the fact that Jesus is the centrum. They were permitted to see, to feel and to touch, and because they did, the truth that Jesus came to proclaim streamed from them as a light in the night—the truth that is not simply *a* truth *alongside* of others, but *the one* central fact of the world that is valid for all men.

But is it not true that what seems to be an advantage
for them is not an advantage over us, for is it not possible for us to have what they had, if we follow them?
For they, too, are but a point on the circle's circumference of which Jesus is the center, just as we are. And
why should not illumination of thought come to other
points of the circumference "now here, now there, in
the East and the West"? Why should it not become
manifest on every point of the circumference, come to
light round the entire earth and burst forth in every
age and in every tongue, that Jesus is Lord? Why
should not the word of the Lord which He gave be
fulfilled, "I will pour out my spirit upon all flesh"?
Why should not all lands once again become full of
the glory of the Lord? Why should not Pentecost
really and finally come again?

Upon first thought it is, perhaps, seldom acknowl-
edged that there might be *one* truth that is given for
all times and generations. But only upon first thought.
For in reality the truth that we human people are
closely bound together through all times and generations is not so strange and so remote. There are great
differences among us, but there are greater similarities.
The remarkable fact is that in considering the similarities we find they are not the successful achievements
of life, but the deep depressions; it is the burdensome,
the serious, the sorrowful and the tragic that we have
in common. These so-called climaxes of life to which
we ascend tend rather to separate us from one another
than to lead us together and bind us with one another.
We need to descend into the valleys and depths of our
lives in order to come to the place where we feel very

near to one another, the place where we belong together and where we find ourselves together; to the place where we feel that we are all sinners, that we all go astray and that we spend our lives in a thousand mistakes and follies. That is such a great similarity which every one experiences and from which no one is excepted. That all of us are passing through hard times which make us despair of an answer to life's riddle— is it not true that this fact is another similarity of ours?

And a fact that includes everything else—we must die—is a fact in which we are all united from pole to pole, from the year two thousand B.C. to two thousand A.D., all of us, "Parthians and Medes and Elamites." Therein we stand together like children in a great circle, hand in hand. I can say: that is also a centrum to which all our eyes are turned, which every one of us without exception knows. A dark and a tragic point indeed. It is no small matter to have death as the centrum of life, death and his premise, sin and sorrow. A short time ago a troup of players in our city produced the dance of death, in which death stood in the center and around him stood all ages and conditions of life. To each he spoke a language like the Pentecostal language, one which every one understood in his own "tongue," and every one understood him and obeyed him—the peasant, the man of the world, the soldier, the beggar, the king, the mother, the aged. There was enacted the mighty fact and all who saw it had to say: "Yes, that is true, so it is, that is our fate, we all must thus obey death." Certainly, it is true. The world has one central point—death. Time

stands still—at the grave. Differences are dropped—
in death.

Now, can we measure what Pentecost means? It
means nothing less than that behind this central point
of death a new, other, central point arises. Behind
death, the Prince of Life; behind the transient, the
Eternal; behind death, the resurrection. What is so
hard to understand about Pentecost is not that something new wants to emerge which is valid for all, which
affects all. That should not make us wonder. Daily
we see in the lives of suffering, sinful and dying people
something which concerns us all and in which we are
all similar. But what makes us wonder and what is
hard to understand about Pentecost is that all this general transiency, imprisonment and chance-existence of
mankind shall be invalidated. That which until now
is called sin shall be forgiveness; that which until now
is called fate shall be called mercy; that which until
now is called transiency and the grave shall be called
eternal life; that which until now is called chance is
called God's will and guidance; that which until now is
called man's wit and wisdom is called God's Word by
which we live!

This great reversal, this great light which arises
upon the people who have wandered in darkness, this
is something it was not possible for us to grasp or to
understand. And it is not easy for us to grasp it. It
is a colossal reversal. Here is proclaimed the miracle
of the Holy Spirit. For when a man comes to the
point where he understands that, he is, as he is, God's
child, elevated to the eternal arms despite, and in the
midst of, all his transiency, so that the grave and judg-

ment do not make him fear any more, and in the midst of his confused walk of life he has an unfathomable hope. In a word: where a person understands Jesus Christ, then it is no longer his own little human spirit, but God's own Holy Spirit who has given him the understanding and who gave his spirit the witness. That is the miracle of the Holy Spirit which makes Jesus Christ contemporary, which places Him and His truth in the center of the truth which is always true, the truth which is applicable for you and me through all times and generations. We, the strangers, we the distant, are able to be stewards with God! Who would not rejoice at that! Who would not worship!

The Kingdom of Heaven is come nigh. But why is it, that we feel and know so little about it? Why is it, that this good news which can burst graves asunder and raise the dead has been so small, so insignificant, so commonplace among us? I shall attempt an answer. Our life is a wandering alongside a wall. But this wall is broken here and there by hidden doors which lead into the Kingdom of Heaven. We are not far from the Kingdom. There is no point upon the circumference of the circle that does not bear a direct relation to the center. There is no moment of time that is without the eternal light from above. There is nothing mortal that can not put on the cloak of immortality. If in spite of these possibilities we have such vacant and dead stretches in our lives, if we stand at the wall and not at the doors, if we merely hesitate and doubt and breathe the air of decay, it need not be so, and it is only right that we should be astonished that we are in such a plight. Would that the sense, the astonishment, as to the distance from God, in which we live, might grow greater among us! We certainly would not complain about our lot, about evil people in the dismal world, if nowhere there were to be found doors that lead from death to life. But we will have to fret about *our* blindness and foolishness, *our* failure to understand our situation, simply because we do not have ears to hear, nor eyes to see, nor lips to proclaim the mighty deeds of God which can be heard and seen and proclaimed in every situation, every place and every hour.

There is where we stumble against the great rock of guilt and responsibility which confronts us in the message of Pentecost. We think of the word of Jesus: who is not for me is against me. Truly, the Holy Spirit seems to be behind a wall, and it seems as if our behavior either adds more stones to it or it takes stones away. For we are doing one or the other every moment of life. Either we are approaching Pentecost, approaching that word which God has for, and wishes to speak through, every situation, or we are departing from Pentecost. Either we are worshiping death, or we are worshiping the power of love. Every moment of life that is sorrowful and empty and cold is an indication of rebellion against God. And every moment of life in which something within us is entranced, in which we become restless, in which we quest and sigh and stretch forth our hands, means a step nearer to that place where one can see again, where tears are dried, where the sighs, sorrows and crying cease. Oh, if we only realized just what life means! If only we would take life seriously, really seriously, if we could only release our members from the slavery of this transient existence and allow ourselves to be taken captive in the slavery of the eternal existence! What shall we do? Stir up that seriousness and that desire for the eternal existence! Struggle for it daily, hourly!

We are guilty of one error, we strangle ourselves in *one* foolishness. We say yes to the low and the common. We open the door to hate or some other passion. In such a situation, what does it mean to take one step towards Pentecost? It does not mean that we resolve that these errors and foolishnesses and sins shall simply be stopped, so as to be done with them at a single stroke. That is not in our power. We are too much imprisoned in this transient existence. It means, rather, that we feel ourselves guilty and that we suffer because we feel it and that we will not consider our precarious situation lightly. Actually we treat it too lightly always. We seem to skim over the surface so smoothly. We do it, perhaps, with a few simple proverbs. We quickly come to the surface only to slide back into the depths again. Is that not something to fear? Something to make one want to agonize, to make one ask, seek and knock? Perhaps, at this very moment we are standing at the door through which the Prince of Life wants to come to us. Nothing else is required but that we place ourselves under judgment and acknowledge that we are aliens, living in a land of estrangement, for then only will we have a longing for home. Nothing else is required of one who would have Pentecost become a reality, except the spirit of supplication which comes when one cannot endure the awful alienation and forsakenness of his soul.

Or, perhaps, we are complaining about our situation. We would like to escape from these hard times. But do we really want to enter into the new times of God? Oh no, we desire only the old days in which we earned and ate in undisturbed freedom. How can God's Spirit speak to us about the age of God which strains to emerge, so long as we are so far from the spirit by which we must wait for it? This is the impediment that must be laid aside if something new and other than now is would burst forth among us. For Pentecost will become a reality only when we come to the point where we find the misery of our situation unbearable, and where it will be possible to see that only God's help can avail. Then it will be Pentecost.

We are always too secure, too easily comforted, too quickly pacified. We utilize every and any method whereby we can minimize and make insignificant that which plagues and weighs us down—our sins, our need, the fact that we must die. But these are not insignificant and trifling. They are immense and burdensome. In fact, they are so immense and burdensome that nothing avails but that *one* thing through which our lives receive a new centrum which is Jesus Christ. When it becomes clear to us that not only for the heathen in far-away lands, but for us as well, yes, precisely for us in the old christendom, only one remedy is great enough—then we will again face Pentecost. For it is the way of Jesus to come to us when our hearts are heavy. When we are at our wits' end for an answer, then the Holy Spirit can give us an answer. But how can He give us an answer when we are still well supplied with all sorts of answers of our own? Nothing blocks God's way more than our profession that goodness, excellence and wisdom creep *up* out of *ourselves*. But when we come to the point where we know nothing, when our breath is gone from us, when nothing more blocks His way, then He can come with power. Our greatest sins, as well as our needs and mistakes of our age, are small matters to Him, if only we are ready to hear Him. The deeper in we stand, the more Jesus helps us. The more deeply we sin, the richer His forgiveness. He beckons the weary and heavy laden to Himself and pours out His Spirit upon those who know it not. He refreshes those who are tired and does not extinguish the flame that burns low.

This is what Pentecost proclaims. It proclaims the break of God's Day. We are deeply sunk in the night of the history of man. Certainly, we have a variety of lights which clarify the way a few steps ahead for us, but they simply cannot attempt to make the night like unto day. Perhaps they even hinder that day that wants to break upon us. But it is necessary for us to acknowledge that these human lights and spirits are far too short in duration. The times through which we are passing are difficult enough. But perhaps we shall learn to thank God some day for these difficult times, for they have served to open our eyes to whom the centrum of life is and who can and wants to take the central place at any and every moment. Come, Creator Spirit, come to us and dwell with us!

"SEEK THE THINGS THAT ARE ABOVE"

If then ye were raised together with Christ, seek the things that are above, where Christ is, seated on the right hand of God. Set your mind on the things that are above, not on the things that are on the earth.—*Colossians* 3:1-2.

It is God's fire cast upon the earth and God's spirit poured out upon all flesh that compel us to *seek* the things that are *above*. We are not voicing ecclesiastical or backstairs truth. We are not offering a so-called religious or ethical or aesthetic truth. We are speaking God's truth, truth from God of whom and through whom and to whom are all things. And because it is God's truth it grips us and holds us firmly gripped. Let the darkness around us be ever so great and complete, and let the light which shines in our darkness be ever so remote and dim, it remains true that for God's sake we must seek the things that are above. For darkness is not too dark for Him, and the night shineth as the day. We may forget this truth in childish disappointment; in bitterness or foolish arrogance we may prick against its goads. For God's sake it is and remains true, nevertheless! Perhaps we have longed that we might live and suffer and die like the beasts of the field which do not know the disturbing antithesis of beneath and above. Perhaps we have endeavored to escape the ominous injunction: "Seek the things that are above!" And the condition of our life is proof of such endeavor. But such desires are vain and cannot be fulfilled. We are bearing the indestructible mark of God's image, even if we have forsaken God and have taken to gods and idols. God's image in man is our remembrance of the things that are above. They will not let go of us but make life a long and restless search and discovery of ever new wants and quests.

Our perverted thoughts and deeds have often enough given the lie to, betrayed and ravished, this remembrance of the things that are above. Our blindness, our troubles and despair have blurred them, yea, all but wiped them away from before our eyes. We no longer knew what were these things that are above; we no longer understood ourselves. But ravished and extinguished, forgotten and all but lost (and is there a man who will deny that we are speaking of him?), because it is God's image that we carry, we cannot be rid of them. The witness of Christ says that we are indissolubly bound from all eternity to this remembrance, in spite of every contrary experience, and in spite of what we know of ourselves. The things against which our whole life from the very depth of our heart cries out in protest are the real, necessary and abiding things in our life, the very life of our life. Because we never seem to know these first things, which it is so necessary for us to know, let this present hour tell us again, not as a matter of human experience or knowledge, but as a witness of Christ: Seek the things that are above! Here is valid truth; the other is not valid, it is untruth. We may and shall ever err. But this truth can never be subverted, not even in our error. God will not be mocked. And God never ceases to be faithful and true!

But what does it mean when we are told: "Above where Christ is, seated on the right hand of God"? Is it not answer enough when we hear that Christ is there? Where Christ is, there God is become man. It means that mercy, which passes all understanding, has visited us in our misery. Here the outcast is again received into a home; here men without comfort are being comforted; our human nature, lost in sin and death, is saved, renewed, and reunited with its Creator. Above, where Christ is is God's miracle. It is not a miracle existing and abiding only within God. Nay, it is God's miracle which He works upon us (and no miracle of God can be greater than this!). Above, where Christ is, is the large, divine nevertheless! We have no tongue for it; but it has been spoken, and is being spoken, to us; and perhaps we may stammeringly repeat it after him as it strikes us and lifts us up from our despondency or our folly, from our presumptuous pride, or from whatever will rise within us against this word of God. Above, where Christ is, there is no devil. The devil is a liar from the beginning. He is a very serious reality here below, in the world of spirits and of the spirit which surrounds us—in the air we breathe, even if the atmosphere is very Christian, very ideal. He, who denies that the devil is here, is a fool,—today more so than ever. The devil is the prince of this world. But he is not above. The reality of the miracle, which God is working upon us, beats back the devil's reality. The right hand of the Lord is exalted; the right hand

of the Lord doeth valiantly. The poison gas, which
we are breathing, is driven off when and where God's
free mercy meets it. And God's free mercy is found
of them who are compelled to seek it.

Above, where Christ is, there is no condemnation
by reason of our sins. Judgment is a fearful life
reality, too. Woe to us for every quarter hour in which
we thought ourselves to be exempt from it on account
of our good intentions or large successes or even on account of a good conscience. In all the world there
is no recoil quite so fearful as the recoil which comes
from this presumption. But not even judgment is
above; it is beneath also. Judgment is whatever comes
to us in life or death *without* Christ. With Christ
alone do we recognize that this is so; and so we stand
free in the judgment. "For God sent not the Son
into the world to judge the world, but that the world
should be saved through him." Above, where Christ
is, there is forgiveness, forgiveness of our unmeas-
ured and ever new sins. And he who receives forgiveness does not remain in judgment, as certainly as
he will no longer seek to make his escape from it or
endeavor to justify himself. For the sake of God's
forgiveness in Christ, "look up, and lift up your heads;
because your redemption draweth nigh!"

Above, where Christ is, there is no death. Death's
dominion reaches as far as our eyes can see. It is in
the beginning and end of all our ways. To kill and
to be killed are our arts and sciences. Death is the
last word and the ultimate fate in our struggle for
existence. We ought not to forget this barefaced
truth. Pagan fear and wisdom of death is sometimes

more Christian than a certain Christian optimism about life. Perhaps they are a bit more aware that, and from what, we must be saved, even if they do not know the Saviour. Death rules on the earth below. It extends over our life, and even our spiritual and religious life is locked in its gruesome embrace. Mankind's history, the history of religion and the church offer no eternal values. They are a part of the earth beneath. And what is earthly at best means want—parable, hope, and pilgrimage. But above, there is no death. Christ lays death as the last enemy at the feet of God, the Scriptures tell us; and our reason pants for breath when it attempts to follow what the Scriptures say.

For immortality we do not need to look, but there will be resurrection, resurrection and life on the battlefield and final resting place of our existence; fullness for our emptiness; truth of our parables; the goal of our pilgrimage; and God's work where our works are at an end. Summing it up, we may say: Above, where Christ is, there is not a God who dwells in impenetrable mystery. The incomprehensible and unsearchable God whom men may worship only in the dust and from afar, as did the publican in the temple, is not there. Let me say it very explicitly: such worship is the rule here below on earth, even if we believe in God. In fact it is the believer who will ever worship Him so. Woe to us, if we shall ever stand before God in a manner different from the publican's in the temple. But God is not inscrutable above, where Christ is. Nay, Christ is the revelation of God's mystery. Above, where Christ is, we see God face to face. In Christ God has stepped forth from behind the veil of His glory and assumed humanity. It is God's miracle, the miracle of this "above," that there our life, as it now lies in the shadows amidst devil, death and judgment, is again received and immersed into the radiant light of divine glory. It is written of the publican who worshiped from afar and dared not lift up his eyes to heaven that he went down to his house justified. Not that our beneath had now become an above; but there is no beneath without an above. We can and ought to seek in our beneath as it is, the things which are above.

But however real and true may be this "above, where Christ is," how shall we ever come to seek it? Are we inclined to do it? Have we faculties for this quest? Are we the creatures who are able to go in search of it? Must we not confess that our every quest is, and shall ever be, a search for the things that are on the earth? We may be able to look for gods and idols, yes;—but for Him who is eternal mercy? We may be willing to fight evil with ways and means of our own, yes;—but with the right hand of the Lord that is exalted and doeth valiantly? We may be yearning for the comfort of a good conscience, yes;—but for the comfort of forgiveness? Perhaps we can search out the origin of mortal life; but shall we find the life which has left death behind? We are quite capable of the Pharisee's justification, yes indeed;—but of the publican's justification, of revelation? Must we not hopelessly drop back to earth in our search, as a man attempting flight? What does

it mean to seek, if these are the things which we are
to seek?

And now see how Paul, as a witness of Jesus Christ,
places God's eternal power into the very heart and
center of our human impotence. He does not merely
say, Seek!; but he says: "*If then ye were raised together with Christ,* seek the things that are above."
You—we "raised together with Christ"! Do you
know what it means? It means that you do not need
to seek the things that are above as you are looking
for things which you do not possess. Nay, here the
search begins with finding. It is not at all a question
of practicing a great art, or of undertaking a daring
flight of the spirit, or of rearing a sky scraping edi-
fice. Such things are done on earth. To seek the
things that are above means to be just what one has
to be, if the things that are above—God's mercy, God's
victory, God's forgiveness—are valid, if the resurrection of the dead is true. It means to take life, the
life here below, seriously in the light of the tender
mercy from on high which has visited us.

Once again—with the gift begins prayer; with the
find, the search; and with stepping into the open
door goes knocking. To be, means here to become.
To be what? To be "raised together with Christ"!
What does it mean? Does it mean to be a hero? A
wise and pious man? A religious personality? To
have sunshine in the heart? To have a good conscience? No, no; and I had almost said, God save
us from these! It means to be simply human here
below; but to be a human being to whom the *word*
has been said—the word which eye has not seen, nor

ear heard, and which has not entered into the heart of man; the word of the things that are above which God has prepared for them who love Him—a man who heeds when he is told, "Behold, I make all things new!" It does not necessarily mean that such a man will live in the sunshine of a beautiful and pure universe; or that men admire his large worth and noble memory; or that he possesses, and effects in others, a feeling of the divine presence. No, perhaps he must be a man who desperately, but vainly, is swimming against the stream, ever wrestling and ever pinned down; perhaps he must be a flickering candle somewhere in a corner, and perhaps it must be so for him lest he forget to seek the things that are above. He may, however, be a different kind of man. He may be or become a man of large importance (in men's judgment). Then he must, as a rich man on earth, seek in his riches the things that are above. And the richer he is, the more difficult will be his task. The quest itself, however, always begins in poverty and want, or rather in God's riches. Its beginning is always our being told and given what is told and given in Christ Jesus to us sinners, slaves and mortal men; that "we were raised together with Christ."

But we must not receive the word and the gift as something that is also true among other truths; but as the one and only and decisive truth; as the decisive weight which turns the scales of our life. It must not come to us as a word and gift from an indefinite someone; but as God's word and gift. He makes them valid, absolutely and finally valid. It means that you cannot consciously, intentionally and of your

own free will and choice enter into a compact with
the devil and the brutal spirits of the earth. You
cannot think and speak as if there were no forgiveness.
You cannot resign yourself to fate at the expense of
hope; to death at the cost of life; to corruptible nature at the cost of God's incorruptible spirit. You
cannot waste your time in vain arguments with the
Pharisees in the temple—to the greater glory of Christianity. You can no longer ignore and deny God's
revelation in favor of what, alas, is only too true without and apart from God's revelation. What we are,
unwittingly and against our will but continually, becoming guilty of, along this line at the expense of
faith and love and hope, is quite enough. What God
has told and given us, is stuck fast in our flesh as a
barbed hook. Provision is made that the flesh lives
on under God's long-suffering; we do not need to help
keep it alive or fatten it. God may indeed be long-
suffering where we must not be. Let the barbed hook
stick; agree to the protest that is being raised here
against us and the world; let the anxiety which it
has created in us do its work!

To seek the things that are above means not to an-
tagonize the established divine fact, but to let it be
in our small and large concerns the *divine* fact as He
has placed it in our weakness and untruth, in our
temptations and falls, on our cemeteries and battle-
fields, in the world of phariseeism and sadduceeism;
placed there not by us and our fathers, not by way of
a discovery which was made by men, not by the church
or tradition; but placed there by God's own word and
the witness of this word. The upright in heart will

give it silent regard, even if it is too large for him to hold; and he will certainly not contradict it. Indeed, the least that all of us can do is not to contradict it; and by all means not contradict it with a Christian pretense. And what then? you may ask. Must not something more be done? Oh yes, a great deal more will then be done. But everything will follow in a natural way; no, it will come from God into whose hands we have then surrendered that He may use it in one way or another, either to make us or to break us. How should we now fail to fulfill life's chief end? But seek ye first the kingdom of God and his righteousness, and all these things shall be added unto you.

Or shall we deny that we are raised together with Christ, and that God has laid His hands upon us? Shall we deny that we have heard it said to us, "Awake, thou that sleepest, and arise from the dead!" Or if we do not deny, shall we say in doubt, I have not *understood* the saying? But what does "understand" mean *here*? That God is the Lord, we have never, and yet long since, understood. Do we need to *consider* and *discuss* this, as if we were met on debatable ground? How unimportant are our views when God's Either-Or confronts us! Or is this the time to wait? And what could we be waiting for? Shall we be differently situated with God, say, tomorrow, or ten years hence, or in the hour of death? The truth stands; it is in force now and demands acknowledgment, "Seek the things that are above!" But it does not depend on me to make it a pressing truth for you; and it does not lie with you to feel its imperiously impetuous urgency. The truth does its own speaking and hearing. It is mouth and ear, light and eye, for the very reason that in the Risen Christ the truth is God and man. Let it stand in the midst between you and me, not as *my* word, and not as directed at *you:* Today, today, if ye hear his voice, let *not* your hearts be hardened!

PASSING ALL UNDERSTANDING

And the peace of God, which passeth all understanding, shall guard your hearts and your thoughts in Christ Jesus.—Philippians 4:7.

The Bible leads us constantly to a point where we ask ourselves the question, Shall we go on or shall we stop and return? We feel like a man who has followed for a time a beautiful and inviting highway toward a seemingly near and easily reached goal. But suddenly he comes to a sharp curve in the road and realizes that the road leads on much farther than he anticipated. Beyond the immediate goal in the forefront, new valleys and new heights are opening up to his eyes. And now we stop and wonder, shall we continue or shall we return? One thing is quite clear to us: the highway on which we are standing leads on. It is quite evident that it passes beyond the point where we stop and hesitate. It means that we should not remain standing still in our tracks. It invites us to seek the faraway yonder which is beckoning us. But are we the people who really dare to undertake the journey to this great beyond? This is the question that is troubling us.

We have read the Bible, perhaps at length and not without profit. We have heard many a beautiful sermon and drawn from them many good and worthwhile lessons. But we have a notion that it is our own business what and how much we care to take to heart. A part of the way we go along gladly and willingly because it so pleases us, or because we are in agreement with what we read and hear. We find it profitable and necessary to hear this or to participate there or to bid welcome to another thing. But we are quite determined to remain masters and lords in our own houses. We are not at all minded to follow through against our socalled better judgment. We reserve at all times the right to say: Now I have had enough; I do not wish for more; this does not strike my fancy, it is too oldfashioned or too modern; I do not find it convenient; it does not fit into my scheme of things; it does not meet my requirements or fit my special need; or we refuse because we are afraid of consequences. In general it is quite true that we deal with matters of the spirit and with religious problems as if they were merchandise. What we need we take along because we can make good use of it. So it has come to pass that the term "religious need" has become a favorite expression in the church of our day. And now the Bible or a sermon may make us aware that we are not lords and masters in our own houses, and that the highway on which we are traveling is not a road of our own choosing, and that we cannot leave it at our own discretion. We are made to face the fact that it is not at all the question whether or not we care to give room to this or that thought. Yes, there are thoughts, spiritual forces and powers which assert their inalienable right to enter our life, even if they are not bidden to come in. We are becoming aware that engaging with God's word and truth is a dangerously large and serious matter. Suddenly we have been caught up by a current which is carrying us far, far beyond our safe havens to new and unknown shores.

When we have reached this point, we have reached the place where the really deep and true and original meaning of the Bible has its beginning. Whatever in the Bible, in Christianity, and in things divine lies before this sharp curve; whatever we take from a sermon without being deeply stirred, challenged and duty bound; whatever does not make us feel that something that is wholly large and wholly strong is meeting us that it might win us; whatever we are able to receive guilefully innocent because we feel it to be a desirable deepening and enrichment of our life as we have lived it until now: all these things are not real and genuine Christianity; it is not the truly biblical content of the Bible; it is not yet the divine itself. On its face it may look to be good and true and even pious; but it is not yet that which is wholly serious and true and pious. It is not that singular fear and adoration of God's glory which is the Bible's chief concern.

Let me repeat: where the highway leads beyond our near and well-known goals to a strange and unknown land,—to that land into which Abraham dared to set his foot because he was constrained to set it there, to that land of which he also knew nothing except as God showed it to him,—there, there alone genuine Christianity has its beginning. Where we can no longer be our own guides; where we must resign our sovereign ways because of One who confronts us with His claim of being our Lord, there indeed begins the

fear of the Lord. Where our need ceases to be the
decisive factor of valid truth, because truth forces
itself upon us in its own right and of its own dynamic;
where we humbly and gratefully open our doors to
it, receive it, and so become one of its least servants;
there is fear of the Lord. For here only do we stand
before the divine itself where we bow and submit.
Here we can do no other than become obedient. Here,
and here only, and just here is the divine, a subject
with its own inherent dynamic which, standing in its
own right, does not live by grace of men. And here
is its sign: it has its beginning where men have reached
their end. Its majesty meets us only at yonder borderline where in our willing and working we are
made to pant for breath. "Where my cunning and
my fortunes can do nothing, cannot help, comes my
God and undertakes to confer His wealth and riches,"
sings the poet in one of our beloved hymns. To bring
us to this point, to this sign of God's highway, to the
borderline of our humanity, to the end of what is
earthly, and so to the beginning of things divine, just
this is the aim of every thought and word of the Bible.
It may well be said that if our churches and chapels
do not bring us to this point; if our Christianity does
not carry in its bosom something of this strong and
dangerous current; if we can listen to sermons only
to be edified, without becoming aware of a keen edge
where matters become grave and serious; if our Christianity leaves us in an undisturbed notion and fancy
that we are our own lords and masters, then so much
the worse for us. We may then possess some good,
discreet, and even religious values; but we have no

genuine Christianity. Something is wanting. In fact,
the chief and decisive thing, the very heart and nature
of Christianity is wanting. Let me put it more simply by saying, The cross is wanting; and therefore
resurrection is wanting also. For the import of the
cross in our Saviour's life is this that there the
boundary between God and man appears with decisive
majesty; there the borderline becomes apparent where
man's extremity, man's impotence, man's failure and
sin, and the mark of death upon his forehead, are
clearly seen. And here also is the import of the resurrection, that on this borderline, and only here, the
sublime majesty of God's will and power, the whole
magnitude of divine forgiveness and reconciliation,
and the glory of the peace of God, are made manifest.

It is not necessary, it is indeed impossible, that we
should reproduce Jesus' ways and works in their totality, and that the whole wide range and extent of
his cross and resurrection—and with them our standing
before God and God's meeting with man—should
become apparent in our life. But at some small point
along this borderline He is waiting for us that He
might reach out for us and touch us. We have not
yet learned to know our life if we do not understand
that its purpose is to bring us to the one point where
God's fullness has its beginning, and where we cease
to live our life in our own strength and authority.
Life tends to make clear to us that another has laid
His hand upon us and that we must become obedient to
Him. Life tends to the point where our humdrum,
freakish little lifelet is sucked up into the powerful
current of an entirely different life whose mighty wa-

ters can do no other than carry us onward toward the point where God becomes our serious concern. Then we shall break forth from our captivities and from the prison houses of our customs and needs and interests into the large freedom of the divine life, where no longer we, but God himself, becomes the center of life. There our eyes shall be trained away from ourselves and from other people and be fixed in full vision upon the work which God's hands have wrought.

Now we have traveled far enough to understand the words of our text: "The peace of God which passeth all understanding, shall guard your hearts and your thoughts in Christ Jesus." Paul does not merely say: "The peace of God shall guard your hearts and your thoughts." It was evidently not clear and definite enough for him. There must have been ears in those days which could or would not hear quite distinctly. They were people who, in the conversation about God, accepted without examination whatever was being said. They were satisfied if only something of a pious and religious nature was being said. It was Paul's intention to roll a stumbling block into their way and to give offense. He meant to direct people with this weak and indistinct hearing to the critical point on which all else depends. He says, therefore, not simply, "The peace of God," but adds, "which passeth all understanding." "Understanding" includes all that we see and experience, understand and feel, will and think, *before* we reach the borderline of our existence and before we touch the edge and meet the point where God meets us. "Understanding" signifies the heights and depths of human experience and comprehension. He does not slur them, does not discredit them. He leaves to them their rightful place. He does not say that they must not be. But he does say that in matters divine we must look and reach beyond this human realm. He says, God—and He is something more than even the best of man; God—and He means more than the loftiest exaltation of your life; God—and you will not strike Him, however deep you may sink the shaft of your soul; God—and He is not the result of a final trial of human strength, not even of your religious capacities; God—of whom you do not become possessed by proofs of logic, neither by high transports of deep emotions, by no trick and plunge of your believing and thinking, even if it were a death leap.

All these things belong to the realm of understanding, as Paul calls it. God transcends all these. When we think of Him we are forced to think a thought which passes all understanding, without being able to do so. We must reckon with the fact—but what does it mean to reckon with *this* fact?—that there is a truth, a world of life which is quite independent of our volition and thought and experience. God—we stand impotently before Him whom we can in no wise touch and handle. We are standing before Him whom we have no means to reach, but whom we cannot hinder from reaching us. God—we may climb the loftiest heights of righteousness and good will, and still fail to come near unto Him; and we may descend into the abyss of human sorrow and suffering and remain unforsaken by Him. He is who He is. We should have escaped Him, slipped through His

very fingers at the very moment when we have made
Him, or even the hem of His garment, subject to us.
But provision has been made that this will not happen.
We cannot escape Him.   He is our Lord and we are
His servants.   He is the Creator and we are nothing
save His creatures.   Here it is, the borderline which
separates us from Him in order to unite us with Him
and to give us completely into His hands.   He hum-
bles us that He may exalt us; condemns us that we
may live only of His grace.   God—it is He into whose
hands we can only surrender ourselves—surrender
without a condition.

But in this surrender lies our peace.   Peace exists
where all differences and contrasts cease.   And where
do they disappear more completely than at the border
line where the unrighteous and the righteous, the high
and the lowly, the gifted and the ungifted, men with
religious experiences and men without them, where
we all, even all, are standing before God as the poor
and little men we are?   Where only one valid word
is heard, God's own word; where we are left with one
last possibility, the possibility that He will lift us up
and not forsake us, because His incomprehensibly large
power of life encloses and engulfs us.

Peace is found where we are made to rest.   On
yonder borderline we are made to rest, because everything depends there on God's will and work.   Where
all depends on this alone, our restless wills and works
must cease.   In fact, we can endure the unrest of our
life, the consuming zeal of our righteousness and the
terrible peacelessness and torment of our unrighteousness only because yonder borderline is drawn also

through our life. As the mighty waves of the ocean come to their rest on their encircling shores, so also does our life find its peaceful end in God's large understanding and forgiveness which dissolves and purifies the problem of our sin and of our righteousness and overrules our "godlessness in evil" and "the godlessness in our good."

Peace is found where there is unity and integration. But where are these to be found? Are they, perhaps, in evidence in our ordinary human life? Are we not rather swayed by a thousand differences of aims and movements of thought and instinct, and by a myriad of opinions and desires? Paul mentions two sources from which these contrary streams and currents flow: our hearts and our thoughts. Our hearts are the fountain of our feelings and passions; and our thoughts are the source of impressions and the views and thoughts proceeding from them. We could not endure their perplexing varieties and would indeed be thrown into hopeless disorder and disintegration, did we not know ourselves upheld by a power of peace, and comprehended and apprehended of a final unity which exists before and behind all our disintegrating strife. God is this power of peace. In God we are apprehended and lifted up in the midst of all disorganization. When we are made to stand before Him, everything, even the most refractory antagonisms, are brought over a common denominator. In judgment and in grace He alone is the center around which our life can become integrated. He guards our life from dissoluteness, as he directs us into His ordinances. In telling us who He is, He

tells us also who we are. We are neither gods nor
demi-gods; but we are men who may go their way
before Him who alone is God, being borne on our
way by His forgiveness and upheld by His statutes.
In putting an end to our own life, He has also set
forth the goal to which we are called. This is our
peace.

Are not these things quite self-evident?   Indeed
not! They are the most astonishing facts of life. They
are a constant intimation of a remarkable crisis. The
last word of our life spells peace, and not war and
strife and disintegration. Who says so?   How do
we know?   Paul gives a last and comprehensive answer to this question as he makes mention of the name
of Jesus Christ in whom our hearts and our thoughts
are being guarded.   Only a divine deed can found
and establish the peace which passes all understanding.
This divine deed of peace was done in Jesus Christ.
He is our peace.   In Him God has condemned our
godlessness, but also expiated and wiped it away.   In
making Himself the center of our life, we have really
and truly been given the center around which it may
be integrated out of its distractions and dissipations.
And this center is not a human idea, neither is it a
human experience; nay indeed, it is He Himself, the
Mediator, who is the center.   In Him our hearts and
our thoughts are guarded.   And this divine deed of
peace is constantly being done anew, as it must be
done if it is to be and remain God's own deed.   As
God opens and illumines our eyes, we behold what we
have in Jesus Christ and see what has been done in
Him for us and all succeeding times.   We can add

nothing to this deed; neither can we subtract anything from it. But our concern is that we ask God to give us eyes to see. And as we ask, we acknowledge that everything is in His hands. To ask God means to vindicate God. There is no real acknowledgment of God that does not lead to invocation and prayer.

This word of Paul is a prayer also, a petition for those whom he would have guarded by God. Is this perhaps the source of our want of peace? Are we dissolute, unsteady, and disintegrated because we do not rightly call on God? Were we to call upon Him again, we would surely be heard. The world would begin to look differently in that selfsame hour. Our hidden union with God could not remain hidden very long. It could not remain a secret that we have peace with God, that we are walking in his commandments and that our life is being integrated out of its disintegration. Men would begin to see our good works and glorify our Father in heaven.

A NARROW WAY

But if any man hath caused sorrow, he hath caused sorrow, not to me, but in part (that I press not too heavily) to you all. Sufficient to such a one is this punishment which was inflicted by the many among you: so that contrariwise you should rather forgive him and comfort him, lest by any means such a one should be swallowed up with his overmuch sorrow. Wherefore I beseech you to confirm your love toward him. For to this end also did I write, that I might know the proof of you, whether you are obedient in all things. But to whom you forgive anything, I forgive also: for what I have also forgiven, if I have forgiven anything, for your sakes have I forgiven it in the presence of Christ, that no advantage may be gained over us by Satan: for we are not ignorant of his devices.—*II Corinthians 2:5-11.*

God's way of grace is like a mountain trail between two abysses, high up above the lowlands. It is for us to find it and walk on it. It does not lend itself to leisurely strolls. If we are looking for this, we must choose one or the other of the two highways in the valleys below us, the one to our right or the other to our left. But then we shall be in the valley and shall never reach our life's high destiny. Neither may we put our feet arbitrarily here or there on God's way of grace. At every moment only one right step is possible for us, and we must take it. Every other possibility is in reality an impossibility which must end with our precipitous fall into one or the other of the two abysses; and the higher we have climbed on our trail, the more disastrous will also be our fall.

Neither can we rest or lounge around; for there are no comfortable spots and no resting places on God's way of grace. Not a single moment of our life offers an opportunity for our ease. Like Elijah on his journey to Mount Horeb, we have so great a journey before us that we cannot afford to be sitting down, but, after we have tasted of the heavenly food, we must go forward forty days and forty nights. We can only incessantly push on, paying strict attention only to the steps we are to take. Our text describes a short step in our forward movement on God's way of grace.

A member of the congregation in Corinth has wronged Paul. We do not know the details. But Paul must have been done a grievous injury. What would we have done? Do you see the two abysses, one to your right and one to your left? Falling into the abyss to our left, we would reply: "I cannot get over it, I have been deeply offended; this man has hurt me to the quick. Henceforth he is a dark spot in my life. My experience with him will henceforth become apparent in whatever I think and say and do; I am through with him." If we take this attitude and rest here, we are fallen into an abyss. For whether the man was quite unjustified in wronging me, or if his wrong was partly in revenge of a wrong on my part, something in me, indeed the very best in me, my immortal soul, remains untouched and free in such an experience; it cannot be hurt to the quick.

There is more to our personality than that such an experience should only grieve and offend us. It may be an occasion to make us see our own wrongs and so lead us to repentance. It may also be that I am

simply called to defend myself. But I cannot im-
prison myself within the cage of a mortal insult to
my person by nursing a grudge. I cannot keep staring
at my injury as an imprisoned bird will stare at a snake.
To do so would be treason against the soul; it is a
fall from grace. This is what Paul thought. He
shakes off the wrong. "He hath not caused sorrow
to me," he says. He will not have a dark spot develop
in his heart. He would remain free. It is God's way
of grace.

To the right of us yawns another abyss. There
we would give another reply to the injury we have
received. "What do I care what such a man says of
me or does to me? I am thick-skinned. I shall
ignore and forget him." Perhaps we have occasionally
wished we could do so. Good friends may have given
us some such advice: "I will tell you what to do. Ignore
it all; what do you care what people say. Leave
them alone. It is nothing to you." But it is so very
difficult to follow such counsels; and this very fact
should tell us that it is not good counsel. "It does
not concern me," has never been great wisdom. The
human heart beats warmly; it is not naturally cold.
We cannot make light of injuries that we have received; we cannot belittle or ignore them. To do
so would be like falling into another abyss or putting
ourselves into another cage. If resentment against
wrongs is extinguished in a man he is living a living
death. The man who can no longer become angry
has lost his soul. It is for this reason that the same
Paul who said "he has not caused sorrow to me,"
does not belittle the sin, but magnifies it, as he con-

tinues, "but to you all." While he will not let the wrong which he has personally suffered put shackles on himself, he is sad and wroth because once again God's work among men has met with a stumbling block. He does not take the personal affront so very seriously; but so much more weight does he attach to the interference with the spirit, communion, and hope which this experience has occasioned and which hovers like a dark shadow over him and the church at Corinth. He is not embittered but exasperated. Shocked? No, but provoked. He does not quarrel, but he does contend for what is right. He shook off the wrong from himself, but only to take it up again as a free man and bear it. Do you see the mountain trail of God's grace high up above the two abysses?

And now evidently something else has happened in Corinth in the meanwhile. As a healthy body defends itself against invading disease germs, so the people in Corinth made the offender understand that he has disturbed the spirit of fellowship and communion with them by what he has said against Paul. They understood that it was not primarily a personal injury to Paul, but much more an offense against the cause of Jesus which was their common concern. It is one of the signs of the vitality of early Christianity that such personal affairs were immediately seen in a higher light. They did not make as much of them as we do; but they took them much more seriously. If a man went astray, as evidently this man did, he was immediately made to feel, "I have gone astray; I am in the wilderness." There was no false acquiescence, no secret covering up of wrongs. They spoke an honest word in those days. Men kept aloof from transgressors; they inflicted punishment, sometimes terribly swift and effective punishment. They could afford to do it; they even felt compelled to do it. There was something new and holy in their midst that leaped almost automatically to a defense against encroaching evil. But for this very reason, Paul could now write them: I am satisfied; the chastisement has served its purpose, and may now be terminated.

We also are accustomed to chastise each other. To be sure, caprice determines very largely our discipline. Most wrongs, and usually the very worst ones, we cover up for each other. But if by chance we feel like it, we take drastic measures and send a man into a wilderness. We differ from those early believers in another aspect. We do not know moderation; we become hard on the spur of the moment. We mete out punishment without giving thought to its purpose; we know no limit in punishing. We keep on making angry faces and shouting harsh words; we cannot keep from maintaining an atmosphere of proud contempt and detachment and indifference until the culprit feels himself in the polar zone. Sometimes such blunderers are stigmatized for years, perhaps ostracized for life, on account of their wrong. And very often they are not the worst men. So we vacillate between hushing up and a blind zeal. Our discipline is not born of life but of death. It is not what is new and holy in us that is rushing forward to vindication; it is much rather our perplexity that drives us on to our fitful actions, because, at bottom, we do not know how to meet evil victoriously. Every chastisement, if it is merely a sharp look, must have a purpose.

Our learned men are disputing whether punishment has for its purpose the reformation of the evildoer or the protection of society against wrong-doing. The early Christians did not need to argue this question. For them such a contrast between society and an individual did not exist. They saw every individual as a member of the one body, and this indivisible whole was destined to glorify its head, Christ. But for this reason, chastisement, if it had to be, could have no other purpose than a re-establishment of the glory of the disgraced head, Christ. We may have difficulty to translate these thoughts for our modern social conscience, because our life does not have the life-pulse of their social conscience. But we divine that chastisement with such an high aim could not be hard, or clumsy, or immoderate. It could have a tremendous and powerful effect, but it could be terminated in the same spirit in which it was inflicted.

Why was it that Paul called a halt here? Because he wished to prevent the offender from becoming consumed by too great a sorrow. His intercession did not spring from weak indulgence. On the contrary, intense zeal for God's glory urged him to take the culprit's part. In this instance, the offender benefitted by his action. He is thinking and speaking, however, from God's standpoint, from within Christ, as he recalls his friends, whom he has previously

urged to severity, from this severity, and commands
them to forgive and comfort. The Bible shows us
everywhere a disinclination to extremities. Extreme
wickedness, extreme justice, extreme power, extreme
joyfulness and extreme sorrow must not be. Extremes consume men; they make them unprofitable
for God and His work. They serve to build a wall
between them and God's will for them, God's salvation, God's forgiveness. Men are to stand and walk
through life, to be sure; but not in too great a security. If need be, they must be broken; and under
some circumstances chastisement may serve this end.
But men must never be completely broken, never
crushed. "A bruised reed will He not break." There
must be no overweening pride but neither complete destruction, Paul means to say. Therefore he orders
a halt and urges love and forgiveness after punishment. In this instance presumption was, perhaps, the
danger which threatened his friends. They had not only
driven their enemy into a wilderness but had a mind
to leave him there. They should not become pharisaical, lest Satan gain an advantage over them with
their good deed, as destruction, bitterness and despair
would have become the portion of his enemy, if they
had continued chastising him; and this would have
been another triumph for the devil. Neither of these
consequences must be, for God's sake. In God there
exists a definite coherence between friends and enemies and therefore also between chastisement and forgiveness. And this bond of unity remains unbroken.
What a salvation it would mean for us and for evil-
doers, were we to return to this coherence in God;

were we to learn again to fear God and therefore
avoid all extremes.

"Wherefore I beseech you to confirm your love
toward him!" This is a remarkable word. And it
will be understood only by him who will walk the
way of God's grace, and by none other. It is remarkable, in the first place, because it offers an opportunity to gain insight into the sincerity of Paul's
contention that chastisement is a part of *forgiveness.*
For this reason it must not be pushed too far. It happens sometimes that we forgive a man his wrong but
are displeased when others also forgive him and
readmit him to their fellowship. We may check our
own resentment but are pleased if resentment against
the wrong-doer continues to thrive in and through
others. It is a proof that our chastisement and forgiveness are true and flow from a pure source, if we
can say to others also: "I, I who have been wronged,
beseech you to love the offender again." To be sure,
we should have to say it not only with words. The
other striking fact in this word of exhortation is this
that Paul presupposes that his readers possess this love
and only need to let it have its course, as when we turn
a faucet and water flows from it. Among these early
Christians there lived an ever-present, never-failing
love, as Paul wrote in another instance; a love which
was ready and prepared to forgive at the very moment
when it inflicted punishment; a love which loved while
it hated, despised and rejected; which merely needed
to cast off a garment which was strange to it in order
to show its true nature. For love is a power which
Christians possess and of which they only need to make

use. Is not all this beautiful and strong, simple and
helpful? God grant us a new access to this love which
rules over men with so self-evident a power.

"To this end did I write to give you an opportunity to confirm that you are obedient in all things,"
Paul says. Here again is one of those words which
come from the very heart of the Bible. He had
previously written them to discipline the offender.
But take note. If they have truly understood him,
they must have been aware that he was not interested
in chastisement merely for the sake of chastising the
man; no, he made it a test of their obedience and
of their readiness for intelligent Christian dealing.
He did not set down before them a peremptory command, You must chastise the man. No, it must occur
only for an instant in the movement of the Christian
on God's way of grace. In another moment something else must take its place; in fact, the very opposite. What he offered them was an opportunity
to learn obedience—not to himself, of course not—
but to the voice of God with its ever-new demands.
Today one part of his lesson may be taken up. They
will prove it today, if yesterday they have learned
yesterday's assignment. So versatile is the biblical
man, and we cannot present him vividly enough to our
minds. His freedom, flexibility and buoyancy will
never let him rust or rot; but these traits will make
him mount up with wings as an eagle.

And now a final word sums up everything. "I
have forgiven, if I have anything to forgive, for your
sakes in the presence of Christ, that no advantage may
be gained over us by Satan; for we are not ignorant

of his devices." It is one of those passages in the
Bible, and of this second epistle to the Corinthians
in particular, which are being passed over with little
attention.   Where lies the secret of its power?   I
believe it is found in the words "for your sakes in
the presence of Christ."   As a soldier of Christ, we
see Paul standing before his King.   His interest is
centered on doing his work well before Him.   In His
presence he must not bungle.   He must chose his way
with care and circumspection because the eyes of his
King are upon him.   Under their constraint he is
bidden now to forgive "for your sakes," i.e., for the
sake of the company of people among whom Christ
will live on earth until He can reveal Himself fully,
that no cause for bitterness, offense or delay be given
among them.   What Paul has to forgive for his own
person, does not play a large role any more.   He does
not forgive because he is goodnatured or indulgent,
or because he has so noble a character.   No, he forgives
"for your sakes in the presence of Christ."

It is to these words that we ought always to return
if we wish to understand Paul and the way of grace
which he pursued as a sinful and imperfect man.   It is
in these words that we are shown the nature and power
of grace; it makes indolent and zealous, severe and
indulgent, watchful against the presumptuous and
merciful toward those who have been humbled; it
produces the love which bears all things, hopes all
things, and suffers all things; from grace flows the
wisdom which asks nothing of a man by asking everything of him.   We are living in a time when collapse
threatens society because men do not know if they shall

forgive one another. And they do not know, because Satan's devices are succeeding. They make men hard and unforgiving. Perhaps the collapse is becoming so complete because we are losing—or have already lost —contact with that power of cohesion which alone is capable of keeping disintegration from becoming complete. May here and there men be found, and find themselves together, who will yearn and quietly lay a new foundation for the way of God's grace. May they dare to take it and remain on it if perhaps they have already found it!

THE FREEDOM OF THE WORD OF GOD

But thanks be unto God, who always leadeth us in triumph in Christ, and maketh manifest through us the savor of his knowledge in every place. For we are a sweet savor of Christ unto God, in them that are saved, and in them that perish; to the one a savor from death unto death; to the other a savor from life unto life. And who is sufficient for these things? For we are not as the many, corrupting the word of God: but as of sincerity, but as of God, in the sight of God, speak we in Christ.—*II Corinthians* *2:14-17.*

No, you cannot make merchandise of the word of God. The revised version translates the Greek text "corrupting it." But Paul's own expression denotes something much more refined, less offensive and more respectable. He means to say, You cannot do with the word of God what we are constantly doing in life, even in our psychical and spiritual life. You cannot make merchandise of the word of God; you cannot handle it as a merchant handles his wares and his customers. A merchant displays and exhibits his merchandise in as faultless and inviting a style as possible. He caters to his patrons and so he induces them to accept his wares. There is nothing dishonorable about it; it is good business. If we would persuade people to buy goods from us, this is the way to make them do it.

It is a very natural desire with us, for example, that people accept our character, acknowledge us, and take pleasure in us as we are. To this end we keep anxiously polishing and smoothing certain fatal spots and wrinkles in ourselves, lest these defects in our merchandise become too flagrantly patent. And quite unconsciously, we are forever busy advertising ourselves a little. We do it to win the good will of our patrons for our individuality. And a childlike happiness comes over us, when we find some one who will buy what we happen to be.

We follow a similar course in persuading others to adopt our point of view. It is gratifying to have other men share our opinions. They are satisfying, if not important, moments in life, when we succeed in convincing men of the worthwhileness of our convictions so that they will make them their own. But in order to succeed in our aim, we must be able to clothe our views in an attractive and convincing form. If we do otherwise, nobody will buy from us. And in addition, we must learn to deal with people so that they will gladly reach for what we offer them. Nobody will buy from a man who does not understand how to be at least a little business-like. If a man wants to move his stock, he must be a bit of a tradesman, a bit of a shopkeeper. If he does not cater to his public, his merchandise will stay on his shelves; and he remains a hermit with his convictions, no matter how good and valuable they may be.

The world follows this course even in the promotion of high ideals. Ideals are called, somewhat indefinitely to be sure, those "higher interests" which stand out above the common and lower levels of life. They surpass ordinary life interests somewhat as church steeples jut over the village roofs beneath them.

For good reasons ideals are merchandise much sought after. Today in particular, when we have become quite aware that we are deeply mired in a morass of earthly and animalistic things, the demand for higher ideals has become quite lively. Ideals of education, politics, and even new religious ideals are eagerly sought. Blessed is the man who can supply even partially this demand. But let him take care that he present what he has in an attractive and palatable form. The so called higher things in life must be presented in a manner which will not make them appear too much out of the ordinary or beyond the reach of the many. In fact, it is much the better way to offer them as the simple fruit of our instinct of self-preservation, as a ripe fruit which may be plucked if this instinct is rightly understood and properly regulated. Christianity must be given such a form that everybody will say, "Oh yes, it is just what I have always thought and felt and wanted in my heart." Political ideals must be passed on so that people will be joyfully astonished as they are made to realize that highest righteousness and their own chief interests happen to be one and the same thing.

The great, silent mystery of most of our great orators, preachers and writers consists in this that they are excellent salesmen. They know the business of catering to their customers and of arousing their desire to buy. They have learned the art of bargaining and of being bargained with. For many a great cause in the world, and for most of the so called spiritual and religious movements, it is not particularly important that they are intrinsically good, or new, or useful;

their chief need is shrewd promoters and able salesmen who can sell them to a pleased public. It is the accepted way of getting things done.

If Paul makes mention of these things in our text, he does not do so to cast reflection on such trade and business practices. He merely says that the word of God cannot be handled in such a way. He tells us that there are many things, more or less good and desirable, about which we may, and perhaps must, bargain carefully and where we must make concessions and allowances. But apart from them all, there is something where bargaining is out of the question. The word of God is not for sale; and therefore it has no need of shrewd salesmen. The word of God is not seeking patrons; therefore it refuses price cutting and bargaining; therefore it has no need of middlemen. The word of God does not compete with other commodities which are being offered to men on the bargain counter of life. It does not care to be sold at any price. It only desires to be its own genuine self, without being compelled to suffer alterations and modifications. It would shine in its own glory to be snapped up of those who would not buy it, but who will accept it as grace, as a gift of grace, just as it is. Until then, it can afford to lie on its shelf and *wait* as if it were poor merchandise. Until then it does not ask whether a grateful public appreciates it or not. Until then it leaves to men their liberty to ignore and refuse it, for the sake of its own freedom.

Yes, the word of God is waiting, and waiting with an impetuous impatience, for men who will give it attention. For it is addressed to men, to men who already belong to God, but who are lost with all their world until they hear what their God has to say to them—until the word of God comes over them, and overcomes them. But it does not care to overcome them save in its own freedom and in their liberty. It will, however, not stoop to overcome resistance with bargain-counter methods. Promoters' successes are sham-victories; their crowded churches and the breathlessness of their audiences have nothing in common with the word of God. Yes, indeed, the word of God has a particular message for every individual; it addresses men quite personally, quite directly. But when a man does not lend his ear to it of his own free choice, he shall not hear the word of God at all. The word of God prefers to remain dumb rather than that a man should after all hear only his own echo and live in an absurd illusion of having heard God speak to him. Yes, the word of God has a persistent and stubborn urge to have its own say in all our conditions and situations; it is eager to put in its word to all the problems and tasks of our existence. We cannot do without it; for it contains final insights and carries decisive instructions. It is not at all contradictory to a sure knowledge of nature and life, because it is itself this sure knowledge. It dissolves contradictions, and it opens new perspectives where we have bitterly bemoaned that vision was denied us. But it disdains to speak where it is made a cheap ephemeral trifle alongside of other views and opinions. This, at least on Paul's lips, is the meaning and virtue of the word of God. "As of sincerity, as of

God, and in the sight of God," he meant to speak it:—
"in Christ." Either so or not at all.

For the word of God, the gospel, is the reminder
of eternity in man. It does not remind us of something which is unknown to us, but of what we know
but have forgotten and must discover anew and learn
again. It speaks to us as we are here and as we are
sitting here, yes; but it tells us how we have come
hither and whither we are to go from here. It speaks
of life, yes; but it speaks of the true life in life. It
speaks of our daily experiences, and of things and
conditions which confront us in our workaday life,
yes; but it speaks of their origin and end. It speaks
of the world, of a world which we have lost but shall
find again. It is you whom it addresses; you, the
very man who is sitting there as you are. It means
you, and to you it is speaking. And yet, it is not
this man after all but the new man, the other man
in you to whom it has given birth, and life, and existence.

You see, eternity is not time and time is not eternity. Time is eternity emptied, pauperized, despoiled;
and eternity is time fulfilled. The very mystery and
meaning of our existence consists in this, that we are
living in time and in eternity. But these two factors
of our existence are not of equal strength. Rather,
eternity is in motion toward, nay, into time. Eternity
is the homeland which is calling us; it is our origin
from which we cannot sever ourselves; it is our real
nature breaking forth with impetuous constancy.
Time is only a wayside station on our journey which
we must leave again when we have reached it; it is

a garment to be laid aside again after it has served for a season; it is like the shadow on a wall which has its existence from a light, only to pass away. Eternity has an advantage over time; and this is its preponderance over time, that it possesses a surer claim and greater power over us. Eternity is like the break of day; it is a dawning while time in its flight is passing on and away. Eternity is above; time is below. Therefore, the light of eternity is constantly falling upon time; but time has no light of its own to throw on eternity. Therefore, something of eternity is ever present in all our temporal thoughts, feelings and endeavors; but we shall never be able to accommodate and subordinate eternity values to our temporal concepts and standards. Therefore, man is never wholly without God; but very often and quite extensively God is without man. "Death shall be swallowed up of life," Paul says; but also at another place he says, "Flesh and blood cannot inherit the kingdom of God," which is saying two different things.

Take heed—the word of God, the gospel, is eternity's spokesman. Therefore it is said of Jesus Christ, "When the fulness of time came, God sent forth his Son"; and we must understand it so. That time was, and is being, fulfilled in this: that God is sending his Son. God would no longer be without man. God would have all men to be saved. Eternity rushes into time as a mountain freshet rushes into its empty bed after a shower. The kingdom of heaven bursts upon earth as an army bursts into hostile territory. "I am come to cast fire upon the earth, and how would I that it were already kindled!" *Thy* name be hallowed—in time where it is not yet holy. *Thy* kingdom come—in time where it is not yet established. *Thy* will be done—in time where it is not yet being done. In this Thine, Thine, Thine in contradistinction to all what is not yet Thine, the word of God, the Gospel, Jesus Christ, lives, moves and has His being. Yes, here is the place where Jesus Christ is standing. They are God's interests which He is minding and of which He reminds us. That we let ourselves be reminded of them is our salvation and our redemption. It is the end to which God's love for us tends. But we cannot be helped except as we help God. Here is God's end; his impetuous message which will meet us, strike us, that we also shall have a part in its fulfilment and that we also shall discover it and become aware and alive in resurrection. *We* are being led to the point where time and eternity meet. *We* are being asked if we will acknowledge eternity's advantage and preponderance over time. *We* are being offered this insight that there is hidden behind all decay and death a greater advent and a larger life. *We* are given a perspective of the victory and perfection toward which our whole existence tends.

Lame and stammering words for these largest things, you say? Yes; but certainly we do not fail to understand that the word of God must be free to go its own way. You see, it has its own source, and also its own course. It is living its own life, with an importance all its own, both in the world and in our own lives. It creates and it destroys, it lifts up and it casts down, by its own power and in its own

order. It will not suffer addition or subtraction. The
new man, who is here being born, must also think and
speak and act in a new way. He is completely severed from the old man and his whole kind. Between
them stands the cross of Christ as an irreducible barrier. The new man lives while the other has died.
The word of God may be small and insignificant as a
mustard seed but it will retain its own kind against
everything that we may otherwise possess or be. It
may well be that we know little, miserably little, of
the new man, of the eternity-man in us; but what
we do know of him is just this that he has a nature of
his own and that he stands in his own right. There
can be no compromises, no accommodations, and no
bargains between him and the old man in us. "If
any man is in Christ, he is a new creature." There
are no bridges leading back from this new man to
the old and no bridges from life to death. Time shall
become as eternity; but never, never can eternity become as time. The earth shall become like heaven;
but never, never even unto the end of time, can heaven
become like the earth.

The Spirit of God can do all things. He can bring
the dead to life; he can raise children unto Abraham
from stones. But there is this one thing which even
the Spirit of God cannot do: He cannot be untrue to
Himself; He cannot change himself into the spirit of
mere man, into men's thoughts, into men's feelings.
He remains ever free, and leaves us free, until we
are able to grasp Him in our newly found, newly
granted liberty, Him who moves where He will. The
word of God which could lose its freedom, the word

of God of which a man could make merchandise, would cease to be the word of God. Of sincerity, of God and in the sight of God it would be spoken and heard—in Christ. Rather not at all than less than this.

Perhaps we understand now also the rest of what Paul is saying in our text of himself as of one who has himself heard, and would speak to others, the word of God. With his powerful hand, God has made him his prisoner and is leading him in chains from country to country and from city to city to the glory of His name, as kings and warlords of old have done with those whom they have conquered. Nothing, nothing of the things in which men glory, remains for Paul. The proclamation of the word of God is not one of those human undertakings in which a man may give himself to self-preferment, self-assertion; and greedy self-aggrandizement has no place here. The word of God promotes itself. Its proclamation is God's own deed. Man merely attends; he is the ear, the heart, and head and mouth, and hand and foot. Paul is just grateful that he may so attend. For this attention has made him free; it has become his liberty. When God made him His prisoner, every other prison-gate was flung open. His care of God's interests saves him from every other care. As human ambition vanishes, human anxiety and diffidence, man's passion and pettishness have disappeared; they have become superfluous. License, his own and that of others, fate and chance, do still play a part in his life. But they are merely playing *along*. The real movement of his life is neither reached, nor touched, nor determined by them. A final residue in him remains free of them, hurries on and tends toward its goal—at all times and in all places.

And such a man simply cannot live in vain, even if he must preach in vain for three and twenty years, as did Jeremiah. If he may no longer be a tradesman, he no longer needs to worry about his patronage or about his public. He manifests a "savor of the knowledge of God." It is not he, indeed, who reveals, but God who makes manifest through him. It is God who makes manifest in all circumstances. The word creates room for itself, if it is the word of God; if it is given its freedom; if a man will make room for the freedom of the word in reverence and in respect. What is born of God overcometh the world. What men do not hear or see, they can be made to smell. They will become aware of what they do not understand. Knowledge of God, eternity in time, is something so new, so strange, so unique and eminent that it is simply not possible for it to remain unobserved. It leaves its mark whatever men may do about it. An atmosphere develops around such men which people must breathe, a temper from which men cannot escape; they compel attention and none can evade. The more such men hear and speak the word "as of sincerity, as of God and in the sight of God," the less they need to be intent on making merchandise of it. The word is at work in its freedom.

To be sure, "to the one a savor from death unto death; to the other a savor from life unto life." So serious a matter is the freedom of the word. He who hears and speaks the word in sincerity need be little concerned about success or effect. And his whole interest need be centered solely in this—that the word be spoken. The freedom of the word cannot be separated from the liberty of men. Not every age is ripe to be fulfilled of eternity; not everything that is old is old enough for re-creation; not every man, and perhaps never the whole of man, becomes free for the freedom of the word. A residue of earthiness will cling to us! The word of God— and he who would speak it—will become "a savor from death unto death" to this earthy residue in men. Unfree ears will hear in the word of eternity only the wisdom of death. Eternity means to them only the end of time and temporal things; destruction of life, limitation of possessions and pleasures, an impossibility in our present existence. Christ is to them only the Christ who died on the cross with the question on His lips, why God has forsaken Him. Such a man finds himself standing before God with his back to the wall; he finds that breath is leaving him, and, not knowing whither to flee, he turns aside from God to make his escape from the impossible. He leaves sorrowful; for he has great possessions which he cannot bear to lose. The peace which is offered to his house must return to him who brought it. To him everything is done in parables. He eats and drinks judgment to himself. For heat has the power to melt but also to wither; light may illumine and cause blindness; wind can bring relief from heat and it can carry on its wings the winter's icy blasts.

The free word of God always has some effect where men face it with their liberty. But it does not have the same effect in every instance, for man's liberty is also freedom. Only in freedom here and there, does God carry on his work. "He chooses whom He will, and hardens whom He will." The judgment which is being pronounced is carried out to the glory of God. But it is quite possible for the other effect to come to pass to the glory of God. Time may be ripe for eternity; the old world may be ready for a new creation; and men may be free for their true liberty. Then the word of God—and he who may be speaking it—becomes "a savor from life unto life"; the word of eternity becomes a message of life; its end becomes a new beginning; downfall is changed to an uprising; and what seems impossible becomes the only possibility for true life. Then the death of Christ gains its importance and power in a resurrection. Then a man will stand before God—but he will not be crushed of the Holy One; nor will he flee from the Righteous One; yea, in joyous obedience he will start on a new way. He dares to make a leap, the great leap! He *finds* peace. He knows the mystery of the kingdom of God. Rejoice, you lonely, unsuccessful and ineffective carrier of the word of God; your life may have also this effect to the glory of God, and perhaps you are a savor from life unto life in a measure, larger than you know.

But either of these two effects is to the glory of *God*. It is not for man to ask the question whether more of this or of the other effect proceeds from him; but it is his concern that whatever proceeds from him shall serve the glory of God. For *we* are not the lords of life and death. Perhaps damnation must proceed from us, but woe to us if we have a mind to sit in judgment. Perhaps salvation radiates from us, but woe to us if we would dish out salvation. The result is in the hands of God. His is the power; and verily His is the will to transform every death into life in Christ Jesus. His is the love which will plumb even the depth of hell. Ours is not the task to set the pace for God; we are but to follow him with our activities. It is for us to be faithful in every given moment to hear and speak the word of God, as it must be spoken and heard, where not yet all that is time has become eternity, and where God is not yet all and in all.

Is the life of a man like Paul too far removed from us? Do we possess the word of God? Or has the Christian church too long made merchandise of it to such a degree that we cannot hear and speak it today when we are in dire straits for it? Yes, we shall do well not to range ourselves beside a Paul too quickly, as if we could apply with a once-over to ourselves what he has said. But neither can we stand quite apart from it. For we are also called to be carriers of the word of God. Secretly, we also carry the chains of our divine captivity. "I cannot bring myself to a living faith!" Yes, I believe, dear Lord, help thou mine unbelief! You mean this, do you not? "I do not have a strong, and high, and superior mind!" Yes, let my grace be sufficient unto thee; for my strength is made perfect in weakness! "The finite is not capable of the Infinite!" Yes, but this corruptible must put on incorruption, and this mortal must put on immortality. "Our sufficiency is from God."

MOSES-TIME AND CHRIST-TIME

Having therefore such a hope, we use great boldness of speech,
and are not as Moses, who put a veil upon his face, that the children of Israel should not look steadfastly on the end of that
which was passing away: but their minds were hardened: for until
this very day at the reading of the Old Testament the same veil
remaineth, it not being revealed to them that it is to be done away
in Christ. Yea, unto this day, whensoever Moses is read, a veil
lieth upon their heart. But whensoever it shall turn to the Lord,
the veil is taken away. Now the Lord is the Spirit, and where the
Spirit of the Lord is, there is liberty. But we all, with unveiled
face reflect as in a mirror the glory of the Lord, and are being
transformed into the same image from glory to glory, even as from
the Lord who is the Spirit.—*II Corinthians 3:12-17.*

Your question is quite pertinent, is it wise to preach
on these words? For this much we have probably
understood that here a quit claim has been given of
something which we had better not relinquish in our
present situation. Moses is being nonsuited. "We
are not as Moses," Paul is saying. And to Paul's
mind, "Moses" does not stand for something petty
but for something large and final. Moses!—we shall
not easily overrate this name. It is much more than
the name of a man. It embodies a power which confronts and conquers the souls of men with what is
good and true. "To be as Moses" means to labor at
rousing men from their indolence and sluggishness and
slothfulness. It means to make men aware that their
life is fraught with large responsibilities. It means to

put before men their glorious destiny, to transfix their minds with those high ideals to which they are called, and to be the voice which incessantly calls and unflinchingly drives them to their pursuit. It means engraving commandments, speaking stern high words of duty and of conscience with which men must not tamper, chiseling laws, as in eternal rock, which will stand through day and night with their curt demand—Thou shalt! Thou shalt not! This is Moses' task; this is his work! And from these pursuits the apostle would call us away? Or perhaps, if not call us away from them, lead us beyond them, as one must leave a lower rung to reach a higher one? But are we far enough along to leave the lower?

Are we not sorely tempted in the break-up and collapse which mark our day to make a loud outcry against the apostle? Must we not insist much rather on more Moses-work, more Moses-men, more Moses-spirit? If our day has need of anything, it is for words with the temper of steel. What is good and true must again be boldly emblazoned! With unbending energy we must impose again the tables of an inexorable law! For is not this the source of the present sad state of affairs that authority and obedience, yea, even the sense of shame, have vanished from our midst? Is not a re-imposition of these lost values and a quick return of another Moses-time, the most pressing need of our day? The shadows of night are settling ever deeper on the hearts of peoples and nations. Must we not give all that we are and have to keep at least flickering a few candles of conscience and duty toward higher things, and if possible relight a few that have been extinguished? We have indeed begun to understand and heed the urgent call of the hour. In the disorder which marks and mars our time, we all are, silently or professingly, hungry for order; we are yearning to re-establish old landmarks and to fix laws to check the hideous corruption of moral integrity and ethical values.

Or have we failed to hear men's clamor everywhere for strong men, for leaders and for leadership, for something that is firm and sure that they may cling to it in their despair? And have we not met with Moses-men—some genuine and some make-believe—who have risen among us in answer to these cries for help? Is their call to repentance and order not an urge to reconsecration to laws of righteousness and peace, once established but now shattered? They are preaching repentance. They ask us to shoulder our share of our common guilt and obligation to atone, to awake from our irresponsible individualism to a consciousness of solidarity with the common weal and woe. They are holding up before us definite aims for which to strive and are giving us definite instructions how we may attain them. Renunciation of brute force is one of those high ideals; peace between nations; new ideals of education; woman's place in our new society; the reconstruction of our economic world-structure—all these are present tasks and lights; and who fails to see them? Our eyes are being opened to the demands of what ought to be and is not. We are living in a bitter recognition of our heavy burden of guilt; we are bearing the heavy sentence meted out to us for our wrongdoing. We know a little better than our fathers that a long, long trail is still ahead of us before we shall reach the goal of our true humanity.

Moses-times are upon us; "to be as Moses" is become our second nature. But what else is there to be done? It really will not do to extinguish the light of laws which sheds a few rays in our twilight hours. It may be that, some time or other, a new day will fully dawn for us. Then we shall dispense with our artificial lights because the end to which they tend and point has come to pass. In the full splendor of that day-to-come we shall discard the makeshifts which served us in our twilight hours. But today we have certainly not reached the point where we can do without them. Today we do not see any more clearly the end of all these transitory things than Israel saw the end of its law. We live in the twilight of an interim, and we do not know whether it is the dusk before an oncoming night or the dawn of a new day. But can we do better justice to the demand of our time than by accepting our present fate, becoming wanderers in the twilight, eating our bread in the sweat of our brows as did our first parents, and by clinging to laws as Israel did in its wilderness-journey? Do you know of a better and more perfect way? What do we know of the goal of our journey, we who are still on the road? Is it not true that our diagnosis of the world and our age must lead us inevitably to some "Thou shalt!", to self-examination and conversion of some kind or other which results in exhortations and resolutions? And ought we not to welcome such a result as the most favorable outcome of our studies? Ought we not to rejoice if a man reaches this point? Is not this the very front-line in the war we are waging today? At any rate, it is the position which all of us have taken who are awake and aware of the critical stage of our times. It is from such a state of mind that we are launching our counter-attacks which are to restore our distracted world.

Do you not see how completely we are living in another Moses-time? Especially we who are of a more serious turn of mind? And beyond it we see and know nothing. We are almost offended if we are told that there might be something larger to be looked for. We are so busily engaged in letting our "lower lights be burning" which are to serve us for the next few years or decades, perhaps even for the next century, that we resent being reminded that another day may possibly dawn which will make our lights superfluous. We even look upon such reminders as devious attacks, launched for the purpose of interrupting and frustrating our work. Do we now understand Paul's word of reproach when he speaks of the veil which he sees hanging before readers of the Old Testament "until this very day"? Heavily, heavily indeed, it is hanging also before our eyes and prevents us from seeing that the front-line position which is held by the most idealistic schemes is only a place of transition, a make-shift, after all. To be sure, we do not care to hear it. Have we not done enough, we ask, if we have finally become aware of the precariousness of our situation and if we feel our guilt and are ready to atone? No, Paul would say, you have really not done enough, even if you have repented, even if you shoulder your guilt and make restitution as best you can; and even if you should go to the jungles of Africa to atone there for the sins of our civilization with a life of self-sacrifice; and if you give your body to be burned and all your goods to the poor. All these things you may do and perhaps you ought to do them; but not enough has yet been done. For none of them atones for your sin; none of them clears the road. All this is "being as Moses," and Moses does not redeem. If you go wrong here, it may well be that you are turning away from God by your very conversion. Your very awareness may be putting you soundly to sleep against God; your ascent may be preparing your descent; that your constructive activities may be really destructive and that your busyness may be merely an evidence that you have come far short of the divine goal.

These are mysterious words, are they not? An objection is being raised here that we do not understand. We are estopped from keeping on thinking as we are confronted by something that we do not understand. But perhaps we do understand something else, namely what Paul is telling us next—that the minds of the children of Israel were hardened at this point. Must we not acknowledge that *we* are meant here? It is *we* who do not understand. We are not *able* to understand because a veil is hanging before our eyes and we do not see beyond what we can see. Oh, that we were being led to think after these incomprehensible words! That we would let their incomprehensibility tell us that we evidently do not yet understand what we ought to understand. That we would let ourselves be shown the veil that is hanging before our eyes, shutting out from our view what really ought to be done! That we were ashamed of our blindness! That, while we are eagerly building our new world, we were made to sigh and groan for something that lies far, far beyond us. Oh, that we would let ourselves be brought to the point where we shall lay aside, not only our folly and sin, but also our conversion, our awareness, all our resolutions and faculties, our whole "being as Moses" with this confession: No, what must be done, if we are to be truly free from our chains and burdens, has not yet been done with all that we have done and are doing. We have lighted candles in the darkness; it had to be done; but the New Day has not dawned with them.

At bottom we ourselves feel that all our efforts to rise again and to be constructive have not gotten us any where. The mysterious deadweight which is estopping our time from getting on has not been really removed. Even the best and noblest in us is so cold; it does not radiate warmth. It is like soggy wood which will not burn; it is like water turned to ice which does not flow. We are always thinking, this or that ought to be done; but we do not succeed in doing it, or something comes from it that we did not intend at all. We aim at a new order of state and a dictatorship results. We proclaim high ideals of peace and liberty and hypocrisy and presumption blossom forth. We champion the restoration of our ancient faith and we produce heretics and inquisitions. We champion the good and true and must declare war on half the world for it. Truly, if we are to be really helped, something quite different must come over us than Moses-times and the Moses-spirit. Something that we cannot acquire from ourselves must be given us; no, not something, but everything; that which is decisive, quite complete and perfect; that which truly helps, burns, shines and radiates warmth. This insight will dawn upon us, if we become truly aware of the veil before our eyes! But perhaps, perhaps it is no longer hanging there, when we have discovered this; perhaps the veil has then been lifted. If, and because, this has dawned upon us, we have indeed received our sight. And now we cannot fail to understand the third moment which Paul mentions—"turning to the Lord." The best must still be given us, and this is it: to turn to the Lord. And here also we may say, *We* are meant; *we* are called; *we* are addressed; before *our* eyes the veil is being removed; and *we* see through and into the mystery of Him who is perfect—into the mystery of our help and salvation!

How shall I describe what we behold when we have truly received our sight? Oh no, the great truth of the Moses-time is not simply invalidated when our veiled face begins to behold a new vision. No, no! Now, if ever, we see how fearfully godless the world is and how necessary it is for her to break away from it. And we shall also be making attempts to bring it to pass. We shall rise from our slumbers. We shall rekindle the candles of faith in a dark world and breathe life into our dead Christianity. But faith, living faith, vital radiant faith, victorious faith which overcomes the world—aye, aye, such faith is something vastly different from our poor and cold Christianity; but for a certainty, it is also something else than *our* being awake, something quite distinct from our attempts to awaken faith. Far, far beyond our faith lies what we cannot take; it must be given us. This is the new vision we behold.

Or, we behold the depth of our moral degradation; we see the morass in which we are mired and we mean to make a struggle for a new purity. Purity, purity worthy of the name, real goodness, is truly something else than our uncontrolled license; but it is also something quite distinct from our feeble attempts at purity and goodness. What is truly pure and good is something holy. Such holiness does not grow in our gardens. It is God's pure grace. This new vision we behold when the veil is taken from our eyes. Or, we see ourselves surrounded by an evil fate and death. We know we ought to take up arms against them, and we do. We make an effort. We excite our courage; we quicken faith in ourselves. But faith is surely not our fear of fate; but it is also something quite distinct from our artificial pulmotored self-confidence. Faith, faith worthy of the name, is faith in *God*. But faith in God is given and not taken; he who has it has received it as a gift.

See, this is what so far transcends our "being as Moses." Here is the coal of living fire; here the living power of life; here is our real help. Here is He, so we must say with Paul and with the whole Bible, for here is the Lord; here is Jesus Christ. He has brought to light what transcends all our good and evil, our capacity and incapacity. He has brought

God to light, Him from whom comes every perfect gift. He is the great light to rule the day of the people who are wandering through the twilight of their times. Through Him we know our goal. Through Him we have reached it while we are still on the way; for through Him we have forgiveness though we are sinners, and eternal life though we must die. Because He is here, Moses has passed away. Because Christmas has come, what we *will* with eager zeal, transitory though it may be, has the promise of a large fulfilment. Before this we are standing; but before this there is no standing still; there can only be an "enter in." To see this means to have it. For "the Lord is the Spirit." And this means that He gives what He is. He works what He promises! For He is not Moses, He is Christ. He is not on the way toward a goal, He comes from it. He is not only God's index finger, uplifted in stern command; He is God's outpouring hand, God's mercy bending low to our misery; He is God's vivifying breath of life. "Where the Spirit of the Lord is," says Paul, "there is liberty." He could not have employed a more fitting word to say all that is to be said here. While we are living in Moses-time, we are prisoners in spite of all our good intentions and resolutions. A prison house is our godlessness, but also the feeble flapping of the wings of our faith. And shall we nevertheless be called the children of God? Yes, but it does not proceed from us; it is something quite new and free that meets us without help from us. The door is being opened from without. We can breathe again; just as we are we may thank God for our liberty. This is faith, but it is a faith which *God* works in our hearts through His Spirit. A prison house is our uncontrolled license, but so are also our fitful, impotent starts toward the good. That nevertheless we do not lose courage and nevertheless need not fling ourselves away in despair, that nevertheless, no, that therefore we are able to make a real fight for self-discipline and purity, this is liberty, liberty bestowed on us in the forgiveness of sins through Jesus Christ. And what of our fear of fate? And what of our fear of death? And what of our convulsive grappling with these monsters? Is it liberty? No; but that you may go on with courage and without fear, through death and devils—this is liberty. "Death, where is thy sting? Grave, where is thy victory? Thanks be to God who giveth us the victory through Jesus Christ our Lord!" Yes, this liberty can be given us. We can do nothing towards it; we can only hear it—and believe it; and in hearing and believing *this*, we who are blind receive our sight.

Do you not also think that the fearful condition of our time is fairly shouting for such ears and eyes? Yes, it is waiting for men who have faith, but not faith in themselves nor in their faith. No, it wants men who have faith in God who can make all things new. It is waiting for men who have learned again what forgiveness is. Forgiveness saves. Forgiveness reconciles. Forgiveness must permeate our politics again; forgiveness and not moral codes; forgiveness and not Moses-zeal! For forgiveness alone makes it possible for us to live together. Forgiveness alone heals wounds. Forgiveness does not make void the laws of God; no indeed, it teaches us to keep them. It is the Spirit who must give life to their dead letter. And our time is waiting for men who dare again to pass through death and devils. Forsooth, for nothing is it waiting more expectantly than for such men. The solution of every question, down to the problem of economics and politics, depends on whether such men will be born—of the Spirit of God. Godlessness certainly abounds today. Moses-zeal and Moses-spirit is not wanting. But there is a dearth of Christ men! Alas, have we not all of us thought and said this very thing? But, if we were to think and say it so that it would pierce our own bone and marrow, then the hour will have struck when it has not only been said and thought, but then it will have come to pass—the veil will have been lifted and Moses-time will have passed away. And we also, with unveiled face, will be mirrors of the glory of the Lord.

AN INDIVIDUAL

But we have this treasure in earthen vessels, that it may be evident that the exceeding greatness of the power is from God, and not of ourselves. We are pressed on every side, yet not straitened; perplexed, yet not unto despair; pursued, yet not forsaken; smitten down, yet not destroyed; always bearing about in the body the dying of Jesus, that the life of Jesus may also be manifested in our body. Yea, while we live, we are always delivered unto death for Jesus' sake, that the life of Jesus may also be manifested in our mortal flesh. So then death worketh in us, but life in you. But having the same spirit of faith (with you), (it turns out) according to that which is written, I believed, therefore did I speak. We also believe, and therefore we also speak; knowing that he that raised up the Lord Jesus shall raise us also with Jesus, and shall present us with you. For all things are for your sakes, that the grace, being multiplied through the many, may cause the thanksgiving to abound unto the glory of God.—*II Corinthians*, *4:7-15.*

Blessed is the man of whom much is required. More blessed is the man of whom more is required than of others. Jesus once said: "To whomsoever much is given, of him shall much be required." You may fittingly invert this saying, and say, Of whomsoever much is required, to him much is given. The proverb, *Noblesse oblige*, may quite properly be changed so that it will read, Obligations are titles of nobility.

When our problems and perplexities threaten to overwhelm us; when we are hard pressed by them, it may help us to remember this. Perhaps a special grace is beckoning us at such times. Perhaps we only need to know this to become deeply grateful in our adversities. The world is always in need of men like Paul of whom more is required than of others. There never are enough of them; and especially men with so large a measure of grace and gratitude are never plentiful. It is not true, however, what I heard a minister say at one time, that such men make their appearance about once in a hundred years. People who bear their burdens with a deep sense of blessedness are found everywhere and at all times. You will find them scattered among folks of small affairs, and occasionally it is a man or a woman involved in the larger interests of humanity. Very often they remain unknown; but it is not necessary that their names be heralded among their fellowmen. Known or unknown, however, such people are necessary and indispensable for mankind, more necessary indeed than the great bulk of people. There could be more of them than there really are; for it does not require special endowments and talents of character and intellect to become such a blessed burden-bearer. By their secret influence, such men hold society together and cause it to make progress. Amidst the sham life of their fellowmen, and for their benefit, they are living the true life that men ought to live.

It may truly be said that all men are capable of, and in fact very near to, becoming such burden-bearing, yet blessed, men. No man is far removed from the point where the special grace and gratitude which marks this kind of people is waiting for him. There we are told from a realm beyond us: Large demands, but also large gifts of grace! Obligations, but also titles of nobility! "Pressed on every side, yet not straitened; perplexed, yet not unto despair; smitten down, yet not destroyed!" For is there a man who is not equally necessary to God, as was Paul? If only a man will understand the divine necessity of this kind of a life,—and engage in living it.

God has need of men who will lend their ears to his call, even if many others remain deaf to him. God needs men who are aroused, even if many others still sleep an undisturbed slumber. This is not a reflection on those others; neither is it a badge of merit and honor for those who are called and aroused of God and so are becoming leaders of God's vanguard among men. It is simply a divine necessity and a law in God's kingdom that there shall be such individuals. God's relation to humanity is not fashioned after the principle of our political states where all citizens are equal before the law. Neither does God follow the rule of the army where a thousand men lift their right feet at the same moment when the regiment begins to march. God's relation to mankind is constituted in liberty. God does not start with mass movements. He begins with a few individuals; and even among them different stages and degrees of preparedness and alertness for divine service are possible.

The great majority is ordinarily not interested in God and the things of God; but there are always a few individuals who are sensitive to God. It is through these individuals that God's movements among men are carried into effect. You know how it is with beautiful paintings or with good music. The man who has an eye for it sees; and the man who has an ear for it hears, while others for the time being see and hear nothing. Through men and women who search and wait for it, God's truth makes its way to men and among men. Or think of the parable of the fourfold soil. Sterile and unproductive soil which is full of rocks, and thorns, and weeds is never wanting. But there is also the good soil where the good seed will bring forth thirty-fold, sixty-fold, and a hundred-fold. In a similar way, these individuals, lonely, alert, and obedient men and women, are necessary in humanity's relation to God. Sometimes they become leaders, heroes, and prophets; sometimes they do not. They are indispensable to God, however, not because God loves them better than their fellowmen but for the very reason that God's eye is on the whole of mankind. The movement between him and humanity must go on; it must always make a new beginning.

No man can be what he is not and no man can give away what he does not possess. And no man is condemned and excluded from God because for the present he is, and has, little that is of value for God. No man is farther removed from God's good will to love him than another, because he is as yet not available for God. But until he surrenders, other men and women who are and possess something because they are at God's service, must be God's servants in His movement toward men. In its inception, God makes use of individuals who stand ready to serve Him, as we make use of a pinch of spice to season the whole dish. As a painter will put a little red color here or there in his painting or as the bassos furnish the foundation in a large chorus—seemingly with a task all their own, but in reality only to render their peculiar service for the benefit of the whole chorus—so God employs individuals who offer themselves to his service; and of them more is required than of others. Their burdens and obligations are multiplied.

Paul's words make you feel his joy in being such an individual. He is in a difficult situation. But he is not unaware of the divine import of his life. It is this insight that makes him so largely grateful. It even makes him quite willing to carry on and continue to live under his difficulties. He has no thought of submitting an account to God:—This I am doing for you! What are you doing for me? He is not asking for sympathy. He does not play the martyr, martyr though he is. In the midst of strong crying and groaning, he is content with God's way. His heart is confirmed in his calling and therefore he does not complain to others:—See, how hard things are going with me! On the contrary, he tells them:—Things keep moving with me. You can detect a secret note of joy, as if he were saying: I would not have matters go differently with me! And you can almost hear him extend an invitation to them, as if he were saying:— Let matters go with you, as they are going with me! He tells them of a precious treasure and of a superabounding power which he is carrying within his bosom. When he, the lonely, alert, and obedient man is driven into a corner, he knows that there is salvation for him; when the task becomes too heavy for his strength, a marvellous help is ready at hand and extricates him from his troubles.

This is what he means when he exclaims, "Not straitened, not in despair, not forsaken, not destroyed!"

Every "Not" is a shout of triumph. As a river, at its mouth, participates in the ocean's life movement, in its ebb and tide, so Paul feels his life linked to God's activity in humanity, with the life and death of Jesus. He participates in them. Now the participant in Jesus dying, he shall have part some day, and in a measure even now, in Jesus' death-destroying resurrection. In this light he accepts the "grace which is given him"; so he fills his office, goes his way and shoulders his task in life. Every man who so understands his life, knows also the reason and destiny of his life. He knows what it is necessary for him to believe, and because he knows what he believes he also speaks. This is the blessedness, the wealth and miracle of a man of whom more is required than of others.

But let us not be blind to the fact that these things are dearly paid for. Paul knows what he is saying when he writes, "We have this treasure in earthen vessels." Everywhere we are hard pressed, forsaken, persecuted, smitten down. We always bear about in our body the sufferings of Jesus. Evidently Paul is speaking here of something that is making his nature, character and appearance very conspicuous. It is quite clear that people saw little of the nobility and blessedness of the God-man in Him. And what little they did discover did not indicate a victorious life; and surely there was little occasion for it. While he was known to be an indefatigable worker, the result of his labours did not clearly and irrefutably indicate what manner of man he was. There was his difficile personality. It did not lend itself to easy friendship, as we know from many passages in his letters. There were times and seasons when everything turned out differently from what he had intended; and oftentimes the turn of affairs was not for the best. He was also suffering under a severe physical handicap which at times completely disabled him. There were limits to his strength; he had his faults; some—we do not know how many—of his undertakings ended in failure; he had enemies.

In short, he was inwardly straitened; and although he was an apostle, he was subject to imperfections and limitations no less than other people. No, not only not less than other people; he was even more hard pressed than others. For the very reason that he was an apostle, he had a particularly hard road to travel. He had to meet many an unpleasant experience and temptation which others could avoid; he had to make enemies of men while others could live in peace with them. Like a magnet, he had to draw to himself a mountain of the imperfections, limitations, and evils of human life from which others could keep themselves free.

The man who is living for God invites attacks upon himself; and, besides, he stands defenseless against them. For his very existence is an attack upon the world and its existing order, on what it prices and values. But he has no weapon like hers to defend himself against her attacks. Childlike, he must stand and suffer. And what is more, his every weakness, fault, defeat, and failure becomes more patent than it does with others. Friend and foe expect him to be masterful, victorious, brilliant. Curiosity follows his every move; suspicion dogs his every footstep; and what he says is scrutinized with an unparalleled care.

"Will God whom he trusts not forsake him?" is a question which becomes much more pointed in men like Paul than in others. The man of whom much is required is always expected to show that much is given him. And if he does not present proof and produce evidence of his high calling by doing large things, and if a close-up view of his life does not stamp him a hero or a prophet, his critics consider themselves justified, nay, even compelled, to ask the question, Where is now your God? And there is another matter which makes his burden still more oppressive. Such a man must make higher demands on himself, on life, on God Himself than others. If no one were to watch him and press him with questions, even if his endeavours were crowned with success and find a complete endorsement among his fellowmen, if he were everywhere loved and applauded, he himself is not blind and deaf to the fact that he only knows in part; he is not mistaken that his eloquent speech is only stammering; and that his purposeful activity is but blind stumbling. He knows that, from the cradle to the grave, his life in the body is really a dying; that his virtues are brilliant vices and his successes only question marks.

This insight is evidence and testimony that a man is where he is, for God's sake. It is God himself who is pressing hard upon him with the question, Where is now your God? It is God who reminds him daily, hourly, that the world needs and wants redemption by reminding him—You also are world. Such a man has asked himself long before others have asked him, Why is not my life more victorious and powerful? Why am I not a better, more engaging and prepossessing

man? Why am I not more successful? Why am I not
more saved? Why does not God's love and glory radiate more gloriously from me?

What has Paul to say to all this? He simply answers that it is so. Yes, he is saying, "We have this
treasure in earthen vessels." If a man cannot or will
not see me in spite of all these liabilities, or if he
cannot close his eyes to what I, Paul, am and have of
myself, he does not need to see anything. I cannot
force him to do so. God does not wish to impose himself on men through me; he does not wish to conquer
through me, but in spite of me. For my own person,
I hide and spoil as much as I unfold and build. In my
own person, I am showing as much unbelief as I show
faith in God. My own person is a question, a problem,
a riddle. I cannot compel a man to see the blessedness, joy, wealth and nobility which I possess. People
may not have an eye for it; in fact, I myself am constantly trying to be blind to them and forget them.
If such things determine your judgment of me, you are
quite justified in asking me, "Where is now your God?"
Paul is putting before us the barrenness, the rough and
bluff jaggedness of his personality. He has nothing
in which to glory, he has nothing to defend, and nothing to justify.

We have first seen Paul's life in its divine setting,
and now we have seen him in his humanity. We have
seen its contradiction: "hard pressed, but not straitened; perplexed, yet not unto despair; pursued, yet
not forsaken; smitten down, yet not destroyed. We
always bear about in the body the dying of Jesus." It
is life's setting for people who are living for God.

Why must there be such men? Of what benefit are they to us? Who is tempted to become such a man?

The dying of Jesus in our body, Paul is saying. It is all that he knows of a man in his situation. But it is not merely an interpretation, or a justification, or an excuse which he offers. It is much more; it is an order, a password, a command under which he is placed. He knows that things are as they are because they must be as they are. For the Lord whom he serves wants them so. "Take it on yourself!" reads the order which he has received. Take it on yourself that things go harder with you than with others. Take it on yourself that you are driven to a more severe self-examination and self-condemnation. Take it all on yourself! Do not try to escape your lot! Do not defend yourself! Do not complain and object! It means the dying of Jesus in your body!—The dying of Jesus! Your dethronement, oh man! You are being dethroned from what is high and exalted among men that God may be high and exalted.

The dying of Jesus means that you must decrease. It is the decrease of your own insight, strength, power, and righteousness; it is the decrease of your works and successes that in the end God's wisdom, strength, and righteousness, God's will and work may grow and triumph. The dying of Jesus is for you most questionable. You must become questionable and dubious that God above you may become more sure, and that the superabounding power be of God and not of you. What else did Jesus do toward resurrection than that He died? What else can you do, if Jesus is your Lord? Can you expect to be led on a road different from His?

Can you desire to be what He would not be? Can you
say except what He said? He has brought life and light
to you as He suffered to become a spectable,—"Behold,
the man!"

So you are demonstrating that you are living for
God's sake when you become a sacrifice with Jesus and
become a man who is tossed about by accusations,
afflictions, doubts, cares, and vexations. When your
inward man is torn asunder and you remain confident,
in spite of all, in the grace that you are who you are in
your imperfections, limitations, and in the evil and
sorrows of this world, in the very midst of death:—
then you are bearing about the dying of Jesus in your
body. That *he* must do it, is the order which *Paul*
has heard.

He has heard it; he has become obedient; he is
already being offered up; he has surrendered. And
therefore he does not live crushed by this contradiction
of human life. Nay, he is happy and possesses blessedness, wealth, and nobility. For he has also heard the
promise which is pinned to the order which he has received. After Good Friday comes Easter! Jesus'
resurrection follows his dying. Exaltation takes the
place of humiliation; decrease makes way for increase;
the question is followed by an answer; the end makes
room for a new beginning; after death comes life; and
in the wake of human sorrow follows the hope of God.
Yes, while we live, we are always being delivered unto
death for Jesus' sake, that the life of Jesus may also
be manifested in our flesh. It is in the making; it is
coming in the advent; it is with God. It is not yet in
any wise visible, tangible, or established. Yes, Paul

would tell us, You unsteady and faltering men, you who are hard pressed here by questions, doubts and troubles, let every one of you believe that life is waiting behind the dying of Jesus where your eyes can see nothing. Whoever would believe, let him believe:— I may believe because I know; because I must believe; for I am called of God and have heard his voice. I have made a start; I have made a leap, because I was apprehended and permitted myself to be apprehended. I have dared, and still dare, to believe—for God's sake.

We who are not Paul ought to let it finally be told us that we all live of what such men have been in the midst of their great blessedness and their great sorrow. For all these things are for *your* sakes. The zeal and the problems of such people uphold the world, even as they are upheld of Jesus and Jesus of God. By hearing, daring, and being apprehended, they are living vital life. We do not know what we should be, if this vital life did not exist. What figures do we cut, we who do not hear, nor dare, and are not apprehended! We who miserably desert and abandon these individuals although our life depends on them. What shall triumph in us:—gratitude that such men have lived; or the restless voice in us which is forever telling us that we cannot and must not belong to the large bulk of those who are only clamouring for support without giving support on their own account?

THE INWARD MAN

Wherefore we faint not [we never lose heart]; but though our outward man is decaying, yet our inward man is renewed day by day. For our light affliction, which is for the moment, worketh for us more and more exceedingly an eternal weight of glory; while we look not at the things which are seen, but at the things which are not seen: for the things which are seen are temporal; but the things which are not seen are eternal.—II Corinthians 4:16-18.

Wherefore we never lose heart! We shall assume without further ado what the text tells us—that there are people who know what it is to lose heart, but they know also a "Wherefore" and a "Not" with which they deliberately and successfully combat their loss of heart. We all know what loss of heart is. But we may not know that it is not a state of mind which can be overcome by merely fostering another and more pleasant state of mind. Loss of heart is a power in our life and a stern necessity in this world; and if we mean to confront it with a "Wherefore not," as Paul is doing it in our text, this "Wherefore not" must needs be a power also, a power transcending the strength of despondency and able to overcome it. It must be a necessity even harder than steel and granite than which no sturdier building and fighting material is found in our world.

Despondency is a frame of mind which comes over men when they become aware of their situation as men among men; as men who are subject to death, yea, as men who are in the throes of death because they are of this world. Loss of heart results from honesty and truthfulness. We well understand why the great majority of people avoid being truthful enough to take a realistic invoice of life. Quite rightly, they are afraid it might cause them to become faint. But their unwillingness to face realities becomes the source of their limitations and fancies.

We are sometimes told that it is better for many people to remain subject to their limitations and fancies than to know the truth. We fear to disturb them lest they become faint. If only the benefit which we are conferring on them by withholding the truth were greater and more effective! For no man escapes despondency altogether, and no man succeeds quite completely in getting away from reality. It keeps trickling through the crags and crannies of our life; for life happens to be what it is. The man who refuses to face it squarely and frankly will in time be made to feel and experience loss of heart without knowing the source of his troubles. It will then overcome him. We may smile and laugh in scorn; we may talk and carry on with an air of security and confidence. But we are only building feeble dikes, unable to hold back the swirling tidalwave. For our dikes are earth-born and earth-built. They are forever breaking down even while we are building them; and fore and aft, everything is being swallowed up of the flood waters.

We may lose heart, for example, when we become aware that we are not accomplishing large and important things, but are condemned to spend our life in little trifling nothings. We are carrying within our bosoms a longing to go on a journey to faraway lands; but we are limited to our constitutional of a few blocks, more or less, from our homes to our offices and back again. And while we are doing it, life is passing on. Does it not make you despondent? We could lose heart were we to know that deep down in us there sits enthroned like a Chinese idol something that will not be taught, or moved, or redeemed. It is our personal self, our selves, what we are for ourselves, our personalities. A very unpleasant thing it is, but it insists on being our inseparable companion. Wherever we may go, it shows its ugly pagoda face in every word and deed. Is it our bitterest enemy or our deepest and most real self? At any rate, the memory of its existence could make us lose heart. It could make us lose heart to find our life's highway strewn with stumbling blocks which in our judgment can never be removed.

We could become despondent because everything in life is in a constant flux, as an ancient philosopher has assured us. It is disheartening to think that our best and noblest endeavours will some day be seen and exposed to have been one-sided and mistaken zeal. To think that the day is coming when we shall be quite forgotten, as if we had never lived and laboured for decent politics or beautiful art, for science or religion, for democracy or socialism or the League of Nations, as if religious experience and Christian activism had never filled our work-a-day life! When the glaciers shall return! Or even before, when Asia's fathomless mystery shall engulf us or America's gold shall have bought us!

Yes, we have reasons to lose heart. Despondency

comes over us when we know that our outward man is decaying. Let us repeat: Faintness overcomes us when we know that our whole existence is subject to death and decay. We could continue and mention reasons without number for faintness. There is the sex problem which conditions and imprisons our very being. But let us stop! There is none among us who does not have his own reasons for becoming faint; and there is none among us who has not at times been ready to close his eyes and surrender in broad daylight to night life and in the very prime of life to death.

Life may still be going on; but its joy, its glory, and its hope are gone out of it, when despondency comes. Expectations and the will to live have perished. Countless numbers are living in such abject resignation; and something of this state of mind clings to all of us. And now, a man is meeting us in these words of Paul, a man who also has known loss of heart. Clearly and distinctly he is telling us of his and our condition, "Our outward man is decaying." But he confronts despondency with a "Wherefore not." And as he is saying it, he is not merely building a tottering sea wall; he is shouting a triumphant battle cry. For it is a cry charged with power against his powerful enemy, steeled to meet his pitiless ferocity, and pregnant with a deep conviction that it will supply men with the one necessity which will turn their losing fight against despondency into a glorious victory over it. He is an honest man; yes, but also a man radiant in triumph. Even if we do not understand at all the how and why? He is a sight to rouse us and to make us straighten our shoulders.

What is it that Paul is saying? Let us listen to him

word for word. He begins by saying, "Our outward man is decaying; but while this is happening, and by the very fact that it is happening, our inward man is renewed day by day." Such words are not merely "Golden texts." When Paul coined them, he was snatching, with a bold and daring hand, at victory in a lost cause. Do we not feel like asking: "Is it really only our outward man who is subject to the decay which we discern upon examination of our life in the light of truth?" Ask the tired and disillusioned among us! Inquire of all those who have lost faith in themselves! Let the inmates of our hospitals and asylums or the care-worn fathers and mothers tell us! Ask those who, after the frightful experiences of our recent past, can see nothing but the decline of our occidental culture! Ask them all if the decay which is making us despondent today is affecting merely our outward man? Is the tragedy of death merely physical and material? Does it merely threaten our external bodies? Alas, you poor comforters!

When you tell us, Yes, *only* our outward man, you would like to have us think of our hearts and souls and spirits, of our "inward man" who is not touched by this tragic decay. Does not our heart suffer when another member of our body suffers? Does not the soul share in the ills of our bodies? Will not the spirit die, if Europe today should go to ruin in things material? Indeed, what do our material wants amount to beside the spiritual misery from which we are suffering? Is not the inner decay the very source of our present despondency?

Of one thing we may be assured, that Paul is not

among these poor comforters. We merely need to remind ourselves that Paul's thinking is centered in Christ, in the Christ of the Cross who cried out in His agony, "My God, my God, why hast thou forsaken me?" And Paul once described his own condition with these words, "Fightings without, fears within." A man who writes such things does not console himself and others like this, "Dear soul, do not become faint. All your afflictions concern merely the outward man. In spite of them, all will be well with your inward man." No, no; such a man knows that the decay of the inward man is chiefly responsible for men's great depression. It is the soul that is facing death; it is the soul that is being destroyed. If Paul says, "Our outward man is decaying," he most assuredly includes what we are accustomed to call our inward man. He includes every thought and experience. Paul knows that nothing in our world is excluded from the reign of death.

Does it not make us lose heart when we become daily increasingly aware that there is not a corner of our whole wide world, either of the world within or without us, that does not bear the scars of the savagery of death? When Paul speaks of the outward man, he means our whole world. "Man" he calls it, because it is man's world, and because it is man who is being done to death here. It is man who feels and experiences its terrible fate. If we wish to know what Paul says of the inward man we must go with him beyond this world, beyond what we are and possess, either externally or inwardly, beyond body and soul, beyond nature and spirit.

We must dare to think with him a thought which we cannot think:—the thought of God. The inward man of whom Paul is speaking is not a still undiscovered corner of our present world, or a last depth within our soul which we must reach in a final trial of strength in the hope of finding our haven there. The inward man is the other in us which is no longer world; it is the depth of God. Physicians and psychiatrists, social scientists and educators have no key to unlock the door to him; neither will their methods be of any avail here. Piety, virtue, and wisdom cannot found, sustain, and complete the life of this inward man. Eye has not seen him, ear has not heard him, neither has he entered into the heart and experience of any man. He has his place on the very threshold of our thoughts, experiences, activities and sufferings. Where we have our beginning, there we also find our end. Time is there no longer time, but eternity.

Where everything finds an end, there the inward man has his beginning. At the point where what we call life is fading away in the absolute mystery of death, there is our genuine life. Where our sight fails us and where we find only an abyss, darkness and the end as our portion in life, there it is where God makes Himself known to man. And yonder, Paul is saying, beyond you tired, fainting, grieving men and women, yonder something is happening, even while the outward man is decaying before your very eyes. On the hither side of this point "finis" is being written; but yonder a new beginning is being made. Here life is being torn down, there it is being builded up. Here is Nay; there is Yea. Here is death; yonder life. Here decay, yonder renewal. Yonder, renewal is daily taking place. Yonder is a bubbling fountain of eternal youth. A new beginning is constantly being made there. Life, a new existence and true being is being created in and from the Yonder out of nothing. Yonder is God Himself. Daily renewal is being made there, and we could continue by saying, "Every hour and every minute it is being done."

There is no time without a touch of eternity; no decay here without renewal yonder; and no aging, weakening, or dying without recreation of new life yonder. And our God-begotten, ever-living inward man is indeed not an unknown stranger and foreigner to us. He is our real self for the very reason that he is our larger self and for the very reason that we ourselves find yonder with him our beginning and our end.

Always and everywhere the Yonder stands hidden behind the Here. The Yonder is only the reverse side, the divine side, of our Here. The inward man who is being renewed is the Yonder side, the divine side of the outward man who is decaying. It is with us that this act of renewing is taking place. For we are this inward man. The depth of God himself, is it not true humanity? A New, New, New is shining into our withering old life, a new life more true than our sadly true decay. Our death is swallowed up in life. Our honest Nay is suspended and changed into a Yea. "Whatever is ailing here below, whatever groans and sighs, shall there be made to shine anew in happy joyous mien." Sown in corruption, it is raised in incorruption.

Do you see the bold and daring victory of which we are laying hold with our "Wherefore not"? We cannot help but feel that it is a daring venture to think the thought of God beyond the world, to make a new beginning where everything has come to an end; to affirm a Yea where we hear only a Nay; to speak of life where we see only death; and to expect everything where commonly nothing more is to be expected. It is a daring thing to posit an "It is," where every "It is" has become impossible. It is a daring thing to unite, as with an iron clamp, our Here and our Yonder, our—alas,—so well-known Here and this—alas,—so unknown Yonder, and to comprehend now our Here from the vantage point of God's Yonder. It is a daring thing to say to oneself and to others, The Yonder transcends the Here; the real man, our real humanity, is indeed the inward man, and therefore, even therefore, we faint not.

No indeed, it is not merely a pious "Golden text." Divine truculence is not a natural gift which we may pluck as a ripe fruit from the tree of our life. It is a daring venture. But in it lies imbedded the power with which Paul is facing despondency.

And now let us listen to a little more of what Paul is saying. We may be wondering, How does a man come to lay hold on this "Wherefore not" that he may use it against despondency? Paul gives a very remarkable answer. He does not say: If you are religiously inclined, you can do it! He does not say, My faith is the power, etc. He does say, however, "Our affliction worketh glory." Let us ponder it a little. What makes me a captive, must serve to make me free. What is killing me, makes me alive. By way of the Nay I arrive at the Yea. My end is the running start of my new beginning. The decay of the outward man is necessary for a renewal of the inward man. He would tell us, for example: "Yes, I really want you to see how trivial are the nothings that you are doing and must do! I do want you to know how unredeemed and unpleasant you are. I want you to see the fearful actuality of the stumbling blocks on your life's way. I want you to know that everything is in a flux and that all is vanity. I want you to have an eye for the decline of the Occident!

Affliction worketh glory. It will rob you of what you ought to lose. It will create doubts and rouse questions in you which need to be roused. It will kill what ought to die. For you have not yet come to the point where everything has come to an end. You have not yet arrived where you are forced to think of God, and only of Him. You are not yet facing the impossible; you have not yet come to the end of the road where a new world has its beginning. You have not yet reached the boundary line of the new life. Affliction is working this glory by pushing you toward this boundary. Your inward man is in need of affliction. It is an immeasurable advantage to know it. It is like capturing guns from an enemy and turning their muzzles against him. Whatever sought to make me faint, must now not only serve to make my heart and mind keep silent and resigned; nay, it makes me take new courage to give battle. It has not only become a "light affliction which is for the moment"; its power to tear down, to arouse questions and create doubts, to drive

me in a corner and kill me, this power must now serve
me. I am happy to be afflicted. I would not chose
not to be afflicted. "Affliction worketh more and more
exceedingly an eternal weight of glory."

But have a care! We cannot simply repeat such
words, and we should not! Let us not imagine that
their reality will come to us without burning personal
questionings, perhaps by virtue of a sudden illumination or of a voluntary decision. If there is one thing
which in our time must come to an end, it is our religious arrogance and presumption, which make us
believe that we are entitled to repeat what prophets,
apostles and Reformers had a right to say, and to repeat their words without a demonstration of the Spirit
and power. Who are they who may take such words
on their lips? Who are they with whom such words
have the ring of truth? Paul answers: "We who look
not at the things which are seen, but at the things
which are not seen, because we know that the things
which are seen are temporal, but the things which are
not seen are eternal." It means a crisis and a trans-
valuation of our life.

Let us not rush in too hastily and say that we are
capable of such a life and that we have the invisible
things in mind. The great majority of those who
claim that they are minding the invisible things would
more likely be stricken with the terror of death if they
were told what the things are which are not seen! A
man is not thinking the thought of God every time
when he is deeply moved. We ought to ask ourselves,
what it was that has moved us so deeply. Let us rather
frankly confess that even in our deepest emotions we

have in mind the things that are seen; and because of it, we do not possess the "Wherefore not" with which we ought to confront our faintness. If we had it, we would be showing a different front and the world would show a face different from what it does. It may be well for us to take note of the far distance which separates us from the world of the Bible. Let us be modestly content to hear that there are people who live courageous lives in spite of faintness, who live something like the knight in Duerer's etchings: Between Death and the Devil. Let us be quite clear on Christianity's chief principle. It is what Paul experienced through Christ, that he was able, nay, was constrained and even willing to close his eyes to the things that are seen and to direct them to those things which are not seen. This complete inversion of life in the direction of unseen things, this is Christianity. Here is the bubbling fountain of courage, of firm and unconditioned and unrestricted courage. The inward man is a man of courage. But he must become awake in us; he must not remain asleep if we are to be helped. Perhaps something of a renunciation of visible things is beginning to shine and glow within us.

Perhaps a dim presentiment is flashing through our whole outward man from beyond ourselves telling us, what is seen is temporal; but the things which are not seen are eternal. Perhaps our inward man is dreaming that he ought to wake up soon. Why should it not be possible? Perhaps we have already thought the unthinkable thought of God. Let God be praised! What we do possess in this life, of light and mercy, and grace and truth, we owe to this Perhaps, to this trifle which links us with Paul together "in Christ." How glorious will be the day when our Perhaps has changed to certainty and our trifle has grown to fullness!

CONFIDENT DESPAIR

For we know that if the earthly house of our tabernacle be dissolved, we have a building from God, a house not made with hands, eternal, in the heavens. For verily in this we groan, longing to be clothed upon with our habitation which is from heaven: if so be that being clothed we shall not be found naked. For indeed we that are in this tabernacle do groan, being burdened; not for that we would be unclothed, but that we would be clothed upon, that what is mortal may be swallowed up of life. Now he that wrought for us this very thing is God, who gave unto us the earnest of the Spirit. Being therefore always of good courage, and knowing that, whilst we are at home in the body, we are absent from the Lord (for we walk by faith, not by sight); we are of good courage, I say, and are willing rather to be absent from the body, and to be at home with the Lord.—*II Corinthians 5:1-8.*

Let us begin the interpretation of these remarkable words with what every one of us can understand quite easily. Twice Paul is saying: "We groan." It does not matter so much whether our groaning is done audibly or silently. Most groaning is never heard. It is known only to one man and God. Groaning is chiefly an inner emotion, an anxious restlessness, almost like panting for breath. It comes upon us when we are about to become faint and have no means of saving ourselves from being overcome by our misfortunes. Groaning is the last stage before faintness. When a dull resignation to an inevitable terror casts its darkening shadows over us, when we are about to say Yea to death, it is at such times that we may have reached the point where we groan. But darkness has not yet completely swallowed us up; we are still yearning for our freedom; we are still inquiring, lamenting, and looking about for the lights of life dimly flickering on the far horizon. I venture to say that every one of us knows these last stages before faintness. But even when we are hard-pressed and sad, let us not overdo. We ought not let ourselves go too easily and surrender too quickly to the thought, So, now I am faint. Fortunately, it is not really so. Despondency is too terrible a state to let go of life altogether, even if we have reached its ragged edge and come to the end of our wits.—But what groaning, this last stage before despondency, may mean, some of us know only too well, and others know it in part.

Paul confesses that he has reached this last stage, and probably he knows it more intimately through long association than any of us. In another place he says that the whole creation groaneth. All existence, even mute and inanimate life, groans. How much more men who not only live, but know that they are living. Paul does not say, "We have groaned," or "We groan sometimes"; he says, "We are groaning." As he is writing he is in the very midst of it, as in a final parting from what he loves. Let us profit immediately as we hear him speak of a great and joyous hope. Let us not see him on some mountain top of triumphant faith and serenity. Let us not think: "Yes, such a hope belongs to people who are in more favourable circumstances than we are today." No, such a hope one may have in the very midst of groaning.

A man may groan and yet be blessed. "We are of good courage," he says a little later. He does not say,

"We shall be of good courage"; he says, "We are of good courage." He says it without an If or a But, as he has previously simply said, "We groan." A man can have good confidence only at a time and in a place where he groans. In the shadows of a great darkness, in the immediate presence of sad and dreary situations where anxiety closes our eyes and ties our hands, precisely there a man may have hope and be of good courage.

Paul is saying something even more remarkable in our text. He says that if we know the real reason for our groaning, we may be of good courage, even while we are groaning. When a man is ill, it is quite an advantage if he knows his ailment. It gives him an opportunity to apply proper remedies. The comparison is not quite pertinent, however. For when we know why we are groaning, recovery has already set in. If we must groan without comfort, in despair and without hope of salvation, it is because we do not know the real cause of our groaning. Here it will be determined whether we are able to follow Paul and to catch a faint echo of what he is saying.

Paul mentions first a mistaken diagnosis of the cause of our groaning. We see, he is saying, that our whole so-called life, with everything that belongs to it, even the things that are great and important and dear to us, is like a tabernacle. It is being erected only to be taken down sooner or later. It is like a hut, as Luther has translated it. It denotes transitoriness. There is a beautiful poem by Johann Peter Hebel on "Transitoriness" in which he says: "Whatever comes, comes young and gay," but all glides silently toward old age

and finds an end.   There is no standing still.—Do you
not hear the brook's unceasing chatter?   Will not the
stars forever twinkle through the nights?—It seems
that nothing moves, and yet—all things do move and
pass away."

This is transitoriness.   One might also compare life
with a play which is really play and not in dead earnest,
as we read it in the same poem: "There I used to play
until my blessed end."   A much more telling and truly
descriptive expression for transitoriness is the word
death.   In the midst of life we are locked in death's
embrace.   In the midst of life, not merely when we
die.   What we call life is in reality dying.   Our body
is a grave, as a pagan wise man has long since told us.
We are standing under a large, all-embracing and all-
destroying Nay.   For a long time and in many in-
stances of our life we may not be aware of it; but
slowly death makes its appearance and its clammy hand
takes an ever firmer hold of us.   We grow older; an
illness, slight or serious, tells us how matters stand and
what is awaiting us.   Unexpected failures overtake us;
we become conscious of our limitations and of those of
other people; the graveyard receives one after another
of those whom we knew and loved; a time like the last
six years comes over us.   We fight it.   Long live life!
we would shout.   We are ever eager to see and experience and have a share in some imperishable and abiding value.   But we do not have much time in which to
do our fighting.   Taps are soon sounded, and the time
of our departure is soon come.   We would be constructive.   But it is all too evident that the last, clear and
unmistakable word of what we call life is not construc-

tion but destruction. Our life is a tabernacle. And therefore we groan until we know what Paul knows.

We are afraid of life's breakdown. For even if it is only a tabernacle, it is in many respects a comfortable dwelling place. Even if there is much to life which is not desirable, we are afraid of the hand which threatens it and which points out to us that we have here no abiding city. We feel almost like a man who is being robbed of his garments in the cold of winter. Here a piece is taken and there another of the things we admire and love. We stand disrobed, naked; we shiver and freeze. Nothing is left except a Nay, Nothing, absolute void. We do not care to stand naked. We have an horror of Nay and Nothing. We dread death. And because we see it coming in spite of our horror, because we see its undisputed reign, therefore we groan.

Or may not our silent and audible groaning and all our problems and laments be reduced to this one cause, that we are disquieted by this large Nay which rules our life? We have seen the truth of our life, in one way or another, and its truth is death. And no amount of groaning will change matters. Just as little as the counsel not to groan and to make the best of our troubles is of any benefit. We are forced to groan. Some time or other it comes upon even the most superficial among us. But we must also see that as we let our groaning run its course unimpeded the more disconsolate and desperate we become. We draw ever nearer the abyss of despondency. Groaning, originating from this source, receives no answer, finds no healing or solution. For here we do not know the true cause of our groaning. And now Paul makes a very bold

assertion. Let us not repeat it too quickly after him.
But we may make a reverent attempt at least to hear
what he is saying. He tells us: You are groaning,
and think you know its cause. But you do not know it.
You are mistaken about yourself. You must learn to
know yourself. Yes, indeed, the meaning of what you
call life is death. But the meaning of death is true
life. You are wanting this true life; you are in
search of it. You have lost it; but you have not forgotten it. It escapes you; and still you are aware that
it exists. You are putting forth much effort in this and
that and the other thing; but you want the true life.
It is within you although you are not one with it.

This true life is your very own, the totally other of
your own life, its eternal and divine side. It is your
origin and beginning of which your reason, your conscience and your peace gives you notice, but so does also
your sin and sorrow. It is the goal toward which your
thoughts and deeds, the tendrils of your heart and
mind are reaching out. Yea, it is the final ground of
all the tempests and terrible crosscurrents in the history
of the world. There is a Yea in you mortals, in you
men who are imprisoned under a large Nay; a Yea
immeasurably higher than your Nay; totally distinct
from your present existence, altogether incomparable
to the tiny Yea which you now possess and strive for;
heavenly compared with what is earthly, and yet not a
strange life; far away, and still not far away, since it is
your most personal portion and inheritance. It is your
very homeland. "We know that we have a building
from God, a house not made with hands, eternal, in
the heavens."

Here is the cause of our groaning. Do you understand now why you must groan? Yes, the present tabernacle must be broken down that the building from God may receive you. And you are groaning now not because the tabernacle is being broken down, but because the building from God has not yet taken you up. It is true, indeed, a large and radical debacle must occur before the true life in our life and the abiding values which we now barely know may appear. But the real source of our problems and groans is not the transitoriness of our life; their reason is the fact that it has not yet appeared what we shall be.

Yes, the way to life leads through death; not only through what we call death—finally also this, to be sure,—but through an extended cancellation, removal, limitation, and discarding of what we call life. True life begins where everything ends. Think of a large number which is preceded by a minus sign. Constant subtraction must be made before you reach zero. And only then appears beyond the cipher the first little number with a plus sign. It is a painful procedure to be sure; it is not cancellation and removal that is hurting us, but that there is such a large sum with a minus sign between us and the redeemed plus beyond the cipher. It is not death that is painful, but that we do not yet live.

Yes, life is a play in which we score no abiding values. But are we not hardpressed by our insight that we are only playing at life? Would we not take pleasure in this play, if we were not aware of something else? For a time we may enjoy playing merchant, and minister, and doctor, church, school, and state, or being genteel and educated. But the cause of our pain is our knowledge that something should be happening and that there ought to be some real accomplishment totally distinct from the best that we can do, and in fact do, even in our best efforts. We are standing under a Nay which suspends everything and gnaws away at the very roots of our human life and growth. Something is coursing through our veins acting like a slow poison. As the Preacher says: "Vanity of vanities, all is vanity." We are suffering from this Nay; and the people, who have lived through the last ten years, will never fully recover from it. But now I say: "The cause of our anxiety is not the Nay; but the Yea which has been pronounced over us even before the Nay has come over us." Why is it that we do not surrender our life in a dull and stupid resignation to this Nay and Nothing? We cannot do it because we know the Yea to be the first and original word of our life; and now that we know it, now that it has come over us as the final and abiding fact of our life, we must suffer from it. See, here is the cause of our groaning, Paul is saying: "We long to be clothed upon with our habitation which is from heaven."

Because we know of life beyond death, life here which is subject to death rests so heavily upon us. Because heaven is our homeland, we feel the strain of the hurried passing of time which is not yet eternity. Because we know the Yea, we are hard pressed to say No so often and to be compelled to live our life of vanity without being able to live in the Yea and to make it the fountain of our life. Not our being disrobed, not death and the Nothing and Nay are terrible,

but that we have not yet passed through them; that
we have not yet overcome them; that their aim and
end has not yet been reached; that we are not yet
clothed upon with our habitation which is of God. If
there were no God and if the heavenly habitation
were not awaiting us, there would be no cause for
groaning. But God has begun to trouble us with an
anxious restlessness. He is the cause of our groaning;
and therefore we must groan. Hosea, the prophet, has
fittingly said: "I will be unto Ephraim as a lion, and
as a young lion to the house of Judah. I, even I, will
tear and go away; I will carry off, and there shall be
none left to deliver." And Paul himself says: "Now
he that has wrought us for this very thing is God, who
gave unto us the earnest of the Spirit." Here indeed
is the Spirit:—our indissoluble communion with God;
our unquenchable remembrance of eternal life; our
uncancelled expectancy of it; its creative power; and
because we have them, therefore we groan while we
are in our tabernacle, Paul is saying. We can do nothing else but groan.

If we have heard and understood this, then we can
perhaps understand a little more. Paul is saying: Because it is God who has wrought us for this that we
must groan in this present life, therefore our groaning
is not done without good confidence. Our groaning
borders very closely on the evil in which despondency
ends. But we shall never reach it. In reality, we are
infinitely far removed from it. We faint not. It is
impossible for us to become faint. We are of good
courage. For the man who understands himself and
therefore knows also that God is the cause of his

groaning, has gained an insight which will make him confident in his greatest and deepest sorrow. He sees death in the light of life. He justifies God who makes him groan while he is in this tabernacle. He understands the necessity of death, and transitoriness, and Nay. Their purpose is to make room for life. As they do their appointed work, true life is drawing nigh; and we come near our goal of being clothed upon with our habitation which is from heaven. The mortal must be swallowed up of immortality; and it is being swallowed up; and to this end that which is mortal must die.

We know that we are not at home with the Lord while we are at home in the body. For we walk here by faith and not by sight. It is an unsatisfying and provisional condition; but it is removed when the tabernacle has been taken down. We do not live the true life; therefore we must die. We do not yet possess true joy; and therefore we must have our sorrows. We still go astray; and therefore we must learn to know nothing. We are not yet at home with the Lord; and therefore we must leave our sojourn in foreign parts. We walk by faith and not by sight; and therefore our old man must be destroyed that the new man who not only believes, but sees, may grow daily. Therefore we are of good courage and are well pleased if we become even more homeless and absent from our body that we may be at home with the Lord. It is the same large crisis and transition of which we have heard already. Affliction worketh glory. And Paul is confident while he is groaning, because he knows it.

Who among us knows this also? We have a bare inkling of it; and therefore we have difficulty in grasping what Paul has told us. And we can grasp it still less that he was really and truly confident in a world where we cannot be confident; that he did not become a hermit with his insights; that he did not lock himself up with a few chosen disciples; that he did not rest, but lived, and fought, and suffered, and fell, and rose again, and triumphed with these insights, and filled the world, this dreary world of death with his victorious deeds and set it in motion to God's glory.

Such confidence transcends our horizon. Once again we may see what Christ, Christ crucified, meant to Paul. He testifies to have seen in Him the crisis of the times; a thrust through the most fearful Nay to a most glorious Yea; the closing of a socalled life in death and the appearance of true life from beyond death; he saw every little light extinguished and a new large light rise out of the darkness. He saw men without God; and then he saw God as he is turning to men: God with us, Immanuel. From this vantage point Paul looked at life. He saw why we groan. He saw the building from God. He saw that the tabernacle must be taken down. He understood that he must be well pleased with what made him also shudder most. He groaned; and yet he was of good courage. He had a vision of the Resurrection.

BEHOLD, NOW!

And working together with God we entreat also that ye receive not the grace of God in vain; for he saith, At an acceptable time I hearkened unto thee, and in a day of salvation did I succor thee: behold, now is the acceptable time; behold, now is the day of salvation.—*II Corinthians 6:1-2*.

"Behold, now is the acceptable time; behold, now is the day of salvation!" What does it mean? Evidently it means that the present time is precious time. It has come to us like a ship with a valuable cargo in its hold. It is standing before us like a tree laden with luscious fruit. Fleeting moments, passing minutes, hours, and days are not empty vessels; they are full of grace, of life, and help, and salvation. They are not merely time; behind the veil of time they hide eternity. We cannot disinterestedly watch the clock strike off the passing hours. The possibilities, opportunities, and hopes which times and seasons hold for us ought to arouse in us an anxious restlessness lest we fail to lift their hidden treasures. It is not time to play, to dream, to drift; we have hard work to do and loads to lift. It is time to be awake, and to rise from our sleep. For our time is not like any other time; it is a special season. Yesterday was not today; and tomorrow will no longer be today. Behold, now! "And working together with God we entreat that ye receive not the grace of God in vain." Thus Paul.

As we read and hear him say it, it becomes almost immediately a burning question with us, if Paul would and could speak also of our time like this. But where in the Bible is it written that the acceptable year of which Paul is speaking has come to an end; or that it will ever cease to be? How depressing that such times should only have occurred many centuries ago! Is not God the same in every succeeding century? Is not every time God's time?—But let us not be too hasty with our answer. Our theology is quick to level everything. In our minds we readily propose to call and make our time God's time. Behold, NOW! We may propose, but God will dispose. In actuality, times are unequal. They differ from each other. In the life of an individual, there may be long stretches of time which can only be called days of vanity, years of indifference, times of dreaming and sleeping. At such times, it cannot possibly be said, Behold, NOW! On the contrary, Behold, not now! And suddenly there may come a few short years, perhaps only a few hours, or even only a fleeting moment when it becomes true, Behold, now is the acceptable time. And when it comes to pass, it is a special season. Probably it does not need to be so; but so it is in actual life.

The larger history of humanity does not differ from the life of an individual in this respect. History shows long periods that have no distinctive color; they have no rhythm and no temper of their own. The nations are as in a deep sleep. Good fortune and ill fortune, even wars and revolutions come over them; but no uplift and no real uprising ensue; no "Forward, march!" is heard; nothing of the old order passes away to make room for a new humanity. People do not even divine that something real could happen. Behold, not now! is the only fitting superscription for such times. And now again, between such colorless times there may come a decade, perhaps only a year and even less, when history's hour strikes, when doors are flung open that have long been barred; when questions and problems of staggering magnitude, tremendous demands and hopes become alive in many hearts. Century-old burdens are thrown off; solutions to age-old problems offer themselves as by magic; and promises of even larger dimensions become apparent. As in the twinkling of a moment, men become aware what the history of humanity really seeks to accomplish. At such times it may become true, Behold, now is the acceptable time!

It is a peculiar and extraordinary happening, when such times come over us. It does not really need to be so; but so it is in actual history. It is the Bible way of looking at times and seasons. The Bible knows that there is a difference in the times. God's activity does not pass over the world like a huge steam roller reducing all times to the same level. From the Bible point of view, God is not the same God at all times; although in theory he is unchangeable. On the contrary, we read of times of ignorance when we can speak only of God's longsuffering, and not of grace and salvation. The prophet Amos mentions a time when the Lord will send a famine of hearing the words of Jehovah, when men shall wander from sea to sea, and from the north to the east; and shall run to and fro to seek the work of Jehovah and shall not find it.

The depressing, and even desperate, thought that the day of grace and salvation has passed or is lying in a far away future is not at all foreign to the Bible. And when the Bible says that the acceptable year is at hand, it does not leave us in doubt about its tremendous implications. Immeasurably large and rare and glorious things will come to pass and serve as unmistakable signs that God's Presence Now is not an everyday occurrence. If we could stand its strain for any length of time? The times are unequal in relation to God. Luther has rightly remarked to our text: "The preaching of the gospel is not an everlasting and abiding doctrine but is like a moving rainstorm. Where it strikes, it strikes; what it misses, it misses; it does not return again and it does not remain motionless, but the sun and heat will follow and lick it up."

At any rate, it is not a self-evident fact that we are standing today in a day of grace and salvation. It may well be that we are passing through a different kind of a season, a season in which we can only wait for showers of blessings, and in which we can only heed God's infinite patience with ourselves and the world. It is by no means a self-evident matter that exactly you, and you exactly now, should be given to find the turning point and the way out of your difficulties; and help and light for your life which you have long sought and of which you have stood in such bitter need. The kingdom of God is not ruled by our needs. It is not a self-evident matter that I, or any other preacher, should at this very moment be given the grace to speak the word of God and not the word of man. And it is not self-evident that you yourself should here and now

hear the word of God and not the word of a man.
The kingdom of God is not fixed by calendars and
ecclesiastical ordinances. It is not at all self-evident
that we are better qualified today to understand God,
and the world, and ourselves, because the world has
passed through wars and revolutions. The kingdom
of God does not take the world's history for its text-
book.

All these things are not impossible, but they are not
self-evident. The things of God are not stacked up
in a stock-room, where we may go and help ourselves
at will. Some one who knew God a little has truly
said that we are not carrying God about in our vest-
pockets to pull him out at will. The Spirit listeth
where it will. If we were to heed the distinctions in
the times, we would perhaps learn to value and treasure God's times when they come to us. If we had the
courage to see clearly that the superscription at times
reads, Behold, not now!

It needs also to be said that times of grace and salvation cannot be manufactured or made to order. We
may compel ourselves to think and say, Behold, now!
In fact, the trials which are harassing our souls today
have led many of our contemporaries to exercise themselves in saying, Behold, now! A friend of mine who,
at least in his thinking, is living in a time of large
fulfillment and of divine presence reproved me for
merely speaking of Paul and for not becoming a Paul
in our day!! Our age is seething with a feeling of
high hope and with a spirit of new life; and in some
finely tempered men these feelings are become so
strong that they are really living under the impression

that something real has now happened. Others again
are busy otherwise; they write books, give lectures,
found magazines and newspapers and societies. Some
men have organized communal congregations and have
a mind to make an entirely new beginning of life with
the clearly defined aim of fashioning life along the
lines of the early Church. A religious association has
been called into being where Jew and Gentile, Mo-
hammedan and Christian are making common cause in
a world-reformation. In the course of this summer,
five different international Congresses are meeting in
Switzerland alone. Who would dare to deny that
tremendous forces are at work behind these movements.

It is a powerful constraint that drives men to think,
to speak, to hope, and to work when they are in the
very depth of misery! But in this very Today it becomes necessary to remember that genuine seasons of
God are not the result of our human endeavors and
movements. God's times come upon us, as it were,
over night. And when they are come, they do not
make themselves known in words and books but in
a demonstration of power and in mighty events. There
is something natural about them, like the ripened fruit
on a tree; they are different from our artificial, ecclesiastical presumptions and self-delusions. If we remind
ourselves of these things, perhaps we shall be a little
more restrained; and even lift up our eyes beyond our
modern artificial trifles, looking beyond them to behold
beyond the lower range of hills in the foreground the
glory of the majestic Alps beyond. Perhaps we shall
learn to wait for a season of which we may say with

more truth and justice than we may say it of our day, Behold, now!

But there is a peculiar driving power in these words of Paul. Even in our own life we prefer not to wait. We like to push on toward our goal, even as we press home the question concerning our present Now: "Why not now?" Is not the whole world alive today? Is it not now that the order for the next fifty or hundred years is being established? Is it not now that money is being earned and spent? Do not men sin and curse and swear now? Do not men suffer and die now? It is now that life asks questions and makes demands. Now, now, now is the motto of life! And the one and absolute necessity on which everything depends and which is basic in a radical renewal, this one thing should *not* be possible now? Can we *really* not understand God, obey him, and live in him now? Are we told to wait, and only wait, for God? No, indeed, we have mentioned it ere this. It is not impossible that even this phase of our life is to come under the divine command, Behold, now! Why should not his Behold, now! be decreed for our poor, wistful, and perplexed age? Why should God be farther removed from us than from Paul and the Corinthians? Why should we not receive grace and salvation today? Why should it not be said of us today, Behold, now is the acceptable time!

See, we must now solve a mystery. If our question, "Why not?" is really and wholly serious, then its "not" may disappear; then it may be said, It is here! If men are wholly alive in their quest for God, His answer is not far away. When men have learned that they can only wait for God, they do no longer need to wait for Him. When men have become quite humble, when they no longer live in the delusion that they have God in their possession and may handle Him at will, then God is near to serve them. When men recoil at the frightful distance which separates them from God, it is then that He is very near to them. When men are become lowly enough to lift up their eyes to God who comforts the faint and feeble, it is then that their salvation has come nigh to them. Such people see at the far end of our human pathways a great light, a light casting its rays over everything; and the name of this light is grace.

Grace is strong; grace is profound; it reaches into the depth and makes all things new. Grace solves every problem. Grace is very near to every man and every age. Grace is what we are all waiting for; grace is what we are all longing to have as our possession, but do not possess; we would have it as *our product,* but are unable to produce it. Men who see and seek it where it may be found; men whose sincere question "Why not?" drives them on until they stand in God's presence, such men will also come to know how near, how very near is grace to us. They know that only a thin wall is standing between God's grace and ourselves. A holy impatience grips such men; a holy impatience with themselves and others makes them cry out: "May not the grace of God be near us in vain! May we not be evasive when the road is straight and narrow! May we not close our eyes to the light in whose radiance we are come to stand." They receive a burden with what they have learned in the presence of God's grace as they must now repeat the word of grace to themselves and to others. And it is this burden that makes them coworkers, working together with God.

When such coworkers with God are found who have been forced to descend into the depth and who have found grace there, at such times it will become true, Behold, now! No, it is not even then a self-evident matter, that such a time is God's time; much rather it is so as by a miracle; not forced, not artificially made, but clear and simple and natural. Then life becomes serious, and time becomes precious, valuable, and full of eternity. The clock has struck God's hour. Paul was such a man. He has learned humility and found grace, in the presence of the Christ. He could no longer endure the vanity of time; he has found eternity there. He pushed into the very presence of God with a large, sincere and upright "Why not?" He became one of God's burden bearers, an impatient coworker with God. "As working together with God we entreat that ye receive not the grace of God in vain. Behold, now is the acceptable time; behold, now is the day of salvation!" When men like Paul come forth from the presence of Christ, God's time has come.

What shall we say of our time? Look about you for such men! Perhaps they have already appeared in our midst, though as yet unseen, unheard, unknown, and not understood by us! Perhaps they are even now speaking to us in humility and divine grace. But have a care lest you be deluded! Not everything that glitters is gold. If such men are now in our midst, why should it not be said of our day, Behold, now! Let it be your concern that we may have such men with us. Render aid to every one who is in fear, in uncertainty; help those who are humble by being afraid, uncertain, and humble yourselves. Perhaps they cannot yet lift up their voice because they are lonely men. They cannot be what they are because they will be misunderstood. When such men may lift up their voices, they will tell us what no man may tell us.

Be such men yourselves, if you can! Why not? Why should we not be taught humility and find grace at the feet of the Christ? Why should not our hearts be consumed by the vanity and emptiness of our age? Why should it not be changed into an abounding fulness? Why should not the righteous wait upon God in joy today? Is not everything prepared? Do you not hear what our time is telling us? Everything is prepared, if only we are prepared. Yes, Paul would call our time with the same call as he called yesterday. Give us again a Paul who speaks thus. A Christ who makes Paul speak as he spoke, we have. Christ removes the difference in the times. Christ fills the desert with streams of living water. Christ touches the dead and they rise. What are we waiting for? For a harvest where no seeding has been done? For fruit that grows by our hands? It is God who worketh, both to will and to do. Therefore work out your own salvation with fear and trembling!

Made in the USA
Columbia, SC
16 October 2020